NEW & UPDATED

DENVER
BRONCOS

The Complete Illustrated History

Jim Saccomano

Foreword by John Elway

MVP
BOOKS

First published in 2009 by MVP Books, an imprint of MBI Publishing Company, 400 First Avenue N., Suite 400, Minneapolis, MN 55401 USA

This updated edition published 2013.

MVP Books are also available at discounts in bulk quantity for industrial or sales-promotional use. For details write to Special Sales Manager at MBI Publishing Company, 400 First Avenue N., Suite 400, Minneapolis, MN 55401 USA.

To find out more about our books, visit us online at www.mvpbooks.com.

ISBN-13: 978-0-7603-4533-7

Library of Congress Cataloging-in-Publication Data

Saccomano, Jim, 1948–
Denver Broncos: the complete illustrated history/Jim Saccomano; foreword by John Elway.
    p. cm.
    Includes index.
    ISBN 978-0-7603-3476-8
      (hardbound with jacket)
    1. Denver Broncos (Football team)—History. 2. Denver Broncos (Football team)—
      History—Pictorial works. I. Title.
    GV956.D37S22 2009
    796.332'640978883—dc22

                                        2009002424

Editor: Leah Noel
Design manager: James Kegley
Designer: Greg Nettles

All cover photos are courtesy of the Denver Broncos, except John Elway circa 1985 (center), photo by Focus on Sport/Getty Images.

Printed in China

For my wife Jo Ann, my children Jennifer and Jeffrey, and my grandchildren Lucas and Rhea.

You light up my life.

CONTENTS

FOREWORD
BY JOHN ELWAY

When you are a young kid playing football with your friends—whether in the backyard, on the playground, or in Pop Warner and high school games—you can't help but fantasize about scoring the winning touchdown or throwing the big pass as time expires. That's part of the fun of playing games.

I was fortunate to develop my skills with great leadership from my father and my coaches along the way, so I was able to look forward to a college career and play the game of "what if" about colleges. And then again, with the kind of success I was able to have at the collegiate level, I started to wonder where I might play my professional career.

But in all these dreams and speculation, I never imagined that I would be fortunate enough to play a career as

Elation and satisfaction: John Elway holds the Vince Lombardi Trophy in the locker room during the postgame celebration for his first Super Bowl win in 1997.

long as 16 years and with just one team. That just is not the way it usually works in professional sports—it usually only works out that way in fantasies and fairy tales.

On top of that, I was as lucky as any player could be to have done this in one of America's great football cities and before fans who truly are the best in the National Football League.

In fact, in a lot of ways the fans in Denver remind me more of a college fan base than a pro one. The fans are passionate, so much so that the team has been sold out entirely for 44 years. It is much more common to find that kind of relationship on a college campus, with the extensive alumni base and the core community support of a smaller city.

That support was one of the first things I noticed in Denver, and it took me a few years to get used to it—especially as the so-called star player on the Broncos. When you play for the Broncos, you learn that you are kind of living in a fishbowl. The interest in the team is so great that your every move is followed by the fans and analyzed by the media. After I adjusted to it, I knew it was all a natural result of the incredible love that the entire Rocky Mountain region feels for the team.

Really, the Broncos are like a religion to a lot of our fans. This is a humbling thing to consider; and, for me, it just made me want to play even harder—if that was even possible.

Mile High Stadium was always sold out, and the excitement level was always palpable. Most fans know that I was able to engineer quite a number of fourth-quarter comebacks, but fans might not realize how big a role they played in those comebacks. No matter what the score was, no matter how late in the game it got, I always knew we had a chance and I always knew the fans would be there for us.

On more than one occasion, friends from the other team mentioned postgame that it was so loud they could not hear their signals, and that it was apparent we were going to come back, even before that final drive.

When I came to Denver, I did not know a lot about Bronco history, but I quickly learned about the tough times of the franchise's early years and about the great players who had such huge roles in the growth of the Broncos.

A few years ago, a poll was taken in which Pat Bowlen was named the best owner in the NFL. As someone who played most of my career for him, I agree completely. When he lifted that Vince Lombardi trophy after Super Bowl XXXII and said, "This one's for John," it was one of the greatest feelings in my life. But when I held the trophy on that stand and looked out at the sea of cheering fans in San Diego, I also knew that it was not just for me but for every fan who ever cheered or cried for the Broncos.

We all reached that pinnacle together, as part of one of the greatest organizations in NFL history. I was honored to have played for such a great organization and a passionate leader such as Mr. Bowlen and before fans who truly are uncompromising in their love and devotion to the Broncos. The city and the team are very fortunate to have him as the Broncos' owner. He is one of the most respected owners in the NFL, and I know I can speak for every player in saying that we all have great respect and affection for him.

The happiness experienced in winning the Super Bowl, and then doing it back to back, was a surreal, out-of-body experience.

But before that moment and after it, win or lose, the Broncos go on as the heart of the city and state. I have a lot of friends who are former players, of course, and many of them do not have the close feeling of kinship that Bronco players have for each other. There is great truth to the saying, "Once a Bronco, always a Bronco."

It is just as exciting for me to be in my new role running the Broncos' football operations now, as the Broncos have always been such an integral part of life for me and my entire family. This is truly one of the classic franchises in NFL history.

With the exciting new path that we all are taking together, this seems like a perfect time for the second edition of this book, a chronicle in words and pictures of the team's complete history.

One of the first administrators I met upon coming to Denver was Jim Saccomano. Jim and I worked together for my entire career, and it seems to me that he is the perfect person to detail the Broncos' history. He, too, is forever Bronco, and is the perfect choice as team historian for the walk down memory lane presented in these pages.

When I was inducted into the Pro Football Hall of Fame, I chose my daughter Jessica to make the presentation. Ultimately, it is all about family, and no one loves us

like our own family members. That's what the Broncos are to me, too. We are a family, including past and present players and the fans. There is no team without the fans who love it. I hope each one of them enjoys this tribute to the Broncos' first 55 years.

Quarterback John Elway was the heart and soul of the Broncos from 1983 to 1999. He led the Broncos to five Super Bowls, finally winning back-to-back titles in 1998 and 1999. He earned the Most Valuable Player (MVP) award for his performance in Super Bowl XXXIII, a 34-19 victory over the Atlanta Falcons. He holds several Bronco records and also is a leader in many NFL record categories, including game-winning or game-saving drives (47). As a result of his stellar career, Elway earned induction into the Pro Football Hall of Fame in 2004. Not only did he become a member of the Broncos' Ring of Fame the fall after he announced his retirement, but his classic No. 7 jersey was immediately retired by the team as well. In January of 2011, Elway joined the Broncos' front office as executive vice president of football operations.

A two-time Super Bowl champion, Elway became a first-ballot selection to the Pro Football Hall of Fame in 2004.

To help prevent child abuse and provide support for child-abuse victims, please contact The Elway Foundation, founded by John Elway in 1987. Over the past 20-plus years, it has been one of the Denver area's most prominent charities, hosting a popular annual golf tournament that raises thousands of dollars for its efforts. To make a donation of your own, or for more information, contact:

The Elway Foundation
6842 S. Netherland Way
Aurora, CO 80016

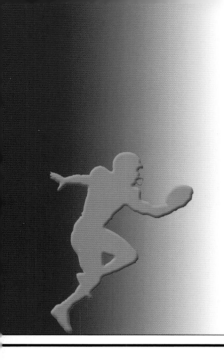

INTRODUCTION

Fans in the south stands of Mile High Stadium cheer on the Broncos. The south stands fans at Mile High were always uniquely passionate and vocal in their support of the Broncos and in their verbal—and sometimes nonverbal—assaults on the other team.

How do you gauge the passion of a city, or more importantly, define its soul? For Denver, the Mile High City, its passion and soul have been defined by the Denver Broncos for the better part of a half century.

From the first nationally televised Monday night game in 1973 through back-to-back world championships and four other Super Bowl appearances, the Broncos arguably have been the face of the Mile High City to those across the country and the globe. For decades, the Broncos have helped transform Denver's image from cow town to major metropolis.

Not only did the Broncos win consecutive Super Bowls at the end of the 1997 and 1998 seasons, but they established all-time pro football records for most wins in two seasons (33), most playoff wins in two seasons (7), and most wins ever in three seasons (46, from 1996 to 1998)—all records that still rank second only to what the New England Patriots have more recently accomplished.

The attachment of Denver's fans to their football team stands out as unusual, even in a city that has a strong affinity for all its teams. "Broncomania" can be judged by a number of factors—the 40 consecutive seasons of sellouts (the last nonsellout being in 1969), the highest overall local television ratings of any NFL city during that time frame, or the impact of Bronco wins and losses on Denver's collective Monday morning psyche.

Denver's love affair for and support of the Broncos certainly helped spawn the eventual arrival of other professional teams in the Mile High City—the Nuggets in the late 1960s and the Rockies and the Avalanche in the 1990s.

When the Broncos became a charter member of the AFL in the 1960s, they were arguably America's first truly regional sports franchise. Since American team sports began with professional baseball in the nineteenth

century, franchises were primarily located in major metropolitan areas, with the heaviest congestion of teams in the East, followed by the Midwest. The Rocky Mountain time zone did not have a major league sports franchise until the Broncos came along. While there was nothing notable about the team's play in its first decade, fans in neighboring states joined Coloradans in having a sense of pride for getting a seat at the table, however unstable the chair. Fans in Wyoming, Montana, New Mexico, Utah, Arizona, western Kansas, and Nebraska finally felt like they were a part of pro sports.

No team ever had a less auspicious beginning. Very few that started life like this one ever reached the heights that the Denver Broncos have scaled, as they became one of the most respected franchises in the most popular sports league in history. Every major public opinion poll taken from the late 1960s to the present has cited pro football as the nation's most popular team sport. The rise of the Broncos has mirrored the sports' popularity, to the point that "all things Broncos" is often referred to as the state religion.

The Denver Broncos played their first winning season in 1973, which was also the year of their first nationally televised game. By 1977, a defense composed of five Pro Bowl players known collectively as the "Orange Crush" propelled the team to its first Super Bowl, validating the faith of the Broncos' loyal and long-suffering fans.

In 1983, legendary quarterback John Elway, the first player taken in that year's NFL draft, joined the team in a blockbuster and controversial trade. With him behind center during the 1980s, the Denver Broncos became the only American Football Conference club to

Don Stone rushes for yardage behind guard Bob McCullough in a 1962 game against the Dallas Texans. The Texans won the AFL title in 1962 before relocating to Kansas City as the Chiefs for the 1963 season.

9

Running back Terrell Davis gives the Mile High salute in the end zone after scoring a touchdown against the Raiders. The Mile High salute became a common celebration for the running backs during the 1990s championship years, and no one did it more often than the magnificent Davis. He was Super Bowl MVP in 1997 and the NFL regular-season MVP in 1998.

appear in three Super Bowls—after the 1986, 1987, and 1989 seasons.

Including the Super Bowl triumphs that the 1990s brought to Denver, the Broncos have won 10 AFC West Division titles, made eight AFC Championship Game appearances, and played in Super Bowls XII, XXI, XXII, XXIV, XXXII, and XXXIII. The team has made a number of other playoff appearances that did not result in titles.

Now an internationally popular team, the Denver Broncos have represented the NFL, the city, and the region in seven American Bowl games since 1987—playing in London, Berlin, Barcelona, Mexico City, Sydney, and twice in Tokyo. However, the Broncos did not start off as being "internationally popular." One could easily argue that the team was not only unpopular in Denver but also completely unknown outside Colorado before nationally televised games brought Rocky Mountain vistas into homes across the country.

This book is about the team's growth from there to here, following the first 55 years of Denver's first, most beloved, and most dominant sports franchise. Decade by decade, this book also looks at those special characters and moments that have made being a Bronco fan so great.

Finally triumphant: Broncos team members hold the Super Bowl trophy after defeating the Packers in Super Bowl XXXII.

ACKNOWLEDGMENTS

I wish to thank a number of individuals for their assistance in the writing and compiling of this book.

Special thanks go out to Denver Broncos owner Pat Bowlen and to President Joe Ellis for their support and cooperation throughout the process, including their willingness to make the entire team historical photo file available for use.

Thanks as well to Rebecca Villanueva for her extensive work in selecting and organizing photos and to Erich Schubert for his editorial assistance in the process.

Many of the pictures were taken by longtime team photographer and friend Eric Bakke, and thanks to Ryan McKee of Clarkson and Associates for his rapid assistance in providing photography whenever asked.

In addition, thanks to my editor, Leah Noel, who took the manuscript and made it better every step of the way.

Thanks to friend, former Bronco, and fellow author Reggie Rivers for the germination that he gave to the entire project.

Thanks also to my mom and dad, who gave me every opportunity to grow. Dad would be very proud.

And lastly, but always first in everything to me, to my wife, Jo Ann, who listened to every idea and always gave me her patience and support.

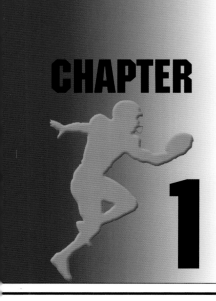

CHAPTER

1

THE 1960S
FROM RAGS TO . . . MORE RAGS

A NEW LEAGUE IS BORN

The Broncos have always played in Denver, but they were born in a Chicago hotel, conceived in a phone call from Dallas to Denver, and came about as the result of a failed effort to create another professional baseball league.

Lamar Hunt, son of a wealthy Texas oil and business family, had long campaigned to get an expansion team in the National Football League for his native Dallas, but he was repeatedly rebuffed by the nation's only pro football league.

Meanwhile, in 1958, the Brooklyn Dodgers and the New York Giants both made moves to the West Coast—to Los Angeles and San Francisco, respectively—leaving no National League baseball team in New York City. This development prompted an idea to create a third major league, the Continental Baseball League, with teams in big American cities that did not have major league baseball, along with a second team in New York.

Denver was to be one of the expansion cities in the Continental League, prompting Denver Bears owner

An early game at Bears Stadium in Denver, with a look at the Broncos' first uniforms, which featured the color combination of seal brown and gold. As was generally the case in the early years, more seats were empty than occupied, with the first season's total attendance just 91,333. That dismal total dropped to 74,508 for the second year, hardly a harbinger of what was to come.

Bob Howsam to build an 8,100-seat addition to the Bears' minor league baseball stadium.

Major League Baseball, concerned about the competition of another baseball league, acted quickly to expand. It returned National League baseball to New York with the creation of the Mets and also brought teams to Houston and Minneapolis, in addition to a second team in Los Angeles. This move scuttled the new baseball league and left Howsam with an 8,100-seat addition to his minor league baseball park.

Meanwhile, in Dallas, Hunt had become increasingly impatient over his rejections by the NFL old guard, notably Chicago Bears owner and NFL founding father George Halas. The scion of the wealthy Texas family decided to take matters into his own hands by founding a second pro football league. He was looking for franchises in major American cities, and Howsam was looking for another creative use for his ballpark.

Hunt and Howsam began to discuss the possibility of Denver joining Hunt's prospective new league, and on August 14, 1959, the first American Football League organizational meeting was held in Chicago. Denver, with Bob Howsam as its principal owner, was named as a charter member along with New York, Dallas, Los Angeles, Minneapolis, and Houston.

Ultimately, the NFL rapidly responded to the creation of the new league with expansion into both Dallas (in 1960) and Minneapolis (for the following season). Hunt's

Texas franchise stayed on course, but the AFL franchise plans for Minnesota were dropped. Oakland took the place of the Minneapolis team, so the original eight of the AFL were Boston, Buffalo, Dallas, Denver, Houston, Los Angeles, New York, and Oakland.

Critics dubbed the eight owners of this enterprise "The Foolish Club." Yet undeterred by the chancy nature of this expansion project, the owners sped forward and found a perfect partner for growing interest in the league: television.

While gate receipts proved to be extremely low for the Broncos and the other AFL teams in the first decade of play, the American Broadcasting Company (ABC) signed an equal five-year contract with the eight teams. As part of the pact, ABC, the only network not televising pro football at this time, would televise every road game back to the home market, while protecting the local gate by blacking out games in the home city.

At that time the NFL and its television partners, NBC and CBS, frowned on road games being televised back to a team's home city, but the AFL-ABC policy was perfect for the fledgling teams. It gave them the kind of exposure they so badly needed.

On November 22, 1959, the AFL's first player selection draft was held in 32 rounds. In that draft, the league made an attempt to keep the playing field in its favor regarding negotiations with new players and thus only announced the selections alphabetically by team. In future years, the

Another angle of venerable Bears Stadium, which was completed in 1948 for minor league baseball. It eventually was remodeled, expanded, given to the city, and re-christened Mile High Stadium.

Broncos team founder Bob Howsam (right) is shown here with quarterback Frank Tripucka upon being honored in a 2002 ceremony at INVESCO Field at Mile High. *Photo courtesy of the Rocky Mountain News*

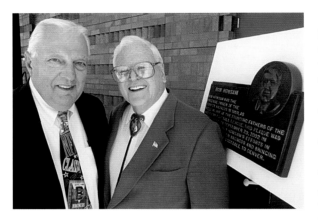

With the birth and christening completed, the team began to form. Griffing had been an executive with the Canadian Football League (CFL), and he looked north for the Broncos' first head coach, bringing fellow CFL veteran Frank Filchock to Denver.

Continuing the theme of calling on reliable old friends, Griffing and Filchock talked former CFL quarterback Frank Tripucka into joining the Denver staff. This move was expected to be the beginning of his coaching career.

At the end of January, the AFL set the Broncos' venue for competition, placing the team in the western division along with the Dallas Texans (later the Kansas City Chiefs), the Oakland Raiders, and the Los Angeles Chargers (who moved to San Diego in 1961). Few at the time could have imagined the four clubs would continue to be in the same division, still fierce rivals, a half century later.

public relations value of high draft choices proved critical both in terms of fan interest and showing top players how desirable they were.

The league was moving so fast that the draft was held before the Broncos even had a general manager. Dean Griffing was not named to that post until December 1.

Denver's very first pick was Roger LeClerc, a center and placekicker from Trinity College in Connecticut. The Broncos were woefully short on cash and couldn't sign LeClerc, who went to play for the NFL's Chicago Bears. In fact, Denver was not able to sign a No. 1 draft choice for its first seven years of existence.

The first order of business as 1960 began was one that truly could not be delayed. The team needed a name.

A contest was held in January of the team's first full year, and the name Denver Broncos was chosen from 500 entries. The moniker was suggested by Ward M. Vining of Lakewood, a Denver suburb. Of interest is the fact that this football team is not the first edition of the Denver Broncos. Albeit less famous, Denver's 1921 Midwest Baseball League entry was called the Broncos.

THE BRONCOS BECOME REALITY

The first training camp opened at the Colorado School of Mines in Golden in July, and it was apparent by then that in a league many would describe as ragtag, the Denver Broncos were the poster children.

Financial backing was subpar, and ticket sales were low. The team had no facilities to speak of, with the Broncos' first headquarters being a Quonset hut on Clay Street near Bears Stadium. An architectural relic, the building still stands, a memory of the World War II era in which it was built and of the first home that Denver's pro football team ever had.

The Broncos played that first season with no playbook of note, and players often have referenced drawing up plays in the dirt, like kids on a playground.

The roster and league attracted a perfect storm of has-beens, wannabes, and never weres. Also among the candidates were some older players who had enjoyed

An original Denver Broncos versus Dallas Texans ticket from October 30, 1960. Note the 1960 Broncos logo on the ticket. The $4.50 ticket price for a sideline seat would be very popular today.

COLORFUL CHARACTERS MARKED EARLY ROSTERS

Every startup league in history has faced the challenge of acquiring lots of players quickly. The American Football League (AFL) was no exception, and with the Broncos as the runt of the AFL litter, Denver's entry into pro football was marked by a colorful assortment of players and hopefuls with some unique backgrounds.

The inaugural 1960 team featured pro football's first black placekicker, Gene Mingo, whose entry in the category of "college" was "no college." Before coming to Denver, he played football in the U.S. Navy—he made the team based on a tryout—and went on to complete an outstanding career that spanned more than a decade. In 1960, he was a do-everything running back and kicker who scored often for the inaugural Broncos.

Another member of the 1960 team was Al Carmichael, who first was a fine halfback in the National Football League (NFL) and the Canadian Football League (CFL). His career wound down in Denver. In the first game in Bronco franchise history, Carmichael and Mingo scored two touchdowns to give Denver a win against Boston. One of the most interesting things about the tough and athletic Carmichael was his offseason occupation—Hollywood stuntman. Later in the 1960s, Al's brother, Paul, played briefly for the Broncos.

That first team also featured the Broncos' first brother combination, with the talented All-AFL tackle Eldon Danenhauer joined by his lesser-known (and lesser-skilled) brother, Bill.

From 1961 to 1963, Denver's roster featured the fabled Ed "Wahoo" McDaniel, a linebacker whose heritage was Native American, hence the nickname. His offseason job turned into a full-time career following his football days—Wahoo was well known on America's pro wrestling circuit.

In 1962, halfback Johnny Olszewski played the last of his 10 pro seasons with the Broncos, and he was known in the Mile High City as "Johnny O." That nickname gave him his uniform number; he remains the only player in Broncos history to wear a No. 0 jersey.

Hardy Brown played for the Broncos in 1960, following stints with Brooklyn and the Chicago Americans in the All-American Football Conference. He made NFL stops in Washington, Baltimore, San Francisco, and Chicago (with the Cardinals). He earned his nickname "Thumper" because many regarded him as the dirtiest player in pro football history. Brown learned his football in an orphanage, the Masonic Home School in Fort Worth, where the players came up with a tackling style that featured hurtling a shoulder into the other player's chest—or chin, if he could reach it. Brown added his own special touch by having a ribbon of steel attached to his shoulder pads, making his tackles memorable.

One of the Broncos' true early stars from 1960 to 1963 was defensive tackle Bud McFadin, an All-American from Texas who came to Denver after a

fine NFL career. McFadin made the ADFL all-star team in 1961, 1962, and 1963. However, in those early years, Denver was always looking for a quarterback, and in 1964 the desperate Broncos traded the stellar McFadin to Houston for the two-year use of Jacky Lee, with one of the terms being that Lee would return to the Oilers after his two-year stay in Denver. Thus one of Denver's early all-stars was dispatched for a quarterback who did not distinguish himself in any way during his Bronco stint, save for being given the nickname of "Lend Lease Lee."

A tough Texan, Bud McFadin was a shining light on the woeful defenses that the Broncos had in their formative years. McFadin was named All-AFL each year from 1960 to 1963.

FRANK TRIPUCKA

QUARTERBACK

1960–1963

Frank Tripucka joined the Denver Broncos as a potential coach in 1960 but was almost immediately called back into service as a quarterback and passed his way into a Ring of Fame selection in 1986.

One of the original Broncos, Tripucka led the team to its first .500 season in 1962 (7-7). He represented half of the Frank Tripucka–to–Lionel Taylor passing combination. The duo went on to set various records together and join the Ring of Fame.

Tripucka, who joins John Elway and Floyd Little as one of three Broncos whose jersey number is retired, recorded his best statistical season in 1960 when he completed 248 of 478 passes (51.9 percent) for 3,038 yards with 24 touchdowns. His 3,038 passing yards led the AFL that year, while his 24 touchdown passes tied for the second-highest total in the league.

He was selected to play in the AFL All-Star Game following the 1962 season. That year, he threw for 2,917 yards to lead Denver to a 7-7 record and a second-place finish in the AFL West. Tripucka's 7,645 passing yards and 51 touchdown passes from 1960 to 1962 marked the second-highest totals in the AFL during those three seasons.

After a half century of Bronco history, Tripucka still ranks fifth in team career passing yards (7,676), attempts (1,277), and completions (662) while standing sixth in touchdown passes (51). He shares the team record for most touchdown passes (5) in a game (an October 28, 1962, matchup versus Buffalo).

His 447 passing yards against Buffalo in a September 15, 1962, game stood as the Broncos' single-game record until 2000 and remains third in club annals.

A former star at Notre Dame, Tripucka joined the Broncos after playing for Detroit (1949), the Chicago Cardinals (1950–1952), and the Dallas Texans (1952).

Tripucka's Denver Broncos Record

Games	Starts	Att.	Comp.	Yards	Pct.	TD	INT	LG	Rtg.
44	42	1,277	662	7,676	51.8	51	85	96t	55.9

Tripucka's NFL Career Record

Games	Starts	Att.	Comp.	Yards	Pct.	TD	INT	LG	Rtg.
75	N/A	1,745	879	10,282	50.4	69	124	96t	52.2

good pro careers and were interested in squeezing out a few more paychecks and taking on one final challenge.

The first set of uniforms, worn for the 1960 and 1961 seasons, was purchased in used condition from a defunct college bowl game, the Copper Bowl, of which no records exist today. The colors were listed in an early media guide as seal brown and light gold (which looked like mustard). The home jerseys were gold, the road jerseys white. Both had brown numerals. The pants were seal brown, home and away, with a brown helmet.

However, the feature that sealed the deal in making the uniform a laughingstock was the socks—brown and gold at home, brown and white on the road, and the only sock in pro football history that was vertically striped like a barber's pole. So unique and shocking were the socks that a pair is on display today at the Pro Football Hall of Fame, somewhat akin to a football version of Ripley's Believe It or Not!

Frank Tripucka's coaching career took one of the strangest turns ever during the team's intrasquad game in Golden. So poor was the passing of the team's young quarterbacks that Coach Filchock implored the old vet to put on a uniform and go in just to give the fans their money's worth.

Tripucka never did coach after that, instead becoming the Broncos' quarterback for the first three-plus years of the team's existence. A star at Notre Dame and a veteran of the NFL and the CFL, Tripucka had strong passing skills—virtually the only factor that kept the Broncos in games during their inaugural season.

All the players were housed together, barracks style, at that first training camp; meals were poor, and weight training was nonexistent. The Broncos played their first preseason schedule just like they trained, losing all five preseason games in 1960 and being outscored 192-53.

When training camp ended, the Broncos began to practice on their regular practice field, which was located on a hillside adjacent to Bears Stadium. Many times, players had to jaunt down the hill to retrieve an errant ball.

The Broncos had high hopes, but everything else was as low as it could get.

Then, remarkably, the Broncos became the first AFL team to win a game. This historic moment was partially due to the schedule makers, who put Denver in the league's very first matchup on Friday, September 9, 1960. The Broncos traveled to Boston where they defeated the Patriots 13-10 before an announced attendance of 21,597 at Boston University Field.

Denver won its second game to go 2-0 and eventually upped its first-year record to 4-2. Then the wheels fell off. Denver did not muster a single win in the final eight games of the season and would not reach the .500 mark in all-time games by the franchise for 36 years.

The first game hosted by Denver was on October 2 against the Oakland Raiders, which led to a 31-14 Bronco win in Bears Stadium before 18,372 attendees. (Bears Stadium holds 36,000.) Tripucka started for Denver, of course, and the Raiders' starting quarterback was Tom Flores, who went on to coach the Raiders to two world championships in the future.

With the season already underway, the Broncos signed NFL castoff Lionel Taylor, who was cut as a linebacker candidate by Chicago. Moving to the wide receiver position, he combined with Tripucka to give the Bronco fans a pass-and-catch show that was the weekly highlight,

Above: Frank Tripucka and wide receiver Lionel Taylor, together one of the AFL's most prolific pass-catch combos. With Tripucka slinging the ball, Taylor caught 92 passes in the inaugural season and then raised the standard to a then-record 100 receptions in 1961. Both men are in the Broncos' Ring of Fame.

Above left: A portrait of quarterback Frank Tripucka, who generously came out of retirement during the first training camp to provide the Broncos' first true leadership and skill at the quarterback position.

Frank Tripucka hands off Gene Mingo. This duo provided some bright spots in the Broncos' first decade. Mingo led the AFL in scoring in 1960 and 1962, and Tripucka bravely soldiered on as the team's first quarterback despite woeful pass protection, throwing 51 touchdown passes in the first four years.

and often the only highlight, of Denver football in 1960. Taylor had a pro record of 92 receptions that first year, as the AFL was a pass-happy league heavy on offense. The Broncos, in particular, had to make up for massive defensive weaknesses by throwing the ball.

Denver also had the first African-American placekicker in pro football in Gene Mingo, who scored the winning touchdown on a punt return in the AFL's inaugural game. He went on to play with the Broncos through 1964.

Overall, the highlights were individual rather than those of team success. By far the most interesting game in that grim 4-9-1 campaign was the tie, a 38-38 matchup played in a driving snowstorm before just 7,785 people on November 27. The Broncos trailed 31-7 at the half, and virtually all the fans departed due to the inclement weather. Then Denver staged a stirring fourth-quarter rally, coming back from a 24-point gap for the tie. The

next day, the *Denver Post* ran a memorable photograph showing two fans—two fans, total—huddled together in the south stands, a far cry from the 8,000-person seating capacity of that section of the park.

At season's end, wide receiver Lionel Taylor, defensive tackle Bud McFadin, and safety Goose Gonsoulin all were named to the first official all-AFL team. Denver had no game sellouts and sold just 2,675 season tickets, never playing before a home crowd bigger than 20,000.

No tale of the 1960 Broncos is complete without recounting an early season moment that illustrated the extremely stingy nature of the organization. As hard as it is to imagine, Griffing—known to all as a notorious tightwad, even in the most flush of circumstances—left his press box vantage point and went down into the north end-zone stands to wrestle a fan for a ball that had been kicked into the seats on an extra point. Griffing came

The first trade in team history brought Austin "Goose" Gonsoulin to Denver. After playing seven excellent years at safety and intercepting 43 passes, he earned Ring of Fame status.

AUSTIN "GOOSE" GONSOULIN

SAFETY
1960–1966

Austin "Goose" Gonsoulin was one of the four original Ring of Fame inductees in 1984, recognized for his splendid play at the safety position for the first seven seasons of Bronco history. The first player acquired by Denver in a trade, Gonsoulin was one of the original Broncos from the 1960 season and was one of three originals still with the team at the start of 1966, his final year with the club. In those days, the Broncos did not have much on defense, but "Goose" was regarded by opponents as one of the best defensive backs in the pass-happy AFL.

At the end of his Bronco career, he was the all-time AFL leader in interceptions with 43, a statistic that still ranks second in club history. His 11 pickoffs in 1960 (his rookie season) are also a Denver record. He shares the team and NFL record for interceptions in a game with four, a feat he accomplished against Buffalo on September 18, 1960. He also had three interceptions in a game against Kansas City on October 11, 1964.

A Texas native, Gonsoulin led the Broncos in interceptions four times in his career, including in consecutive seasons (1962 and 1963). He still ranks fifth in club history with 542 career interception return yards.

He was an All-AFL choice in 1960, 1962, and 1963 while also being named to the AFL All-Star Game from 1961 to 1964 and in 1966. His amazing durability and toughness enabled him to start 61 consecutive games at one point in his career. Gonsoulin played one season with San Francisco in 1967 after his Broncos career was over. Before joining the Broncos, he was captain of his college team at Baylor University.

Gonsoulin's Denver Broncos Record

Games	Starts	Sacks	Int.	Yds.	Avg.	TD
94	N/A	1.0	43	542	12.6	2

Gonsoulin's NFL Career Record

Games	Starts	Sacks	Int.	Yds.	Avg.	TD
108	N/A	N/A	46	551	12.0	2

away with the ball but did so in full view of the fans and the press corps. Not surprisingly, he was bombarded by boos and bad press, and at a subsequent game he had to make both a ball and ticket presentation to the victim of his tussle. Certainly, this was one of the most embarrassing moments in franchise history.

GROWING PAINS CONTINUE

If the first season was bad, the second season was even worse. With little fan attendance came little revenue, and in May 1961 Bob and Lee Howsam, the original principal owners of the team, sold their stock to a new syndicate headed by local businessmen Cal Kunz and Gerry Phipps. Kunz was named president and operating head of Rocky Mountain Empire Sports.

The group comprised 14 prominent Denver citizens who often offered their financial support to projects deemed good for the city's growth, which is how they saw the young football team. In a few years, most of them would tire of this investment, but one would save the team and play a major factor in the development of Denver as a professional sports city.

Denver plummeted to a 3-11 record in 1961, and the home attendance went from bad to worse. Not a single crowd was larger than the paltry 14,500 that showed up to watch the Dallas Texans dispatch the Broncos by a relatively respectable 19-12 margin on October 8.

Lionel Taylor caught 100 passes this year, becoming the first pro football receiver to crack the century mark. He joined Bud McFadin in being named to the all-AFL team for a second consecutive season.

A portrait of president and former Broncos owner Allan R. Phipps, chairman of the board Gerald H. Phipps (also former owner), and Broncos general manager Fred Gehrke.

The early Broncos had their share of one-year wonders. Al Frazier accounted for 1,644 all-purpose yards and scored nine touchdowns in his 1961 rookie campaign, but he was out of pro football entirely, partially due to injury, just two years later.

Frank Filchock was released as the Broncos head coach as soon as the season ended. His next head coaching job was for St. Joseph High School in the prep Denver Parochial League.

Most of the Broncos' first decade saw the team sharing not just a minor league baseball park, but also the employees of the minor league Bears, in both public relations and ticket operations. The concept of a marketing department was more than two decades in the future. A portion of training camp at the Colorado School of Mines conflicted with the baseball season, so the PR people would be in Golden for practice and interview sessions. Then they would make a late-afternoon drive to Bears Stadium to handle the baseball game.

In fact, no consideration was even made for a separate pricing structure for the baseball and football tickets in those early years, in part because there was common ownership of the two clubs. Thus, the Broncos tickets were the same price as that of the minor league baseball team in town.

Nevertheless, it was apparent to the ownership that the team lagged badly behind its peers and needed a

Jack Faulkner was named AFL Coach of the Year in 1962 after leading the Broncos to a 7-7 record. Faulkner gave the team its first playbook and pushed for the uniform color change to orange and blue, burning the gold and seal brown uniforms at a public bonfire as part of the team's scrimmage-ending training camp.

new direction. New head coach Jack Faulkner was hired February 1, 1962. He saw the chaos and quickly realized that his direction and Dean Griffing's were not the same. Griffing was released as Broncos general manager as summer began, and Faulkner was named to a dual post as head coach and general manager.

This move would be the Broncos' first measure of stability, however fleeting. Faulkner put the team's first playbook into use and then made one of the most dramatic changes in franchise history.

OUT WITH THE STRIPES, IN WITH THE ORANGE

One look at the uniforms was one too many, so much so that Faulkner ordered a public burning ceremony of the Broncos' notorious vertically striped socks at the August intrasquad game.

Before that, a small committee of club employees had watched a private uniform fashion show and decided the franchise should have its own identity, rather than the standard versions of red and blue common in the game. Orange was selected as the Broncos' primary color, giving the club a fresh, new look for 1962 and beyond.

Like a lot of early Broncos, halfback Frank Bernardi played at the University of Colorado, where he teamed with fellow running back Carroll Hardy in a combo that earned national attention. This picture is a good example of the "huck and buck" promotional photo style of the era.

Hardy Brown closed out his legendary career in Denver. Depending on the generosity of whoever was describing him, Brown was known as either the toughest or dirtiest player in pro football.

Due to baseball stadium conflicts, Denver couldn't play preseason games at home to try to stimulate local interest in the upcoming season. So the Broncos ended 1962 exhibition play with a streak of 14 consecutive road games over three preseasons, having played in such remote outposts as Rochester, New York; Little Rock, Arkansas; Midland, Texas; Spokane, Washington; Mobile, Alabama; and Stockton, California. Unhappy with having to start every season on the road, Faulkner negotiated a deal for the Broncos to open the 1963 season at the University of Denver Stadium, where they defeated the Chargers on Friday, September 7.

The Broncos charged out of the gate in 1962 and built their record to 7-2 before the league caught up with them. Denver finished 7-7 for the first .500 record in team history. Faulkner was named the AFL coach of the year for his quick rebuilding job, and Gene Mingo set the pro record (at that time) of 27 field goals in a single season.

For the first time, Denver's fans tasted respectability, and it appeared that better times were ahead.

However, the success of 1962 disappeared as fast as it came, and the Broncos got no closer to that first winning season in the team's first decade.

DÉJÀ VU, ALL OVER AGAIN

Denver slumped back into its old ways for a 2-11-1 record in 1963. The seemingly ageless Frank Tripucka called it quits midway through the season. The Broncos lost by scores that included 59-7 (opening night against Kansas City, to which the Dallas franchise had moved that year), 52-21 at Kansas City (allowing 111 points to the Chiefs in two games), and a 58-20 loss at San Diego (to which the Los Angeles Chargers had relocated in 1961). In all, the Broncos allowed 473 points in 14 games.

The one historically significant note from 1963 was a 50-34 win against San Diego at home on October 6. Mingo kicked five field goals in that game. To this day, it is the only contest in franchise history in which the Broncos scored 50 points—an extraordinary oddity, considering the tremendous long-term success to come.

Taylor won his fourth straight AFL receiving title that year, heading toward being the first player ever to catch 500 career passes. Fullback Billy Joe earned AFL rookie-of-the-year honors for his stellar first-year performance.

Unfortunately, the 1963 season, not the previous successful one, proved to be a harbinger of what was to come.

Other AFL teams were beginning to build powerhouses, most notably Kansas City, San Diego, and the Buffalo Bills, but the Broncos were mired in the cellar of an expansion football league. Desperate to make personnel moves that could impact the club, the Broncos completed a historic nine-player trade with the New

Goose Gonsoulin helps a teammate put on his jersey while Gene Mingo prepares in the background in a circa 1962 photo. Pro football locker rooms were small and dingy in the early 1960s, and everyone just had to make do.

Quarterback John McCormick engaged in a back-and-forth battle with Mickey Slaughter for the starting job from 1963 to 1966. McCormick engineered the only 50-point game in Denver history, a 50-34 Bronco win over San Diego in 1963.

Mickey Slaughter was the first Denver quarterback to wear a No. 7 jersey. Given the lack of success those early teams had, no one would have guessed that decades later a starting quarterback wearing that number would take the Broncos to five world championship games.

Lionel Taylor makes a one-handed catch against the Chargers. Not fleet of foot, Taylor still ran great pass patterns and was one of the most sure-handed receivers in pro football during the 1960s. He finished his Denver career with 543 receptions.

York Jets in January 1964. It was the largest ever made in the AFL. Denver sent Gene Prebola, Wahoo McDaniel, Gordy Holz, and Bob Zeman to New York for Dick Guesman, Ed Cooke, Charlie Janerette, Jim Price, and Sid Fournet.

The most notable of these players was McDaniel, whose given name was Ed, but he preferred the nickname "Wahoo" due to his Native American heritage. While with Denver and continuing far after his gridiron career was over, Wahoo worked the professional wrestling circuit, which was, at the time, considered seedy at best.

TEAM MIGHT NOT BE FAST, BUT IT GETS SPEEDIE

The Broncos went 2-11-1 in 1964, and with dust barely gathering on his coach-of-the-year trophy from two years earlier, Faulkner was fired after a 0-4 start.

Popular assistant Mac Speedie—formerly a great receiver with the Cleveland Browns club that won 10 consecutive titles in the 1940s and 1950s—was named interim head coach.

The fired-up Broncos won the first game under Speedie, defeating Lamar Hunt's franchise by a 33-27 margin. However, the talent was not there for Denver, and there would be only one more win in the final nine games of this woeful season.

The best player on the team by far was cornerback Willie Brown, who had nine interceptions and was named to the all-AFL team. Two years later, he would be traded to the Oakland Raiders. Ultimately, he would be recognized as one of the game's greatest defensive backs, earning an induction into the Pro Football Hall of Fame.

In the next two years, the Broncos had a 4-10 record each season, but their terrible performance on the playing

LIONEL TAYLOR
WIDE RECEIVER
1960–1966

An original Bronco, Lionel Taylor also was one of the original Ring of Famers, inducted in 1984. He finished his seven-year Bronco career (1960–1966) as the franchise's all-time leader in receptions (543) and receiving yards (6,872), records he held until 1999, when he was eclipsed first by Shannon Sharpe and most recently by Rod Smith.

In addition, he set a Bronco record for career touchdown receptions with 44, a mark that still ties for fourth highest in team history. Taylor caught 92 passes for 1,235 yards (a 13.4-yard average) with 12 touchdowns in Denver's inaugural 1960 campaign, and his reception total that year stands as the fifth best by a second-year player in NFL history. In addition, Taylor's 12 receiving touchdowns and 1,235 receiving yards that season were Bronco single-season records until 1981 and currently rank fourth and sixth, respectively, in club annals.

Taylor followed his impressive 1960 campaign with 100 receptions (for 1,176 yards) in 1961. That mark stood as the franchise record until 2000 and is now fifth on the single-season chart.

Regarded by many as a guy with the best hands in pro football at the time, Taylor led the AFL in receiving for five of the league's first six years. He never caught fewer than 76 passes in a season over those first six years, averaging 84.7 catches from 1960 to 1965 for the highest six-year total in football history at that time.

A superb route runner, he totaled AFL/NFL bests in receptions (508), while ranking third in receiving yards (6,424) and tying for eighth in touchdown receptions (43) from 1960 to 1965. A three-time All-AFL selection (1960, 1961, 1965) who played in the league all-star game in 1962, Taylor registered four 1,000-yard receiving seasons and 24 100-yard receiving games during his Bronco career. Both of these rank second in the club's record book for their respective categories.

He played collegiately at New Mexico Highlands and entered the NFL with Chicago in 1959. He played linebacker for the Bears for one season before joining the Broncos in 1960. Taylor tried out for the Broncos while the team was on its first East Coast road trip two weeks into the inaugural season. He made his first appearance as a Bronco that week against the New York Titans in the Polo Grounds, and he was an immediate sensation. He caught six passes for 125 yards and snagged a 31-yard touchdown pass from Frank Tripucka in his first game as a wide receiver.

He finished his brilliant professional career playing two seasons with Houston from 1967 to 1968.

Taylor's Denver Broncos Record

Games	Starts	Rec.	Yds.	Avg.	LG	TD
96	N/A	543	6,872	12.7	80t	44

Taylor's NFL Career Record

Games	Starts	Rec.	Yds.	Avg.	LG	TD
121	N/A	567	7,195	12.7	80t	45

field was insignificant compared to the franchise-altering events that took place in boardrooms from Denver to New York City at the end of the 1964 season.

By then, it was apparent to anyone interested enough to notice—which certainly included the Denver businessmen who had been part of the 1961 investment—that the team was floundering in every way possible. It was a financial disaster with no apparent possibility of success, and the performance of the team itself was dismal.

The ownership group had had enough, and a group of Atlanta businessmen had inquired about purchasing the team and relocating it there. During the first two weeks

of February, the Denver dailies reported what seemed like the Broncos' imminent departure. The football team was finally getting a lot of local attention, but for all the wrong reasons.

A GREAT MAN STEPS FORWARD

Often noble citizens step forward at the absolute worst of times, and Gerald H. (Gerry) Phipps was one of those.

In 1961, one year after professional football arrived in Denver, Phipps became a major owner and assumed duties as chairman of the board of Rocky Mountain Empire Sports, Inc. His involvement in Denver sports

A photo of the first known Broncos cheerleader group, the Broncoettes. Their costumes reflect the styles of the early 1960s for college cheerleaders.

began in 1947 when he became part of the organization that owned baseball's old Western League Denver Bears. Over the next few years, the Bears set minor league attendance records that stood unchallenged for many years.

The son of a Colorado senator who made his fortune in the East before relocating west, Phipps was born in Denver and raised to uphold the ideals of citizenship and responsibility. He volunteered for the navy during World War II, and after serving, he returned to his beloved Denver. There, he formed his own construction company, helping to build the postwar Mile High City.

Gerry Phipps could see the direction of the ownership group. While he understood their desire to drop a soured investment, he was not going to let the Broncos leave on his watch. During a break in the board meetings on February 15, 1965, he excused himself and went to a nearby bank, where he borrowed a million dollars. He returned to the meeting, and along with his brother, Allan R. Phipps, purchased virtually complete ownership of the Denver Broncos and saved the franchise.

Up until that time, the local football team had been the object of local derision, more ignored than taken for granted. But the Phipps brothers' show of commitment, coupled with newfound public awareness that another city somewhere might actually desire this team, completely transformed Denver's attitude about the Broncos.

The Mile High City responded to the Phipps' move with the kind of passion and love that could be described as that toward the return of a prodigal child.

BRONCOMANIA IS BORN

Season-ticket sales for the Broncos totaled 2,675 in 1960, followed by figures of 5,775, 5,042, 7,624, and 8,002 in the following four campaigns.

On March 5, 1965, the Broncos had a record sale of 941 season tickets in one day. By April 1, they reached the season-ticket sales drive goal of 20,000, amazing for a team that to date had been completely woeful on the field. The only thing that had changed was how the city viewed the Broncos. The entire city now knew that Gerry Phipps had saved the Broncos, a franchise desired by other cities. For the first time, the Broncos were valued and appreciated by locals, and the seeds were being sown for what would eventually come to be known as Broncomania.

Cookie Gilchrist at the team's Colorado School of Mines training camp in Golden in 1965. One of the most colorful characters and greatest all-around players in history, Gilchrist had two stints with the Broncos. As a fullback, he chose the unusual No. 2 jersey because he was obtained in a trade for Billy Joe, who wore No. 3 with Denver. Of course, Cookie wanted to be one digit lower. He wore the more traditional No. 30 in his 1967 encore with the team.

The season ticket sales figure reached 22,000 by May 1, and later that month Allan Phipps was named president of Rocky Mountain Empire Sports, Inc. Gerry Phipps was renamed chairman of the board.

Not much changed on the field, however. But in a December 12 loss to the Boston Patriots, Lionel Taylor made the 500th catch of his career, becoming the first AFL player to top this figure. Taylor, tackle Eldon Danenhauer, and fullback Cookie Gilchrist were named to the all-AFL team. Taylor also won his fifth pass receiving crown, and Abner Haynes led the AFL in kickoff returns.

Individual honors were about the only accolades the Broncos could claim in another grim 4-10 campaign. Yet home attendance had skyrocketed, with six of the seven home games drawing more than 30,000 fans to Bears Stadium.

General manager and head coach Lou Saban (right) sells a ticket to a fan in a promotional photo before the watershed 1967 season. Saban was brought in to truly make the Broncos a professional team, and he left no stone unturned in dealing with the public.

Undoubtedly, the most colorful character on that team was Gilchrist, who had come to Denver in a trade for Billy Joe and arrived at training camp in a gold Cadillac. His infectious smile matched his car. But Gilchrist, who had played pro football in Canada right after high school, was a shrewd negotiator who knew that what separated pro football from amateur was money. He had been a tremendous defensive player and placekicker in the CFL prior to playing on championship teams for the Buffalo Bills, but the Bills had tired of his financial demands and thus sent him to the Broncos for Joe.

Gilchrist said that in addition to playing fullback for his new team, he would be happy to play defense and kick as well—but he wanted separate contracts for each. The Broncos declined that offer and used him exclusively at fullback, where he rushed for 954 yards, leading the team.

Meanwhile, the battle for players between the AFL and the established NFL proved to be a financial bloodbath for everybody—except the Broncos, of course. They were essentially incapable of competing in the battle of the highest dollars. Many teams were the victims of high spending and bad judgments in the race for the finest college talent. The Broncos did not succeed in signing very much of that talent pool, so they had by far the least competitive team at that time.

The Broncos were a "have not," but the "haves" had had enough, and secret meetings were taking place between the two leagues. The merger of the National and American Football Leagues was announced on June 8, setting the stage for a period of unimaginable development in American sports history.

On the field, the Broncos' 4-10 mark in 1965 begat a 4-10 mark again in 1966, and Mac Speedie was replaced by assistant Ray Malavasi as head coach by week three.

Five different quarterbacks took snaps for Denver in 1966, including the once-legendary Tobin Rote, who

came out of retirement at what appeared to be many pounds over his announced 211-pound weight. Those five passers combined for an astonishingly bad 41.3 completion percentage, throwing just 12 touchdown passes compared to 30 interceptions.

THE PRO FOOTBALL STONE AGE ENDS IN DENVER

Attendance remained strong, but Gerry Phipps had seen enough. He wanted the tide to turn toward respectability for the Broncos.

Up to this point in franchise history, the Broncos had always hired whoever was available at their price, both in terms of players and coaches. Invariably, the Broncos had been settling for far less than mediocre, while powerhouse teams were being developed in other cities. One of those cities was Buffalo, where the Bills won back-to-back AFL titles in 1964 and 1965 under Lou Saban. He was named

coach of the year both seasons, because he developed one of the most formidable teams in pro football.

Phipps had watched those Buffalo teams play their way to those titles, and he identified Saban, now coaching at the University of Maryland, as the man to guide the Broncos out of their deep morass. After winning the AFL title for the second straight year at Buffalo in 1965, Saban decided to return to college coaching at Maryland. The Phipps brothers persuaded him to return to the AFL by offering unprecedented power and authority, to say nothing of the promise of longevity.

In the most significant hire in Denver sports history to that date, Saban joined the Broncos with a 10-year pact that named him both general manager and head coach, with sweeping powers over the entire organization.

A taskmaster of the highest order, Saban was a man who quickly recognized the two-fold challenge of building a solid organization while winning football games.

Lou Saban coaches players at training camp in 1967. He made it very clear that his style was "my way or the highway," and the young players were attentive to their tough and intimidating leader.

Halfback Floyd Little poses after becoming the first first-round draft pick to sign with the Broncos. Little came to Denver as the first consensus three-time All-American halfback since Doak Walker and quickly earned the moniker "The Franchise."

The winning would come slowly, but the organization changed overnight.

Saban signed his contract on December 19, 1966, and immediately announced that a new era was underway. He was going to build this team into a respectable organization, and he began with the physical building that housed the club.

The Broncos immediately began construction for new suburban executive offices in Adams County, complete with practice fields and locker room facilities for both preseason and regular-season training. The new facility was just 10 minutes from downtown, but light years from where the Broncos had first begun football life.

THE BRONCOS AND "THE FRANCHISE" ARE UNITED

Now that the AFL and NFL were one league, there was a common draft in 1966. As a result, the Broncos were able to sign their No. 1 draft choice, Syracuse All-American Floyd Little, for the first time. The first three-time consensus All-American running back since Doak Walker at Southern Methodist in the 1940s, Little was one in a line of great Syracuse backs to wear No. 44. During his career with the Broncos, he would be a nine-time team captain and become known to the fans as "The Franchise." The Broncos eventually retired his number.

Little signed in May, and in a six-month period the team had signed its first significant coach and its first truly great player, and moved into facilities competitive with those housing other teams.

Saban was relentless in his desire to change the image of the team and build a stable franchise. He cut or traded without remorse veterans who had been less than productive and he had a steady stream of free-agent tryouts.

No detail escaped Saban in his quest to advance the Broncos toward true major league status, and the uni-

form was one more item on the checklist. He decided to stay with the orange jersey but emphasized the secondary color, blue, by changing the helmet color. The Broncos went to the now-traditional blue helmet in 1967. Initially, Saban could not decide on a new logo for the franchise, so the team played that season with solid blue helmets devoid of any markings, save the center striping. In 1968, he settled on the charging horse that identified the Denver Broncos for nearly 30 years.

The brightest spots in the 1967 season came before the regular season even began. For the first time, AFL teams played NFL teams in preseason games, with the Broncos slated to host both the Detroit Lions and Minnesota Vikings at old Denver University Stadium.

The excitement was palpable as the Broncos hosted Detroit. The game meant next to nothing to the veteran Lions, but everything to a franchise that was held in virtually no esteem and trying to take those first evolutionary steps out of the swamp onto dry land.

Overall, the city of Denver had very little in the way of national media attention in the early 1960s—very few national media datelines originated there. Arguably, the greatest amount of press coverage to come from the Mile High City in the entire century had been when President Dwight Eisenhower suffered a heart attack while in Denver for a visit with his wife's family in 1955. Daily reports updated the country on his recovery.

In terms of sports, Denver had the minor league Bears and the Broncos but nothing more. The annual National Western Stock Show and Rodeo was a huge event, but that cemented outsiders' opinions of the Mile High City as a western cow town.

Hence, the significance of the Broncos' games with Detroit and Minnesota—teams from the actual National Football League—was gigantic for a city hungry to grab its place at the pro sports world table.

The Broncos defeated Detroit 13-7 for the AFL's first win over an NFL team, and Lou Saban was carried off

Lou Saban and quarterback Steve Tensi in a 1967 sideline strategy session. Note the helmet, which had no logo or number on either side. Saban remodeled the entire organization upon his arrival in 1967, and the changes included going to a blue helmet. However, he did not settle on a logo for his first Denver campaign, so that remains the only year in Bronco history in which the helmet was plain on both sides.

Saban built his defense first. Here, defensive end Pete Duranko makes a hit on Oakland quarterback Daryle Lamonica as defensive tackle Jerry Inman jumps to block a pass during a November 5, 1967, loss (21-17) to Oakland.

the field on the shoulders of players and fans. For this franchise, it was like winning a championship, and it represented as much.

Just before the Vikings game, Saban acquired quarterback Steve Tensi from San Diego for first-round draft choices in both 1968 and 1969. Tensi had a nondescript career with the Broncos, largely due to injuries sustained by running for his life behind a poor offensive line. But this trade once again signaled that the Broncos were at least initiating the process of competition on the player personnel front.

Three days after the Tensi trade, Denver defeated Minnesota by a 14-3 margin. It was an electric moment, but it masked the reality that Saban would keep 22 rookies on his final regular-season roster, trimming fat and

deadwood at every position in favor of young legs and minds attentive to his demands.

The record, naturally, reflected that, and the 1967 Broncos finished 3-11. Some of the scores that season were atrocious (51-0 at Oakland, 52-9 at Kansas City), as Saban played his youngsters. Yet for the first time, leadership was resolute and focused on future goals, and the fans knew it.

Saban made six trades in 1967 alone, nearly as many as the team had made in its previous seven years of existence. One brought future standout defensive end Richard Jackson to Denver from Oakland. Another acquired the enigmatic Cookie Gilchrist, who had played on Saban's great Buffalo championship teams. Two of the players traded in all this action were the

Defensive end Richard Jackson came to Denver in a trade from Oakland and became one of pro football's most fearsome pass rushers. Here Jackson chases the Raider quarterback during a game in Oakland. Jackson became both a Ring of Famer and an all-pro defensive end, with 43 career sacks.

popular Lionel Taylor and the supremely gifted Willie Brown, who would go on to win a world championship in Oakland.

During the 1967 season, Floyd Little led the AFL in punt returning with a 16.9-yard average, and punter Bob Scarpitto, who got plenty of work, repeated as the league's punting leader with a 44.9-yard norm. The only Bronco All-AFL player was wide receiver Al Denson.

In an ironic twist, one of Saban's many moves brought Denver's first No. 1 draft choice to the team; Roger LeClerc played briefly with the team in 1967, while his career was playing out. On October 8, against Saban's

Marlin Briscoe warms up before a game in 1968. The first African-American quarterback of pro football's modern era, Briscoe was a rookie pressed into service due to teammates' injuries and responded with a fine performance. He passed for 1,589 yards and 14 touchdowns while rushing for 308 yards and three additional scores.

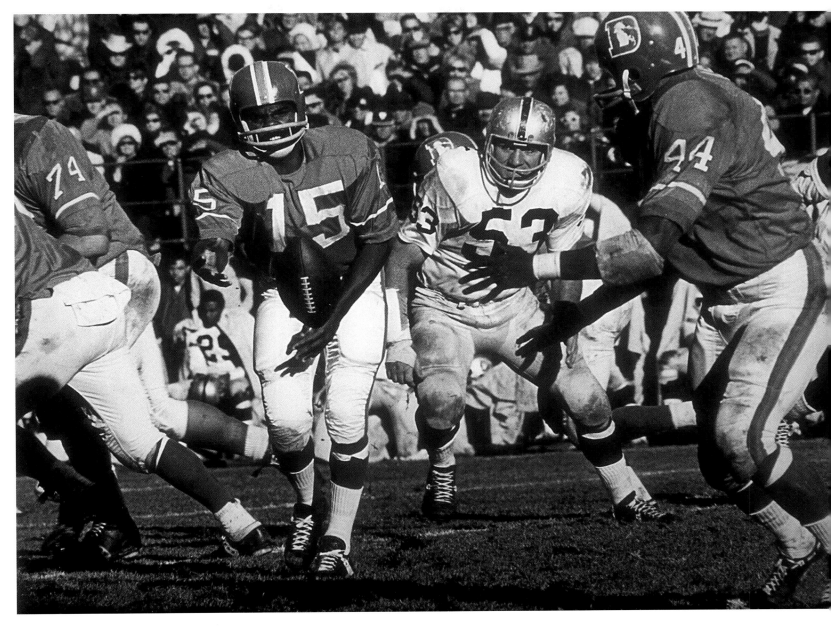

old Buffalo team, Denver lost by a one-point margin, 17-16, as LeClerc missed field goals of 48, 47, 42, and 45 yards. The symbolism was supreme.

DRIVING FOR THE FUTURE OF FOOTBALL IN DENVER

The home attendance at the game versus Buffalo was sold to capacity at 35,188, but that wasn't enough for the Broncos to be competitive in the new world of pro football. As part of the agreement to merge into the NFL, every franchise had to have a stadium that seated at least 50,000 fans by the 1970 season. While Denver's attendance had boomed, Bears Stadium still only seated 35,000.

In March 1967, metropolitan Denver voters turned down a bond issue for a new stadium, but Bronco fans immediately organized a fundraising drive to improve Bears Stadium and keep the Broncos in Denver. Local fans came to the rescue by forming a nonprofit group called the "DOERS" and raised $1.8 million to purchase Bears Stadium from its private owners and present the deed to the city. This fundraising effort included donations from everyone, including housewives and college students. The money was solicited door-to-door and through a telephone campaign that was a precursor to today's telemarketing calls. Dollar by dollar, the money was given to the Phipps brothers, who eventually presented it to the city.

Floyd Little takes a pitchout from Marlin Briscoe and prepares to scamper for some of his 1,825 all-purpose yards in 1968.

RICH JACKSON
DEFENSIVE END
1967–1972

Rich Jackson was also one of the four original Ring of Famers inducted in 1984, recognized for his six outstanding seasons with the Broncos from 1967 to 1972. He was considered by many to be the best defensive end in professional football during his prime. He entered the AFL in 1966 by playing five games with Oakland. Then, he spent the next six seasons in Denver after the Broncos acquired him in a trade.

Known as "Tombstone," Jackson was the first Bronco to be named to the All-NFL first team in 1970. His 43 sacks as a Bronco were the most by any player in club history at the conclusion of his career, and it still ranks ninth. Jackson posted his career high in quarterback sacks in 1969 with 11, and he had 10 sacks in both 1968 and 1970. He was voted All-AFL in 1968 and 1969, and he started in the 1970 Pro Bowl. He made the Pro Bowl again in 1971, despite the fact that he'd played in only seven games due to a knee injury—one that eventually forced him out of football. That season, he was graded by the Broncos' coaches as the team's most efficient tackler, as he made the stop on 97 percent of his opportunities.

Tabbed the Colorado Sports Hall of Fame Pro Athlete of the Year in 1970, Jackson played the first four games of 1972 season with the Broncos before being traded to Cleveland for a 1973 third-round draft choice (Paul Howard, who eventually was a starter on the Broncos' first Super Bowl team).

Jackson played in each of the final 10 games for the Browns in 1972, his final NFL season. In college, he was a standout end at Southern University on both sides of the ball and also was the NAIA shotput champion.

Jackson's Denver Broncos Record

Games	Starts	Sacks	Int.	Yds.	Avg.	TD
67	52	43.0	0	0	0.0	0

Jackson's NFL Career Record

Games	Starts	Sacks	Int.	Yds.	Avg.	TD
82	N/A	43.0	0	0	0.0	0

Pete Duranko (No. 55) closes in on Jets quarterback Joe Namath in a September 21, 1969, Denver upset win, 21-19, over the defending world champions. The Broncos were beginning to build their reputation as a team to be taken seriously.

In February 1968, the civic drive ended successfully, and construction began on a 16,000-seat upper deck that raised seating capacity to 50,000 for the 1968 season. After the expansion, Bears Stadium was renamed Denver Mile High Stadium on December 14, 1968.

The Broncos had officially moved into their new administrative building earlier in the year, and like that original Quonset hut, the Logan Street building still stands today. At the time of this book's publication, the building still featured the original wallpaper in the entry lobby. Actually, it was not wallpaper at all but a series of NFL team posters pieced together in an artistic football patchwork by Fred Gehrke, an art major and halfback during his college days at the University of Utah.

Gehrke joined the Broncos as director of player personnel in 1965 and was one of the very few employees Lou Saban retained. In retrospect, this was a brilliant decision, considering both Gehrke's previous background and the dramatic impact he would have on the franchise in the following decade.

Saban's vision always started with defense and the running game, and the Broncos ended the 1960s fashioning that type of team—a tough, physical group, always fighting to win a low-scoring game.

Denver improved dramatically to a 5-9 record in 1968, and the physical Broncos were beginning to grow into the team Saban wanted. They still lost, but both the defensive line and Little were garnering attention. Dave Costa earned a spot in the AFL all-star game at defensive tackle, as did Rich Jackson. After coming over from Oakland, Jackson moved from playing linebacker to defensive end, coupling natural athleticism with a menacing field presence. His skills quickly marked him as one of the game's best pass rushers, regardless of league.

Little was everything a coach could want: a team captain, a leader, and a self starter who would not let the lack of blocking deter him. He was named an all-star for a glittering performance that included 1,825 all-purpose yards in 1968. Not only did he lead the team in rushing, but he also led the team in both punt returns (261 yards and a 10.9 average) and kickoff returns (649 yards and an excellent 25.0 average). He also led the game in combined yards two years in a row, in 1967 and 1968.

In 1969, Little averaged an even 5 yards a carry and again had more than 1,000 all-purpose yards. He was named to the first team All-AFL along with Jackson, although the team improved just slightly, to a 5-8-1 record.

Nevertheless, respectability was at hand for the Broncos. The 1969 defense gained the addition of rookie Billy Thompson, who started his career as an acclaimed cornerback; he later moved to safety with equal success. Thompson made his mark on pro football immediately by becoming the first player to lead the league in punt returns (25 returns for 288 yards and an 11.5 average) and kickoff returns (18 for 513 yards and a glittering 28.5 average) in the same season. He still holds the record as the only player ever to accomplish that feat. Thompson also led the 1969 Broncos in interceptions with three, including a 57-yard return for a touchdown.

The Broncos started off 2-0 before injuries doomed them to another losing season. But the biggest win of the season came in a week-two contest that, for the first time, gave Denver at least a dot on the national pro football map. Denver recorded a stirring 21-19 win over the world champion New York Jets and its quarterback, Joe Namath. The following week a national magazine cover featured a Bronco for the first time, with a shot of Dave Costa leveling Namath on a quarterback sack.

The Broncos won their final game of the season at home against the Cincinnati Bengals, 21-16, ending a three-game, late-season losing skid. The game was played before 42,198 people, the last nonsellout the Denver Broncos ever had at home.

The games were a lot closer by the end of the 1969 campaign, but getting yards and wins still was difficult. The intense Saban was becoming frustrated with the time it was taking to build a winner in Denver, which closed out the decade never having posted a winning year.

Dave Costa was a free spirit and a menacing presence for the Broncos when their defense took shape as one of the AFL's best in the latter part of the 1960s.

1960s
DENVER BRONCOS
YEAR BY YEAR

1960	4-9-1
1961	3-11
1962	7-7
1963	2-11-1
1964	2-11-1
1965	4-10
1966	4-10
1967	3-11
1968	5-9
1969	5-8-1

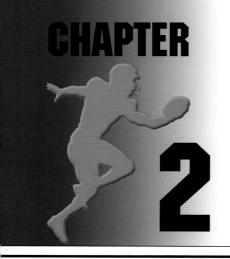

CHAPTER 2

THE 1970S
A CITY COMES OF AGE

MERGER BRINGS DENVER CLOSER TO THE BIG TIME

As the new decade dawned, the Denver Broncos and pro football were on the rise. The AFL and NFL had officially combined into the National Football League, with American and National conferences. Not only had the merger ended any remnants of the war between the two leagues, but television was proving to be the perfect venue for the continued blossoming of the game.

Reflecting a trend that started to develop in the late 1960s, every Gallup and Harris public opinion poll taken in the 1970s showed Americans choosing pro football as their favorite sport. This popularity begat a level of money and status that would have been unthinkable for the game's pioneers, including those behind the 1960 founding of the Broncos.

Denver had been placed in the AFC's western division, along with longtime rivals Kansas City, Oakland, and

An aerial view of Mile High Stadium. The Broncos started their fabled sellout streak there in the first game of the 1970 season. While the stadium has changed, the streak goes on, now concluding its fourth full decade.

San Diego, Buffalo, Boston, the New York Jets, and Miami went into the AFC East with NFL transfer Baltimore, while Houston and Cincinnati joined original NFL clubs Cleveland and Pittsburgh in creating the AFC Central.

In league meetings, the owners agreed that three original NFL teams needed to move over to the American conference with the former AFL clubs. However, deciding which three teams became so contentious that Commissioner Pete Rozelle asked his secretary to pull three names out of a hat to finalize the selection. Baltimore, Cleveland, and Pittsburgh were chosen.

The new decade was as dramatic for the Broncos as the old one was stagnant. Season ticket sales hit a record number of 43,584 in 1970, and in 1971 voters approved a $25 million bond issue to expand the stadium to more than 75,000 seats. This was the final leap for the city to have the necessary seating capacity to allow the Broncos to compete and thrive financially. It also would accommodate an ever-present, passionate fan base, beginning one of the greatest sellout streaks in American sports history.

The streak began on September 27, 1970, for Denver's home opening win against the Pittsburgh Steelers. In the entire NFL, only Washington has had a longer streak in one city, playing before the power brokers and football fanatics in the nation's capital.

Defense was the Broncos' forte again in 1970, mounting just enough offense for another 5-8-1 campaign. However, this time Floyd Little got over the hump and led the entire AFC in rushing with 901 yards. The great back played in all 14 games and gave Denver its first rushing crown. In his fourth season as a pro, he was the team's captain and unquestioned team leader.

Still, one of the recurring themes among fans and media in the early 1970s had not changed from the Broncos' early years—whether the Broncos would *ever* be a winning team. It had not happened thus far, despite Little's efforts.

After leading the AFC in rushing while playing for a last-place team in 1970, Little led the entire NFL in rushing yards again in 1971 with 1,133. Little became the third back in pro football history to hold the title while playing with a last-place team. He remains the only player ever to win back-to-back rushing titles with last-place teams, and he did it with a club that had slipped into total chaos.

LOU TEMPERS TEMPER AND MOVES ON

Lou Saban had had enough. In spite of the five full years remaining on his historic 10-year Bronco pact, he called it quits with five games remaining in the 1971 campaign. The losing record and criticism had become more than the fiery Saban could tolerate. Offensive line coach Jerry Smith moved up to finish out the season as interim head coach.

A two-sport star at the University of Colorado, Bobby Anderson was Denver's No. 1 draft choice in 1970, but played just four years with the Broncos due to injuries. Despite that, he ran, passed, received passes, and returned kicks to the tune of 3,031 all-purpose yards as a Bronco.

Floyd Little runs the ball behind tackle Mike Current. During the six-year period from 1968 to 1973, Little led the NFL in rushing with 5,185 yards and also in yards from scrimmage with 6,940. He remains the only NFL running back to win consecutive conference rushing titles (1970 and 1971) on last-place teams.

The Broncos finished 4-9-1, and the hallmark game for the season came on opening day against the Miami Dolphins. Don Shula was building his Dolphins into perennial Super Bowl contenders. They made the playoffs with a 10-4 mark in 1970 and went into the new season with the favorite tag firmly attached. They proved the pundits correct by advancing to Super Bowl VI before losing to the Dallas Cowboys.

Saban knew his team was badly outmatched against Miami and played a defense-oriented ball-control game all day, trying to work the field position to his underdog advantage. The game was tied at 10-10 when Denver got the final possession. Instead of calling any daring passes downfield, favored by the booing fans, Saban played it safe and ran out the clock, afterward invoking the old adage that half a loaf of bread is better than none. He could not have expected that during the next week the front lawn of his stately Denver home would be littered by half loaves of bread or that the mantra he uttered would follow him with every step he took, on the field and off, all season long.

He would have one great, final moment before becoming overwhelmed by his own frustration and the criticism aimed in his direction.

One of the franchises that had not wanted to move into the AFC was the Cleveland Browns. Prominent owner Art Modell even vowed that if he had anything to say about it, a loser like Denver would never play in venerable old Cleveland Stadium, which had seen so many championship games in Browns' history. However, the Browns joined the AFC, and on October 24, 1970, the Broncos made their first visit to Cleveland. At the time, no one could have predicted how the two franchises' stars would cross 17 years later.

Saban and his Broncos absolutely shocked the Browns and their fans on that perfect fall afternoon, downing Cleveland 27-0. Denver took the opening kickoff 92 yards within 15 plays to use up more than 10 minutes for the first quarter. The Broncos never looked back as Little ran for 113 yards on 25 carries to dominate both the clock and the game.

It was the first time the Browns had been shut out since 1952, but it also was Saban's last victory as Bronco coach. Denver lost at Philadelphia to a horrible Eagles team the following week, then followed up with consecutive home defeats against Detroit and Cincinnati.

With five games remaining, Saban gave up. He had been given more than a hint that the Bills wanted him back. As the losses mounted, he concluded that he wanted Buffalo as much as the Bills wanted him. His entire career was marked by movement and wanderlust, and this time it found him wandering out of Denver.

Still, Saban had brought a toughness and respectability to Denver's pro football team for the first time.

FLOYD LITTLE

RUNNING BACK
1967–1975

Floyd Little is one of the four original Denver Broncos' Ring of Fame inductees from 1984 and joins John Elway and Frank Tripucka as one of three Broncos whose jersey number is retired.

A first-round (sixth overall) draft choice in 1967 from Syracuse University, Little was the first No. 1 draft pick ever signed by the Broncos. He was widely known as "The Franchise" during his nine-year career, in which he established himself as Denver's first serious threat at running back. During the often-dismal early years of the Broncos, Little was a shining light for the fans and the entire organization. His performance was as much of substance as it was symbolism as the Broncos built a respectable reputation.

A Pro Bowl participant in 1970, 1971, and 1973, Little twice played in the AFL All-Star game (1968 and 1969) and was named the Colorado Sports Hall of Fame Pro Athlete of the Year in 1972. He finished his Bronco career ranked first on the franchise's all-time list for rushing attempts (1,641), rushing yards (6,323), and rushing touchdowns (43); he now ranks second in each behind Terrell Davis.

Among professional football players from 1967 to 1975, only O.J. Simpson totaled more rushing yards than Little. Little led Denver in rushing for seven consecutive seasons from 1967 to 1973, marking the longest such streak in club history, and at the time of his retirement, he ranked seventh in NFL annals in career rushing yards.

In 1971, Little led the NFL in rushing with a career-best 1,133 yards after capturing the AFC rushing crown a year earlier with 901 yards. He set a Bronco career record with 54 total touchdowns (43 rushing, nine receiving, and two by return), a statistic that currently ranks fourth on the team's all-time list. Little finished his career third on the all-time scoring list with 324 points (currently ninth).

He also set a team record with 12,173 career all-purpose yards, a mark that stood until Rod Smith passed him three decades later

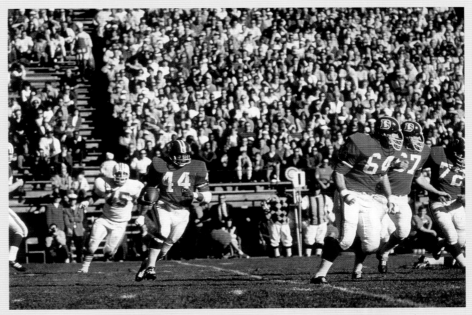

Floyd Little runs against the Dolphins in the 1971 10-10 tie that became known as the "Half a Loaf" game and precipitated Lou Saban's eventual resignation as head coach and general manager.

(in 2006). In addition, Little finished his career as the Broncos' all-time leader in career kickoff return yards (2,523—currently second).

In college, Little followed in the footsteps of Jim Brown and Ernie Davis as a superstar tailback for the Syracuse Orangemen. He was the first three-time All-American at running back since the 1940s and shattered most of the records set by his predecessors. He rushed for 2,704 yards, totaled 582 receiving yards, returned punts for 845 yards, kickoffs for 797 yards, and recorded 19 passing yards—for a total of 4,947 yards.

He is under consideration by the veterans committee for induction into the Pro Football Hall of Fame.

Little's Denver Broncos Career Record

		RUSHING					RECEIVING					KICK RETURNS			
Gms.	Starts	No.	Yds.	Avg.	LG	TD	No.	Yds.	Avg.	LG	TD	No.	Yds.	Avg.	LG	TD
117	93	1,641	6,323	3.9	80t	43	215	2,418	11.2	74	9	104	2,523	24.3	89	0

Coupled with the new headquarters and training facility, the team's new coach would be inheriting a franchise far different from the one Saban had been handed a mere five years before.

A NEW COACH, POSITIVELY A NEW ATTITUDE

Jerry Smith finished out a nondescript campaign in which the Broncos actually won two of their last four games. However, the city was focused on the new coach, and the buzz of uncertainty and speculation filled the Denver dailies.

While the Broncos were finishing last in 1970 and 1971, Stanford University was winning consecutive Rose Bowl games under the enthusiastic guidance of head coach John Ralston. Known for his pro-type offense, Ralston had eight straight winning seasons and won two Pacific Eight titles in his nine years in Palo Alto.

Coach John Ralston gives a speech to a group of team boosters. Ralston was detail-oriented and positive to the ultimate degree, and he brought a fresh level of confidence to the organization.

His boundless enthusiasm captivated Denver owners and was a stark contrast to the drill-sergeant attitude that Saban brought to the position. Fresh from Rose Bowl wins over Big 10 powers Ohio State and Michigan, Ralston very quickly energized the interview process and was offered the job. He was named head coach on January 5, 1972, and later added the title of general manager.

Ralston was a certified Dale Carnegie instructor—an absolute believer in the power of positive thinking. He proved to be exactly what the Broncos needed as the franchise and community still sought that first winning season.

Fan support continued unabated. For the first time in the history of Denver professional football, there was no public sale of season tickets, as ticket holders renewed 46,500 of the 47,500 available season tickets and further exercised their option for 8,000 additional seats.

One brick at a time, the team was building a foundation in pro football and the city's identity was beginning to be molded around the Broncos.

This was an era when the draft was paramount in the building of a team, many years before the free agent era. Luckily for the Broncos, Ralston proved to be an astute judge of college talent who laid the foundation for greatness in Denver. Ralston's first No. 1 draft choice was tight end Riley Odoms, who went on to be a perennial Pro Bowl player and a force in the lineup for the Broncos' new offense-minded coach.

A PIONEER GETS HIS DUE AT LAST

Before the 1972 season began, the Broncos got their first connection with the Pro Football Hall of Fame when Fred Gehrke was honored in Canton as the first recipient of the Daniel F. Reeves Memorial Pioneer Award (named for the late owner of the Rams, not the future coach of the Broncos). Gehrke was recognized for innovative off-field contributions to the game.

A former art major and halfback at the University of Utah, he had a seven-year NFL career, with a four-year interruption for wartime military service. He then became the Broncos' director of personnel. He played most of his career with the Cleveland Browns and the Los Angeles Rams—during the time when the postwar Rams played before sellouts in football's first golden age. At one time in L.A., Gehrke was the Rams' starting halfback, and his reserves were Heisman Trophy winner Glenn "Mr. Outside" Davis and Hall of Famer Elroy "Crazylegs" Hirsch.

While with the Rams, Gehrke helped develop the prototype of the helmet facemask, preventing countless broken noses. He also invented the net that placekickers and punters have used ever since to warm up in the bench area. And he first painted the logo on the sides of

the helmets—his most significant visual contribution. The helmets were still leather then, and in fact Gehrke himself carried the nickname "Leather," due to his reputation as one of the toughest players in the game.

After getting approval from the owner, he hand-painted every Rams helmet. He watched in amazement at the ovation the team received when players took the field with their new helmets—before a sellout crowd of more than 92,000 in the Los Angeles Memorial Coliseum.

For those three contributions, Gehrke became the first Bronco to enter Canton. It would be awhile before others followed. Of course, his Canton ceremony was not the last that football would hear of Fred Gehrke. He would have a key role in changing the course of Bronco history just five years later.

John Ralston's Broncos only produced a 5-9 record in 1972, but it did move up to third place in the AFC West. To the delight of Denver fans, the offense made real strides in his first year, finishing fifth in the league overall and third in passing.

Floyd Little scored 13 touchdowns to pace the team. The brilliant back was so loved by his adopted city that a special Floyd Little Day was held on October 29, 1972, for his numerous contributions on and off the field, even though he was still three years from retirement. The Broncos dropped a tough one to Cleveland, 27-20, on Little's day of recognition, however, and callers to Denver's major sports talk show continued to lament that it looked like the Broncos would never have a winning record. Many fans felt it would take a miracle for the team to ever have a winning season, never mind staking a claim to a championship.

Tight end Riley Odoms (left) congratulates wide receiver Jack Dolbin as they leave the field after Dolbin caught a touchdown pass.

A GREAT STEP FORWARD, FINALLY WINNERS

Then came 1973, a watershed year in which the Broncos and the city changed forever. Ralston had one of the greatest draft classes in Denver history that year. The team now boasted a group of future starters that included running back Otis Armstrong (first round), defensive end Barney Chavous (second), guard Paul Howard (third), linebacker Tom Jackson (fourth), and six other players who contributed in significant reserve roles.

The Broncos thus began 1973 with limited but realistic expectations, but at the start of the season it appeared these hopes would amount to nothing once again. After an opening day win over Cincinnati, Denver fell to San Francisco, losing a classic offensive battle, 36-34, in the final moments. The Broncos looked particularly lethargic the following week in a 33-14 defeat at the hands of the Chicago Bears. The Broncos had opened at home with three straight games and were 1-2. The following week they lost another close one, 16-14, at Kansas City, and their 1-3 record suggested they were on the road to nowhere.

The following week, Denver played the Houston Oilers in the Astrodome, and the team entered the so-called eighth wonder of the world in disarray. Those three consecutive losses suggested a losing season that would be their 11th in succession and the club's 13th

Above: Otis Armstrong proved a worthy successor to Floyd Little and led the league in rushing twice as Denver began to establish its tradition of excellent running backs.

Right: Guard Paul Howard helps with the annual U.S. Marine Corps Toys for Tots Drive.

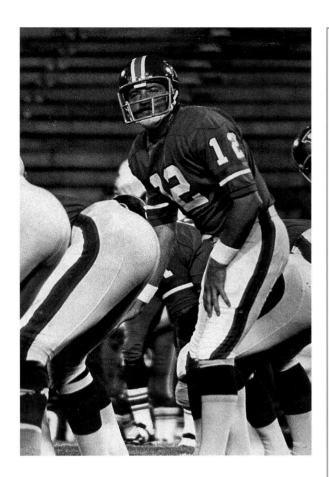

Quarterback Charley Johnson calls a play from scrimmage during a game at Mile High Stadium. Johnson was the quarterback for the 1973 season, the Broncos' first winning campaign. Talking about the signal caller, wide receiver Haven Moses said, "He taught us how to win."

sub-.500 campaign. At the time, the Broncos held an all-time record of 54-126-6. They were 72 games below .500 for their history—but they would drop no further. The Broncos defeated the Oilers 48-20 that day and really began to turn the franchise's fortunes around.

Thirty-one of Denver's 48 points that day came as a result of Houston turnovers. The Broncos had a sharp offensive showing that yielded 435 yards from scrimmage and no giveaways. Charley Johnson became the 18th quarterback in pro football history to go more than 20,000 lifetime yards as he connected for 214 yards. Three of his passes went for touchdowns to wide receiver Haven Moses.

From that moment on, though no one knew it at the time, the Broncos were on their way to becoming one of pro football's premier franchises. It would take 23 more seasons for the Broncos to actually reach the .500 mark in franchise history, but from that game on, Denver's record steadily went up instead of down.

CHARLEY JOHNSON
QUARTERBACK
1972–1975

Charley Johnson was one of three inductees into the Denver Broncos' Ring of Fame in 1986, along with fellow quarterback Frank Tripucka and defensive end Paul Smith. Johnson came to Denver in 1972 from Houston in exchange for a third-round draft choice, and at the time, the trade was regarded as the most important in franchise history.

He quarterbacked the Broncos to their first winning season (7-5-2 in 1973), a landmark moment in the first 14 years of franchise history. In 1974, Johnson set a Bronco record for passing accuracy (since broken) by completing 55.7 percent of his attempts. He made the All-AFC team picked by UPI and *Pro Football Weekly* after the 1973 season, and he also was chosen by his teammates as the Broncos' most valuable offensive player.

Johnson once threw for 445 yards in a game (versus Kansas City on November 18, 1974), marking the fourth-highest single-game passing total in team history. He recorded four 300-yard passing games in his career. He also threw a touchdown pass in 10 consecutive games in 1973 and 1974, a Bronco record at the time and a streak that still ties for the fifth-longest in club history.

He finished his Bronco career with 7,238 passing yards, which currently ranks sixth in team history, and 52 touchdown passes, which currently ranks fifth in club annals. He had a 20-18-3 (.524) record as a starter with Denver and averaged an impressive 7.46 yards per pass attempt, the third-best career mark by a Bronco. During the 1974 campaign, Johnson averaged a career-best 8.07 yards per pass attempt (244 passes for 1,969 yards), which is still the fourth-best single-season mark in Bronco history.

Selected in the draft by the St. Louis Cardinals, Johnson played his first professional season with the Cardinals in 1961 and set many passing records during his nine years with the team. He was traded to Houston before the 1970 season and played for the Oilers for two years before joining the Broncos. In college, Johnson was a star quarterback at New Mexico State, where he led his team to two Sun Bowl titles.

A man of remarkable accomplishment, he now is Dr. Charley Johnson, professor of chemical engineering and assistant to the president of New Mexico State University in Las Cruces, New Mexico. He earned his doctoral degree while playing in the NFL and even served two active duty years as an officer in the U.S. Army without interruption of his career as a professional quarterback.

Johnson's Denver Broncos Record

Games	Starts	Att.	Comp.	Yards	Pct.	TD	INT	LG	Rtg.
54	41	970	517	7,238	53.3	52	52	90t	73.1

Johnson's NFL Career Record

Games	Starts	Att.	Comp.	Yards	Pct.	TD	INT	LG	Rtg.
165	124	3,392	1,737	24,410	51.2	170	181	90t	69.2

PRIME TIME IN THE MILE HIGH CITY

Eight days later, the Broncos and Denver reached a milestone together: Monday Night Football came to the Mile High City.

Monday Night Football had quickly exploded onto America's sports scene. It was absolutely must-see TV. But when Bronco fans watched, they could not help but notice that, first, the Broncos were never playing on Monday night, and, second, the Broncos were virtually ignored each week when announcer Howard Cosell narrated the Sunday games highlights. So pronounced was

Billy Thompson started his career at cornerback but shifted to safety, where he was both team captain and an integral cog in the Orange Crush.

Denver's exclusion—at a time when the city deservedly had a complex about the networks ignoring the Rocky Mountain time zone—that a bar in suburban Glendale had a weekly contest in which the winner would get to throw a brick into a television set just as the halftime highlights aired.

With "Orange Monday" banners waving, the Broncos played the most important game to date, one that placed the Mile High City on the national stage for keeps, against Oakland. First, there had never been a live telecast out of the state that had an audience that large. Second, Ralston was known for his exceptional motivational skills, and he was in perfect form as he whipped his squad into a frenzy, extolling the significance of showing the whole nation what type of ball club they were.

The game was a classic Monday night matchup in which the drama came early and late. Billy Thompson returned a fumble 80 yards for a Denver score to give the Broncos an early lead, but the Raiders surged back to score 13 second-quarter points and take a 13-7 halftime advantage.

Floyd Little scored on a one-yard third-period run, and kicker Jim Turner, who played in the very first Monday-night game (Cleveland versus his New York Jets), added a field goal to keep Denver in the game, 20-17, going into the fourth quarter. He added another field goal to tie the score, but ancient George Blanda kicked his third field goal of the night to give Oakland the lead and apparent win, 23-20, with just 36 seconds remaining.

The sellout crowd was standing, electrified, as they watched Charley Johnson complete a 13-yard pass to Little, fullback Joe Dawkins dart 12 yards on a draw play, and then Little carry one last time for 9 yards to place the ball at the Oakland 28 yard line with seven seconds remaining.

Turner trotted onto the field in his trademark black hightops, the last man in football to still be wearing that type of shoe, and calmly connected on his third field goal of the second half. The 35-yarder gave the Broncos one of the most significant ties in football history.

In late November, Denver defeated Kansas City, 14-10, to take first place in the AFC West with three games to go in the season. The game at Houston had launched the Broncos on a seven-game winning streak that turned the 1-3 start into a 6-3-2 mark heading into December.

The winning streak came to an end the following week versus Dallas, but at San Diego on December 9, the Broncos defeated the Chargers 42-28, becoming winners at last. With the victory, Denver had seven wins, finally assuring the club a winning record.

The Broncos went into the final game of the season against Oakland knowing that a win would give them

JIM TURNER
KICKER
1971–1979

Jim Turner, a 1988 inductee into the Denver Broncos' Ring of Fame, ranks as one of the most prolific kickers of all time in professional football. He never missed a game as a pro. He finished with a streak of 228 consecutive appearances, including 130 in nine seasons (1971–1979) as a Bronco. He also scored 742 points to establish himself as Denver's all-time scoring leader until Jason Elam passed his mark in 1999.

Turner also ranks behind only Elam in Broncos' history in career field goals made (151) and extra points made (283). Turner's 151 field goals with Denver from 1971 to 1979 marked the fourth-highest total in the NFL during that period, and his 742 points scored were the fifth most in the league over that span.

In 1977, Turner helped Denver post a 12-2 regular-season record to earn the franchise's first playoff appearance en route to advancing to Super Bowl XII against Dallas. Turner was a key part of Bronco squads that earned a total of three playoff appearances (1977–1979) and two division titles (1977–1978). He posted his Bronco single-season high for field goals made with 25 in his first year with the club in 1971 and added a 100-point season (106 points) in 1973.

Named the Broncos' special teams MVP in 1975, Turner joined Denver in 1971 after the club acquired him in a trade with the New York Jets. He played seven seasons for the Jets (1964–1970), helping lead the club to a victory in Super Bowl III against Baltimore. At the time of his retirement, Turner ranked second in NFL career scoring with 1,439 points (currently 16th), as well as second in field goals with 304 (currently tied for 17th). Turner kicked 521 career extra points (15th in NFL history) and was the fourth player to ever reach the 500 mark. Before entering the NFL, Turner was a three-time letterman as a quarterback at Utah State University in the early 1960s.

Jim Turner earned a place in the Broncos' Ring of Fame and legendary status as one of the game's great placekickers.

Turner's Denver Broncos Record

	PAT CONVERSIONS			FIELD GOALS			
Games	No.-Att.	Pct.		No.-Att.	Pct.	LG	Pts.
130	283-301	94.1		151-232	65.1	53	742

Turner's NFL Career Record

	PAT CONVERSIONS			FIELD GOALS			
Games	No.-Att.	Pct.		No.-Att.	Pct.	LG	Pts.
228	521-543	95.9		304-488	62.3	53	1,439

Defensive tackle Paul Smith takes a breather during a game at Mile High Stadium. Smith joined the team when the Broncos were perennial losers, but he was a force at the defensive tackle position as the franchise pushed its way to supremacy. Smith is in the Broncos' Ring of Fame.

PAUL SMITH

DEFENSIVE TACKLE

1968–1978

Paul Smith was inducted into the Denver Broncos' Ring of Fame in 1986 along with quarterbacks Frank Tripucka and Charley Johnson.

This defensive tackle recorded 55.5 sacks with the Broncos from 1968 to 1978, finishing his 11-year career in Denver ranked second in that category (currently seventh). He posted 10.5 sacks in 1972 and 11 sacks in 1973, propelling him to back-to-back Pro Bowl selections. He registered a career-high 12 sacks during the 1971 campaign.

Smith did not miss a game during five consecutive seasons from 1969 to 1973, appearing in all 70 contests. He saw action in 12 games during the 1977 campaign, a season in which the AFC West Champion Broncos reached the playoffs for the first time in club history and went on to play in Super Bowl XII against the Cowboys. Smith was one of the team's defensive leaders during the years when Denver was building the foundation for defensive excellence with the famed "Orange Crush."

His head coach, John Ralston, once said that Smith was "the finest defensive tackle in pro football," and the lineman was known for being one of the quickest defensive tackles in the NFL.

Smith's 11-year career was the longest in Bronco annals until he was surpassed by fellow Ring of Famer Billy Thompson. Smith finished his professional career by playing two seasons with Washington from 1979 to 1980. He passed away on March 14, 2000.

Smith's Denver Broncos Record

Games	Starts	Sacks	Int.	Yds.	Avg.	TD
133	72	55.5	1	6	6.0	0

Smith's NFL Career Record

Games	Starts	Sacks	Int.	Yds.	Avg.	TD
164	N/A	55.5	2	14	7.0	0

the division title—a loss would leave them out of the playoffs. Denver played the Raiders close before losing 21-17, but Denver finished with a 7-5-2 record that marked the first winning season in history and served as a harbinger of things to come.

Floyd Little, Haven Moses, Riley Odoms, and defensive tackle Paul Smith were invited to play in the Pro Bowl. Odoms had been the NFL's dominant tight end all season long, catching 43 passes for 629 yards (an excellent 14.6-yard average) and 7 touchdowns. The big tight end was named All-Pro by the NEA.

Little led the NFL in rushing touchdowns with 12 and the AFC in overall scores with 13. He was the offensive cornerstone once again, and in the four-year period from 1970 to 1973, he led the AFC with 35 total scores. He also continued his stardom as a role model and leader in the Denver community, in 1973 winning the National YMCA Brian Piccolo Award for Humanitarian Service.

However, the most significant football honor went to John Ralston, who was named AFC coach of the year.

SOMETIMES CHAMPIONS COME FROM CHAMPION

An astute planner who organized every aspect of the Broncos organization, Ralston was aware that more talent was needed to get Denver to a true championship level, and his first-round draft choice in 1974 came to him from Champion, Ohio.

Seldom was a hometown name more fitting than that of Randy Gradishar's. During an illustrious 10-year career with the Broncos, Gradishar was a seven-time Pro Bowler and Denver's all-time tackle leader with 2,049 tackles from his inside linebacker position. He was an immediate anchor for the Broncos' defense and a crowd favorite to the highest degree. Indeed, Gradishar still would be on any short list of the

Ohio native Randy Gradishar wraps up a sack against the Cleveland Browns. One of the NFL's all-time greats at linebacker, he always seemed to make the big play for the Broncos.

RANDY GRADISHAR

LINEBACKER

1974–1983

In recognition of his outstanding 10-year career at linebacker with the Broncos, Randy Gradishar was the only Ring of Fame inductee in 1989. He was among 15 finalists for the Pro Football Hall of Fame balloting in 2003 and 2008, as well as one of 25 semifinalists for the class of 2005, 2006, and 2007. He now is under consideration by the veterans committee of the Pro Football Hall of Fame.

During his career, Gradishar earned seven Pro Bowl selections, a total that was the most by a Bronco when he retired (it currently ties for third). He is the Broncos' all-time leader in tackles with 2,049. A consummate professional and team leader, he led the Broncos in tackles for a franchise-record nine consecutive years from 1975 to 1983 and averaged 222 tackles per season during that stretch. His 286 tackles during the 1978 campaign still stand as the Broncos' single-season record.

Selected by the Broncos in the first round (14th overall) of the 1974 NFL Draft, Gradishar never missed a game, playing in 145 in a row.

He accounted for 33 turnovers in his career (20 interceptions and 13 fumble recoveries), which tied for the fourth most by an NFL linebacker during his 10-year career, and he was voted the Defensive Player of the Year in 1978 by the AP, UPI, *Pro Football Weekly*, and NEA (as a recipient of the George Halas Award).

The linebacker was a defensive force in leading the Broncos to four playoff berths (1977, 1978, 1979, 1983), two divisional titles (1977 and 1978), and an appearance in Super Bowl XII following the 1977 season. His teammates also voted him defensive MVP in 1978 and 1980.

While at Ohio State, Gradishar was referred to by head coach Woody Hayes as "the best linebacker I ever coached at Ohio State." A three-year starter for the Buckeyes and a consensus All-American as a senior, Gradishar also received Academic All-America honors in college. He was president of the Denver Broncos Youth Foundation from 1982 to 1992 and was inducted into the College Football Hall of Fame in 1998.

Gradishar's Denver Broncos Career Record

Games	Starts	Tackles	Sacks	Int.	Yds.	Avg.	TD
145	134	2,049	19.5	20	335	16.8	3

most popular athletes ever to play for a Denver pro sports team.

At a time when Little's career was winding down, and with Otis Armstrong in place as the successor at running back, Ralston deftly made the selection that would be the cornerstone for the other side of the ball. Gradishar had been a three-year starter at Ohio State, was named to every All-America team following his senior season, and was an Academic All-American as well. He was the embodiment of every value held high and true, and Bronco fans knew it from the start.

As the 1974 season got underway, Denver voters passed a $25 million bond issue to expand and improve Mile High Stadium to more than 75,000 seats, with the stadium projected to be finished in time for the start of the 1976 regular season.

Also during the offseason, the NFL owners voted to have an overtime period that would greatly reduce any

possibility of a tie, and in week two of the season the Broncos wrote another note in football history when they hosted Pittsburgh in the league's first matchup that went into overtime.

The new conference rivals put on a dizzying offensive show in a stunning 35-35 tie, as Armstrong scored twice on passes of 45 yards from Charley Johnson and 23 yards from Steve Ramsey. Each quarterback threw an additional scoring pass in spectacular passing displays. Rookie fullback Jon Keyworth from the University of Colorado also rushed for a touchdown. Not to be out-done, Pittsburgh's Joe Gilliam completed 31-of-50 for 348 yards himself.

Billy Thompson blocked a field goal that would have given Pittsburgh the win, and neither team scored in the first sudden-death period in NFL regular-season play.

Bronco fans' excitement just continued to build, and the city was relishing the newfound attention it was

Jon Keyworth runs the ball. He stampeded his way to 10 touchdowns in his 1974 rookie campaign and was a key player at fullback during the 1977 season. Keyworth dabbled in singing, and in 1977 he released a single, "Make Those Miracles Happen," that achieved hit status locally.

BILLY THOMPSON

DEFENSIVE BACK

1969–1981

Billy Thompson, certainly regarded as one of the best defensive backs in Denver Broncos' history, was the only Ring of Fame inductee in 1987. A third-round Bronco draft choice (61st overall) in 1969, Thompson was the first player in team history to play 13 seasons with Denver (1969–1981). That total ties for the sixth highest in franchise annals.

A team captain for many years, Thompson finished his career with more starts (178) and games played (179) than any player in Broncos' history and currently ranks 3rd and 10th, respectively, in those categories. He also had the longest consecutive starts and games played streaks (156 games) in Bronco history at the time of his retirement, marks that still rank first and third, respectively, in club annals.

Thompson was a three-time Pro Bowl selection (1977, 1978, 1981) who earned All-NFL honors twice (1977 and 1978) while establishing himself as one of the game's top ballhawks. He finished his career with a club-record 61 takeaways (40 interceptions and 21 fumble recoveries) as a member of clubs that reached the playoffs three times (1977–1979), won two division titles (1977 and 1978), and appeared in one Super Bowl (XII in 1977). His 40 career interceptions are the third most by a Bronco in team history, and Thompson stands near the top of the Broncos' career interception return yardage list with 784 for a 19.6-yard average, second best in club history.

The safety scored seven defensive touchdowns in his career, reaching the end zone three times on interception returns and four times on fumble recoveries. His three interception return touchdowns tie for the second-highest total in Bronco annals, while his four fumble recovery touchdowns stood as the NFL's career record for many years and currently tie for second in league history.

As a rookie in 1969, Thompson became the first player in pro football history to lead his league in both kickoff (28.5-yard average) and punt return (11.5-yard average) averages in the same season. He finished his career with the second-most punt return yards (1,814), seventh-best punt return average (11.56), and third-best kickoff return average (25.1) in Broncos' history.

Thompson enjoyed a brilliant career at Maryland State (now Maryland-Eastern Shore), earning All-CIAA honors three times as a defensive back and being named team MVP as a senior. He also twice earned NAIA All-America honors and made All-CIAA three times in baseball as a centerfielder.

Thompson is now the Broncos' director of community outreach, and in that role he works with the Denver Broncos Alumni Council and former Broncos players to encourage their involvement in the club's community outreach programs, which focus on youth, health, and hunger initiatives.

Thompson's Denver Broncos Career Record

Games	Starts	Sacks	Int.	Yds.	Avg.	TD	Fum. Rec.	Fum TD	Def. TD
179	178	4.0	40	784	19.6	3	21	4	7

KICK RETURNS					PUNT RETURNS				
No.	Yds.	Avg.	LG	TD	No.	Yds.	Avg.	LG	TD
46	1,156	25.1	63	0	157	1,814	11.6	60	0

receiving due to its pro football team. One year before, the Broncos had played their first nationally televised game as an NFL team, and this year they had two.

On Monday night, November 18, the Kansas City Chiefs visited Mile High Stadium, and the national audience saw another tremendous display of offensive football. The Chiefs recorded a 42-34 win with future Hall of Fame quarterback Len Dawson. However, Keyworth ran for three touchdowns and Johnson put on a scintillating show, completing 28-of-42 passes for 445 yards and two scores. Denver amassed 564 yards to total offense, but it could not prevent Kansas City from making the big plays necessary to win.

Then, before a television audience estimated at 35 million, the Broncos riddled the Detroit Lions 31-27 on Denver's first Thanksgiving Day game, in Detroit. Armstrong ran for 144 yards, and the lithe running back also contributed five receptions for 33 yards and returned a kickoff for 22—giving him 199 yards in a brilliant display. Keyworth also scored twice on 1-yard runs, as Ralston valued the rookie's power in short yardage situations. In all, the Bronco offense racked up 240 yards.

This was the year in which Little began to play a different role for the Broncos, as Otis Armstrong demonstrated the fresh legs that had made him an All-American at Purdue. On December 8, Armstrong set the Broncos' single game rushing mark of 183 yards as the Broncos downed Houston, 37-14 (assuring Denver its second consecutive winning season). Armstrong scored on runs of 10, 12, and 15 yards, and when he remarked on the sideline that he was getting tired, Little told him to go back out on the field to set the record. It was the greatest rushing day Bronco fans had ever seen.

Armstrong finished the season with 1,407 yards and the NFL rushing title. He became one of just six players in history to average more than 100 yards per game in pro football at the time (when a 14-game season was still in place).

The Broncos gave Ralston a contract extension, which was announced to the team in the locker room before the final game at San Diego. The Broncos promptly went out and got shutout, 17-0, prompting some media speculation about the players' relationship with their coach. The team's final record was 7-6-1.

Odoms again led the team in receptions with 42, this time for an average of 15.2 yards per catch (an amazing per-catch average for a tight end). He paced the club in touchdown receptions as well, with six total. He joined Armstrong to represent the Broncos at the Pro Bowl. Keyworth scored 10 touchdowns in his rookie year and was a fine addition to a blossoming offense.

While the number one rushing job clearly belonged to Armstrong, Little continued to be recognized for his community excellence. In 1974, he was named the Byron

Safety Billy Thompson (No. 36) in pass coverage against the Chargers. Thompson finished his career with 61 turnovers for the Broncos.

Defensive end Lyle Alzado (left) and defensive tackle Paul Smith (middle) talk with running back Otis Armstrong on the bench during the latter moments of another Denver win.

Cornerback Louis Wright returns an interception for a touchdown. Wright's cover skills were so feared that opponents often went the entire game without throwing at his receiver. A Ring of Famer, Wright was a physical player with dazzling speed, and he also excelled on special teams.

Below: Riley Odoms rambles for yardage at Kansas City. Odoms was named All-Pro three times and made four Pro Bowl appearances for Denver.

White Humanitarian Award winner by the National Football League Players Association.

Expansion began on Mile High Stadium the following year, and John Ralston's roster expansion continued as well. He continued to demonstrate his draft prowess by making first-day selections of Louis Wright, who would go on to become a superb cornerback for the team, along with wide receiver/return specialist Rick Upchurch and nose tackle Rubin Carter. The foundation was being laid for a tremendous team, especially on the defensive side.

On day two of the draft, the Broncos, like every other team, took some chances, and one of Ralston's hunches was that a quarterback at Tulane University might be able to transition to defense and play safety. In the eighth round, with the 199th overall selection, the Broncos chose Steve Foley, who had never seen action on defense for the Green Wave. But the Broncos put him down on paper as a safety, and when he moved to that spot on the field, it was as if he had been there all his life.

SOME HUMBLING AND GRUMBLING, BUT THE FUTURE COMES CLOSER

The team dipped to a 6-8 record in 1975, and the fan base grumbled, as it expected continued improvement. Conditioned to years of losing, the fans had no way of knowing the kind of success that was around the corner. For the moment, they were unhappy, and Ralston was being labeled as a coach who was too "rah-rah," now sustaining criticism for his boundless enthusiasm and optimism.

Keyworth led the Broncos in rushing with 725 yards and in receptions with 42 for 314 yards. Armstrong was limited by a hamstring pull that nagged at him all year long, and the noble warrior Little was playing his last season, still putting up great figures, even at the very end. In a career noted by leadership, excellence, and versatility, he closed it out with 445 rushing yards and added 308 on 29 receptions while still returning 16 kickoffs for 307 yards—1,060 yards total in his final pro year.

On December 14 against Philadelphia, Floyd Little played his final game before the adoring Denver fans, and when it was over he left the fans with searing memories of that game, as well as of his whole career. He ended his last game being carried off the field by his legion of fans. In the matchup, the ageless All-American wearing the historic number 44—never worn again by a Denver player—scored two touchdowns against the Eagles and accounted for more than 150 yards from scrimmage. His exploits included a 66-yard scoring run that began as a screen pass that required a leaping catch on the run, which then evolved into a classic bob-and-weave down the west sideline until he reached the end zone. Naturally, the fans erupted into euphoric cheering.

His final score was on a short run very late in the game that everyone knew was coming, and by then the fans were overwhelmed with joy. They stormed the field in 18-degree weather and carried Little off in a celebration befitting the team's first truly great hero.

Little finished as the seventh all-time leading rusher in NFL history with 6,323 yards. During the six-year period from 1968 to 1973, he led the entire NFL in rushing yards with 5,185, also amassing the most total yards from scrimmage in that time frame with 6,940. He reached those totals despite playing on what was indeed one of the league's worst offensive teams of the time. During his career, the Broncos never made the playoffs despite their brilliant all-purpose halfback. He was named to the All-NFL team of the 1970s by the Pro Football Hall of Fame selection committee, and his rushing total remained the team record for 23 years until Terrell Davis surpassed it.

Rick Upchurch was absolutely spectacular as a kickoff return man in his first season, with a 27.1-yard average and 1,084 yards. His total overall yardage for the season totaled 1,929, and he was the runaway winner of the AFC Rookie of the Year Award.

Gradishar led the team in tackles with 106 and was inheriting the mantle of fan popularity from Little, although the superb linebacker would have much more company among teammates being showered with fan affection. Gradishar and Odoms both made the Pro Bowl, and the Broncos were improving.

Ralston became the Broncos' winningest all-time coach in 1975, but that was indicative not only of his vision and drive but also a sign of how far down the team had been for years. But with respectability had come a new challenge and a new demand from the fans—they were no longer pleased just to watch individual players excel in a torrent of losses. More was expected, and Ralston was beginning to be labeled as a great personnel man, but one whose sideline leadership and coaching was under increasingly greater negative scrutiny.

Rick Upchurch made the NFL's all-decade team of the 1970s as a kick return specialist and was named All-NFL four times (in 1976, 1978, 1979, and 1982). He retired as the leading punt returner in NFL history.

The glow had worn off from 1973, and any future expectations for the team now carried a foreboding chill.

Charley Johnson had given the Broncos a fine level of play at quarterback during their growth seasons from 1972 to 1975, but he decided in the offseason to retire so he could finish off doctoral studies in chemical engineering and move into the next phase of his life. His career spanned 15 years, and in addition to PhD study in several offseasons, he also had served full time in the U.S. Army while quarterbacking for the St. Louis Cardinals at one point. One of the Renaissance men of pro football and a superb leader for Denver over the last four years—including the first two winning seasons in team history—Johnson walked away, and the Broncos' quarterback job went to journeyman Steve Ramsey in 1976.

The year began as sour as possible in Cincinnati, less for the 17-7 defeat than for the fact that defensive end Lyle Alzado tore up his knee and now would spend the entire year on injured reserve. The year prior, the fearsome pass rusher had been one of the finalists for the NFL Man of the Year Award.

Broncos defensive tackle Lyle Alzado wraps up Raiders quarterback Ken "The Snake" Stabler during a November 3, 1974, loss (17-28) to Oakland at Mile High Stadium.

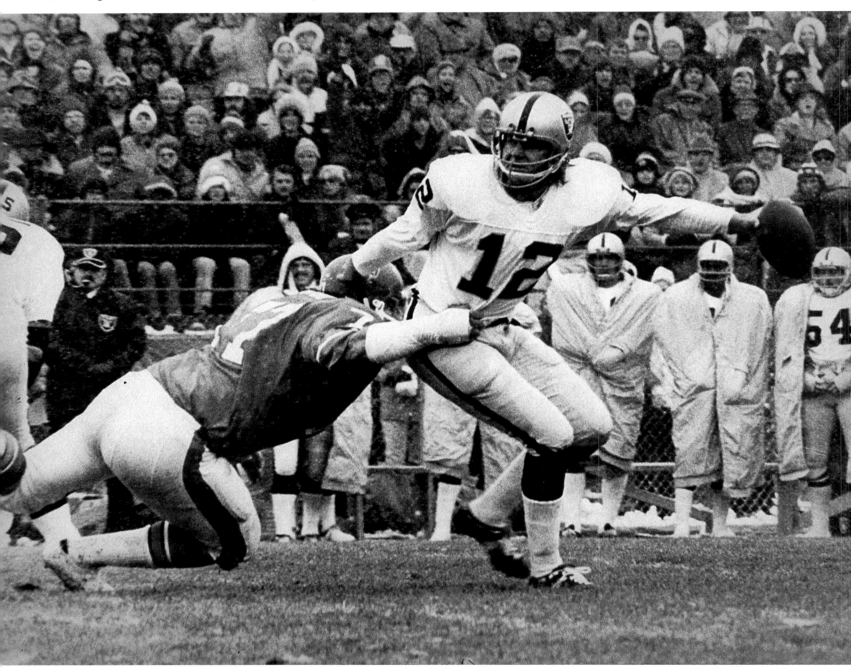

While the team was licking its wounds from the Cincinnati defeat, defensive coordinator Joe Collier had to figure out a way to compensate for the loss of one of Denver's biggest defensive stars. In a few short weeks, Collier ultimately altered the course of the season, the Broncos' future, and the way defense would be played in the NFL.

ENTER THE "ORANGE CRUSH"

The NFL in the 1970s was much more of a run-oriented game than pro football is today. The 4-3 defense that the Broncos and all other teams played required more players up front than at linebacker, and the defensive ends had to be athletic enough to rush the passer. Collier had just lost his best pass rushing defensive end, but as he studied his situation, the veteran coordinator decided to take full advantage of his superb linebacking crew. Just like that, Collier changed the entire Denver defense to a 3-4, with no offseason or training camp preparation.

The defense had actually been around since Bud Wilkinson popularized it on the collegiate level with his powerhouse teams at Oklahoma. However, it was not in use as a pro defense when Collier was spending those long nights in front of his projector looking for solutions.

The 3-4 defensive system is one in which the linebackers are expected to make a lot of the tackles. These four linebackers have to have enough speed to drop back and cover a zone in pass defense, but they also have to roam sideline to sideline to bring down the ball carriers. With four linebackers up front, the quarterback has a harder time determining when a defense might blitz on any given play. In an extremely fast, physical game, the nose tackle needs to clog the middle, the linebackers have to be able to run better than those in a 4-3, and the corners need the skill to jam receivers hard at the line of scrimmage if necessary. One advantage of the 3-4 setup is that a team doesn't need to switch to a prevent defense when guarding a late lead. Since the four linebackers theoretically are talented enough that they can all play pass defense, they can become part of the eight pass defenders in zone coverage without the need to make a substitution.

However, there is always a concern when making the switch that a team might not have the talent necessary to make the 3-4 work. Four strong linebackers, plenty of defensive backfield talent, and a physical nose tackle are all needed. The Broncos had all the pieces to the 3-4 puzzle. Their linebacker foursome and secondary were top notch, and Rubin Carter was as physical as any nose tackle in the game.

Rubin Carter was a fifth-round draft choice in 1975, overlooked by many teams because of a relative lack of height—Carter packed his 256 pounds on a frame that reached just six feet. But he had tremendous strength and

Tom Jackson was the unquestioned emotional leader of the Orange Crush defense, as well as one of the most popular fan favorites in club history.

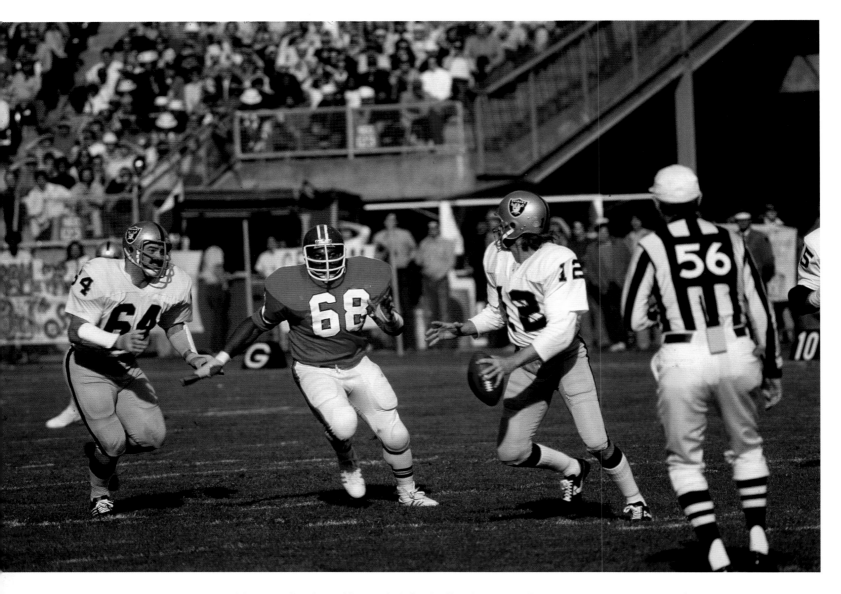

Nose tackle Rubin Carter—who became the face of the 3-4 defense in the NFL during the 1970s—rushes Ken Stabler in one of the legendary Bronco-Raider matchups.

quickness and anchored Denver's defensive line throughout the decade. The Broncos made the switch to the 3-4 in 1976, and just one year later Carter's glowering stare graced the cover of *Sports Illustrated* for an article about the rage that the 3-4 defense had become.

Randy Gradishar was arguably the finest linebacker in the game during his playing career. The first defensive player to be taken in the first round by Denver since the AFL-NFL merger, he was key to the complex 3-4 defense. Strong enough, fast enough, and smart enough, he had been labeled the finest player ever coached by Ohio State legend Woody Hayes.

Joining Gradishar at inside linebacker was Joe Rizzo, one of the most unheralded players ever to start for the Broncos. A free agent in 1974 from the Merchant Marine Academy, Rizzo proved to be one of the steadiest yet underrated players on that fine defensive unit. The

Broncos had no expectations for him when he signed on three years earlier, but Rizzo just quietly kept outplaying the guys around him until there was no place left to put him except the starting lineup.

One of the outside spots was manned by Tom Jackson, who earned his reputation as a team leader and big play member of the defensive unit. Certainly one of the most exciting players in Bronco history, he was the most vocal inspirational leader of the team. Where Gradishar was modest and shy about his brilliant accomplishments, the 5-foot-11 Jackson stood defiantly at the line of scrimmage and stared down the other team's offense, daring them with his attitude, speed, and mobility. A Cleveland native, he was the prototypical streetwise city kid.

At the strong outside position was Bob Swenson, who played his college ball at California and who, like Rizzo, came to Denver as a free agent. A college defensive lineman who embodied a "cool" West Coast persona, Swenson never flinched when others suggested he couldn't be a pro linebacker. He had great range, quickness, and speed to go along with plenty of swagger.

This superb linebacking tandem had behind it a secondary that included the heady Foley, who had only been playing safety since joining the Broncos a year earlier, and two all-time Denver superstars in Billy Thompson and Louis Wright.

Thompson had come to Denver as the third-round draft choice in 1969, and the 1970s were all prime years for this brilliant athlete. He initially played cornerback, and by 1976, he made the switch to safety. In both roles, he earned Pro Bowl selections.

And Wright had almost no parallel in the game at the cornerback position. The Broncos' first-round selection one year earlier, he was an imposing physical presence at 6 feet 2 inches and ranked as Denver's fastest player with his documented 4.4-second time in the 40-yard dash. Possessing uncommon athletic gifts, he was very strong against the run and a solid tackler, as well as a great pass defender. In many games over the course of his career, the opposing quarterback did not even attempt one pass in Wright's direction.

John Ralston brought all these players to Denver. Gradishar, Jackson, Thompson, and Wright went on to be among the best and most popular players in franchise history.

With the 3-4 scheme instituted by Collier, the Broncos defense of the 1970s became one of pro football's greatest.

The team rolled to an easy 46-3 win over the New York Jets in Denver's home opener. The following week drubbed Cleveland, 44-13, as Upchurch tied an NFL record by returning two punts for touchdowns in that win over the visiting Browns. On October 24, Upchurch set a new NFL record with his fourth punt return touchdown of the season in a 35-26 win over Kansas City in Arrowhead Stadium.

The rest of the special teams unit was having a great year as well. In a subsequent home win over Tampa Bay, placekicker Jim Turner connected on two field goals and six extra points to become just the fifth player in pro football history to surpass 1,200 points for a career.

On November 14, Denver shut out San Diego on the road by a 17-0 count, marking the first time the team ever recorded two shutouts in one season. The overwhelming Bronco defense had blanked the Chargers by a 26-0 count in Mile High Stadium earlier.

The defense was putting on a tremendous show every week. However, the offense failed to score 20 points in more than half the season's games, including a dismal four weeks in a row. The Broncos closed out the season

with a 28-14 win at Chicago for the team's ninth win of the season, the highest win total in Denver history.

Otis Armstrong rushed for 116 yards against the Bears to give him 1,008 yards for the season. This was his second 1,000-yard campaign, earning him selection, along with the mercurial Rick Upchurch, to participate in the Pro Bowl game again.

Led by Randy Gradishar's 137 tackles, the defense allowed the fewest points in Denver history—206—and

Bob Swenson was a superb linebacker and an integral member of the Broncos' legendary defense of the 1970s. Swenson had his career curtailed by a devastating knee injury, but he went to both the Super Bowl and Pro Bowl as a Bronco defender.

Bronco owner Gerald Phipps congratulates running back Otis Armstrong after a sterling performance.

GERALD H. PHIPPS

TEAM OWNER

1965–1981

Gerald "Gerry" H. Phipps became the first and only nonplayer to be inducted into the Denver Broncos' Ring of Fame in 1985. After he purchased the club on February 15, 1965, Gerry and his brother, Allan, guided the Broncos from their less-than-auspicious beginnings to the top of the American Football Conference.

Gerry's purchase (his brother was out of town, on vacation) saved the Bronco franchise from being sold to an investment group that would have moved the team. Though the brothers owned the club together, Gerry was the principal guiding voice in team matters.

Under the Phipps brothers, the Broncos became one of the NFL's most stable franchises after recording the first winning season (a 7-5-2 record) in club history in 1973. In 1977, the Broncos posted a 12-2 regular-season record and advanced to the playoffs for the first time in franchise history, en route to the team's first

AFC Championship and first Super Bowl (XII versus Dallas). Denver won the AFC West title in 1977 and 1978, and the club made three consecutive playoff appearances from 1977 to 1979.

With the success of the Broncos, the doors opened for other professional sports teams in Denver. Following the takeover by the Phipps brothers, Denver Bronco season ticket sales improved from 8,002 in 1964 to 22,905 in 1965. Bronco season tickets were sold out for every season under the Phipps brothers from 1970 to 1981 and grew to 73,380 in 1981. Denver's yearly home attendance grew to 598,224 as the Phipps were in their final year overseeing the club, 1981.

Before purchasing the Broncos, Gerry was the president of the Gerald H. Phipps Inc. Construction Company, which he continued to operate while owning the team. Phipps was born March 4, 1915, in Denver. He passed away August 6, 1993.

---

finished second in the AFC in fewest rushing yards per game. Tom Jackson was a force as a tackler, third on the team with 77 tackles. He capitalized on his speed and coverage skill to have the most single-season interceptions ever by a Denver linebacker, with seven to lead the team.

DISSENT IN THE MILE HIGH AIR

Still, overall the offense suffered badly from the retirement of Charley Johnson. Steve Ramsey struggled throughout the 1976 season, finishing with just 11 touchdowns compared to 13 interceptions and a dismal 47.4 completion percentage. Despite Armstrong's productivity, the offense was not able to capitalize on it or the defensive performance that Denver put forth.

Worse still, there was widespread locker-room dissatisfaction with Ralston as a coach. Players grumbled among themselves and aired off-the-record complaints about strategy and leadership to many members of the press. Gerry Phipps was aware of this, and at season's end, he informed Ralston that he had to choose between being head coach or general manager. He could not do both, citing a growing trend around the league in splitting the roles.

Ralston chose coaching, and Fred Gehrke was named to the general manager post on December 18. Just as he

impacted all of pro football with his bold design of the Los Angeles Rams' helmet nearly three decades earlier, he was now within a few weeks of casting a new mold for the Denver Broncos.

First, though, the ugly dissent was about to go public. A number of players, unhappy that Ralston would remain as coach, scheduled a late December news conference at which they intended to call for the coach's ouster. While the total number of players involved remains uncertain, the group that actually showed up for the press conference was labeled by media as "The Dirty Dozen." When word reached Phipps and Gehrke of the players' intent, the two executives showed up at the site of the press conference, a hotel away from the team complex, and convinced the players to soften their scheduled public statement.

According to published reports in the *Denver Post*, the original statement expressed the players' concerns that they didn't believe it was possible to win a championship under the guidance of John Ralston. "He has lost the respect of the players, and we don't believe he is capable of coaching us to a championship," it read.

But after Phipps and Gehrke intervened, the full news conference then became just Billy Thompson reading a general statement of support: "The players will support Fred Gehrke completely, and we are looking forward to a championship season under his leadership. We also

Coach Red Miller signs autographs for fans at the 1978 Quarterback Club. His fiery enthusiasm infected fans as well as players and paved the way for the team's magical 1977 campaign.

Never at a loss for words when fighting for his team, Red Miller gives an official a piece of his mind.

give our full support to the owners in their attempt to bring this about." No mention was made of Ralston.

One of the new general manager's first projects was to meet individually with every player to get a feel of the team's attitude. When Gehrke finished listening to the utter negativity expressed by the players, he made up his mind that the only course of action was to fire Ralston. He informed the Phipps brothers of his plans and received the owners' blessing on the action, which

altered the team and city forever. John Ralston resigned as the head coach of the Denver Broncos on January 31, and Gehrke already knew who he wanted for the job.

MILLER, MIRACLES, AND THE M&M CONNECTION

When Gehrke started his Denver career in personnel, one of the assistant coaches was Robert "Red" Miller, who by now had 17 years in the pro football assistant-coaching

Quarterback Craig Morton tries to quiet the crowd during a 1977 game at Mile High Stadium. His talent and leadership proved the final ingredients to making the Broncos a championship team and annual playoff contenders.

ranks and most recently had directed a high-powered offense with the New England Patriots.

Miller was tapped for the Denver job and took full advantage of his first opportunity as a head coach, making as big a first impression on the game as any first-year coach in NFL history. The fiery redhead was known as a "player's coach" for his leadership skills. He knew that the table had been set for future success, but there was a glaring weakness at the quarterback position. The son of a coal miner who had worked his way through college and up the coaching ladder, he had a hands-on attitude and dynamic interpersonal skills. He and Gehrke worked in tandem to evaluate the roster, and as the offseason settled in, Denver completed a trade with the New York Giants to bring Craig Morton in as the final piece of the puzzle.

Known for having one of the best throwing arms in the game, Morton had been a No. 1 draft choice of the Dallas Cowboys in 1965 and had been the target of verbal assaults in his stay with the Giants.

Miller knew the defense was tremendous, and if he had a skilled veteran quarterback to manage the offense, controlling the ball and striking at key opportunities, the Broncos had a chance to be something special. His philosophy on offense would be to play to the defense and take a sack rather than risk a mistake. Morton's talent was matched by his experience, and he embodied that philosophy to create Denver's greatest season.

For the first time in the history of the Broncos, all the stars aligned. The 1977 season proved to be one of the greatest in team history and the first truly one-of-a-kind season in all of Denver sports. Before it was over, Miller took the Broncos to their first playoff game, their first division title, their first conference title, and, the miracle of miracles, a berth in Super Bowl XII.

The Broncos started off with a 7-0 home shutout over the St. Louis Cardinals, holding the powerful Cardinals to just 12 first downs as St. Louis was befuddled all day by Denver's 3-4 defense. Then Denver followed that up with another Mile High Stadium win, this one a 26-6 thumping of Buffalo. In the game, the Bills mustered just 8 first downs and 129 total yards against a dynamic unit that was rapidly attracting national attention. Morton threw a touchdown pass to Riley Odoms and scored himself on a 1-yard naked reverse. Part of the play's success was due to no one expecting the old quarterback with bad knees to be carrying the ball. Miller liked to keep his plays conservative and then do something surprising. As a result, Morton ran this reverse play successfully a number of times throughout the year.

The fans and community were becoming crazed with support, not even realizing how much Broncomania would grow as the season progressed.

Denver took to the road the following week and posted a relatively easy 24-13 win at Seattle, with the

CRAIG MORTON

QUARTERBACK

1977–1982

Craig Morton was one of three Broncos' Ring of Fame inductees in 1988, along with fellow teammates Haven Moses and Jim Turner. Morton came to the Broncos in a trade with the New York Giants in 1977, and his arrival was the finishing touch on a team primed for its first championship season.

He was Denver's starting quarterback for most of the years from 1977 to 1982, and he led the team to its first postseason and subsequent Super Bowl berth in 1977. That year he guided the Broncos to a 12-2 regular-season record and won home playoff games over Pittsburgh and Oakland.

Morton—who also played for the Cowboys from 1965 to 1974—earned a variety of awards for his performance in 1977, including AFC Most Valuable Player honors, after ranking fourth in the league in passer rating (82.0). He and wide receiver Haven Moses were labeled by rabid Bronco fans as the "M&M Connection."

During his career with Denver, Morton led the team to two division titles (1977 and 1978) and three playoff berths (1977–1979).

He finished his Bronco career ranked first in passing yards (11,895—currently second), touchdown passes (74—currently second), pass attempts (1,594—currently fourth), completions (907—currently fourth), and total offense (12,155—currently fourth). His 41 regular-season career wins as the Broncos' starting quarterback mark the second-highest total in club history, and his .641 winning percentage (41-23) as Denver's signal caller is the third best in franchise annals.

In 1981, the veteran led the NFL with an 8.50-yards-per-attempt average, a figure that stands as the second-highest single-season total in Broncos' history, and he threw for a career-high 3,195 yards. He also tied a personal best with 21 touchdowns in 1981, a total that was the second highest in club history at the time (currently 10th).

Morton once completed 16 consecutive passes in a game and had a streak of nine consecutive games with a touchdown pass. He was a consensus All-American at the University of California, where he also starred in baseball.

Morton's Denver Broncos Record

Games	Starts	Att.	Comp.	Yards	Pct.	TD	INT	LG	Rtg.
72	64	1,594	907	11,895	56.9	74	65	95t	79.1

Morton's NFL Career Record

Games	Starts	Att.	Comp.	Yards	Pct.	TD	INT	LG	Rtg.
203	144	3,786	2,053	27,908	54.2	183	187	95t	73.5

expansion Seahawks never really a threat as the Broncos amassed 330 yards of offense. Fullback Lonnie Perrin and Morton each scored on 1-yard runs, and Morton threw a pretty 47-yard strike to Rob Lytle too.

The Broncos returned home to face division rival Kansas City and moved out to a 23-0 lead before the Chiefs scored their only touchdown as the fourth quarter ran out. Once again, the opponents were held to just 166 yards and proved no match for the now 4-0 Broncos.

The first major test of the season came the following week at Oakland, where the Broncos faced the defending world champions in the intimidating Oakland Coliseum. In the 14 years from 1963 to 1976, the Raiders had a commanding 24-2-2 mark against the Broncos.

Denver absolutely shocked the Raiders, 30-7. Oakland scored first before the Broncos took complete control

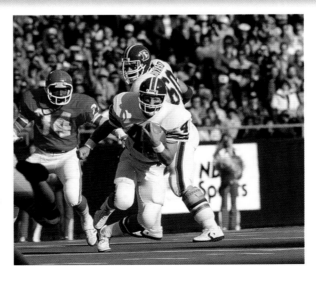

A great player in college, Rob Lytle had a career hampered by injuries. He still was key in gaining tough yardage on the 1977 Super Bowl squad.

of the game, making seven interceptions and a shocking 25-yard touchdown pass on a fake field goal just before the half. That score put the Broncos up 21-7. The defense completely controlled the second half, even picking up a score of its own when the acrobatic Louis Wright made a leaping sideline interception and returned it 18 yards for Denver's final touchdown.

The Broncos pushed their season record to 6-0 at Cincinnati the following week and then returned home for the rematch with Oakland.

By now, fans had dubbed the Morton-to-Moses combo the "M&M Connection," and houses were being painted orange. Used cars were selling better if they happened to be orange, and the defense had become known as the "Orange Crush" (partly because the popular soft drink was bottled in Denver).

The Raiders scored early and often to remind the Broncos and their fans that they were still world champions. It was 24-0 before the Broncos scored twice in the fourth quarter, and the 24-14 loss took some of the bloom off Denver's rose, at least temporarily.

Rick Upchurch returned a punt 87 yards for a score in the first quarter the following week against Pittsburgh, setting the tone for a 21-7 Denver win at home. The next week the Chargers gave Denver all it could handle in San Diego, holding onto a 14-3 lead into the third quarter. However, Morton connected with Moses for a 33-yard score to bring the Broncos within three. Then on the final Denver drive, the M&M Connection again hooked up, this time for an 8-yard touchdown that provided the winning margin.

The following week in Kansas City, a stirring goal line stand on the Chiefs' final drive preserved a 14-7 win, and the wins were looking more miraculous with each passing week. By now, thousands of fans routinely met the team at the airport when it returned from road games. Catching up with the city's frenzied attitude, fullback Jon Keyworth, an aspiring singer, came out with a record single called "Make Those Miracles Happen," local sales of which skyrocketed.

In a November 27 showdown in Denver of the two best records in the NFL, the Broncos got an electrifying 73-yard interception return for a touchdown by Tom Jackson in the fourth quarter to dump Baltimore, 27-13, and run the team's record to 10-1. The Broncos won despite just 11 first downs of their own as Baltimore's Bert Jones led a furious passing assault before the Jackson theft.

The following week, the Broncos won a playoff berth, the first in the club's history, with a routine 24-14 victory at Houston. Later in the day while the team flew home, team members got word that the Raiders had fallen to the Los Angeles Rams and Denver had clinched the AFC West Division championship.

Denver defeated the Chargers at home the following week, 17-9, before losing at Dallas in the regular-season finale, 14-6. Despite the loss, the Broncos posted the best record in the history of the franchise, 12-2, and were tied with the Cowboys for the best record in the NFL.

The defense had allowed just 148 points all year, the lowest mark in club annals, and finished number one in the NFL in fewest yards allowed rushing. Gradishar was a devastating force on short yardage plays and was credited with 219 total tackles by the defensive staff.

MERRY CHRISTMAS TO THE MILE HIGH CITY

Christmas Eve, 1977, gave the victory-starved denizens of the Mile High City the present they had long hoped for but almost didn't think was possible. The Broncos were in the playoffs and would host the fearsome Pittsburgh Steelers before the largest crowd ever to see a sporting event in Colorado.

Denver jumped out to a 7-0 lead after running back Rob Lytle broke through the Steelers' defense to score on a 7-yard run midway through the first quarter. The score came four plays after a punt was blocked by John Schultz and recovered at Pittsburgh's 17 yard line.

Pittsburgh pulled even in the second quarter when quarterback Terry Bradshaw scampered in from 1 yard out. Later in the period, linebacker Tom Jackson recovered a fumble at Pittsburgh's 10 yard line that set up a 10-yard touchdown run by Otis Armstrong on the next play to give Denver a 14-7 lead. The teams went into the locker room tied at 14 after Franco Harris scored on a 1-yard touchdown run late in the half.

The Broncos once again regained the lead, 21-14, after Riley Odoms hauled in a 30-yard pass from Craig Morton for a third-quarter touchdown. Pittsburgh answered early in the fourth quarter with a 1-yard touchdown pass from Bradshaw to Larry Brown. The game had now been tied at 7, 14, and 21, and the Mile High Stadium crowd of 75,011 was in a frenzy.

Midway through the fourth quarter, Denver went on top to stay on the strength of a 44-yard field goal by Jim Turner. On their next drive, the Broncos opened a six-point lead when Turner hit a 25-yard field goal with just under six minutes left in the game.

Euphoria exploded on the Bronco sideline when Morton put the game out of reach, tossing his second touchdown of the game on a strike to Jack Dolbin from 34 yards out. The score was set up after Jackson intercepted his second pass of the game, giving the Broncos the ball on Pittsburgh's 33 yard line.

Morton finished the game completing 11 of 23 passes for 164 yards with two touchdowns as the Broncos racked up 258 yards of total offense against one of the NFL's top defenses. Odoms led the Broncos with five

catches for 43 yards, and Moses chipped in 45 yards receiving on two catches.

The "Orange Crush" defense kept the Steelers off balance all game, holding Bradshaw to just 177 passing yards on 19-of-37 attempts and intercepting him three times. The Denver victory, 34-21, set up a third game between the AFC West Champion Broncos and the AFC Wild Card Raiders in the AFC Championship Game. The teams, of course, had split the two regular-season games earlier in the 1977 season, and as usual the Broncos would be facing a battle-tested defending world championship team accustomed to dominating Denver and expecting nothing different this time.

The long season had taken its physical toll on Morton. He had a nagging hip pointer injury that had been seriously aggravated in the regular-season finale at Dallas then battered again by the Steelers. Unbeknownst to all outside of the organization, including the media, Morton spent the entire week leading up to the AFC title game in the hospital. Miller visited him daily and brought him the game plan to study, but the veteran signal caller was not at all optimistic he could play against the Raiders.

Finally, he made a Sunday-morning decision to go to the stadium and take a chance on playing in the biggest game in Bronco history, knowing that one wrong hit would likely end the season. Before the game, Miller told the offensive

Linebacker Tom Jackson is congratulated by special teams coach Marv Braden, left, while a trainer checks him out on the bench during a game at Mile High Stadium.

Wide receiver Haven Moses pushes forward for extra yardage against the Raiders. Moses was acquired in a trade with Buffalo and was a key to the passing game during his 10 seasons with Denver.

linemen in no uncertain terms that Morton had to be protected at all costs for the Broncos to have a chance.

The game was on January 1, 1978, and every football fan in Denver had a common hope for the new year—a win, securing the team a trip to its first Super Bowl.

The Raiders scored on their initial possession as Errol Mann kicked a 20-yard field goal to end an 18-play, 54-yard drive at 10:34 of the first quarter. Morton hit

wide receiver Haven Moses for the Broncos' first touchdown two plays later on a 74-yard scoring pass, giving Denver a 7-3 advantage.

Despite several Raiders comeback attempts, Denver did not surrender the lead for the remainder of the contest. The Broncos took advantage of two costly Oakland turnovers to increase its lead in the second half. Defensive end Brison Manor recovered running back Clarence Davis' fumble at the Oakland 17, and Jon Keyworth scored from the 1 yard line to increase the Broncos' lead to 14-3 at 6:23 of the third quarter.

Oakland quarterback Ken Stabler hit tight end Dave Casper on the first of two scoring passes to narrow the Denver lead to 14-10 with 39 seconds elapsed in the final quarter.

Bob Swenson had dogged Casper throughout the day, hitting the great tight end at every opportunity, and on Oakland's next possession, Swenson intercepted a Stabler pass and ran to the Raiders' 14. Morton then threw 12 yards to Moses, who made a superb diving catch for the Broncos' final touchdown at 7:17 of the period. Oakland finished the scoring on the next series as Stabler threw 17 yards to Casper for the game's last touchdown.

Denver controlled the ball for the final 3:08 and gave Red Miller the AFC title in his first year as head coach. Moses, a 10-year veteran, led all receivers with 168 yards on five catches (33.6-yard average) with two touchdowns. On the ground, Denver used a balanced attack to gain 91 yards with Lonnie Perrin leading the way with 42.

The Denver defense, number one against the rush in the NFL during the regular season, held the Raiders to 94 yards on the ground and limited Oakland to just 204 passing yards while picking up one interception and one sack.

With great protection from the line all day, Craig Morton was never sacked and connected with his M&M Connection partner twice for scores as the Broncos defeated the defending NFL Champion Raiders, 20-17. Morton completed 10-of-20 passes (50 percent) for 224 yards with two touchdowns that day and had one interception, steering the Broncos to their first Super Bowl berth.

The win was the Broncos second against the Raiders in its three meetings with the club during the 1977 season, and no win in history had ever been sweeter. Many of the 74,982 fans in attendance charged the field to tear down the goalposts, one of the few times that college tradition has happened at a pro venue.

Taking his cue from the decade-old refrain that a Denver appearance in the ultimate title game would be miraculous, radio play-by-play announcer Bob Martin said at the final gun, "The miracle has happened. The Broncos are going to the Super Bowl."

HAVEN MOSES
WIDE RECEIVER
1972–1981

Haven Moses was inducted into the Denver Broncos' Ring of Fame in 1988 as part of a three-member class that included quarterback Craig Morton and kicker Jim Turner. Moses played 10 seasons for the Broncos from 1972 to 1981 as one of the team's primary wide receivers. He played his first four professional seasons with Buffalo. His smooth professionalism on the field and polite, classy manner in his numerous public appearances made him one of the fan favorites in the Mile High City.

He finished his Broncos career ranked third in receptions (302—currently eighth) and receiving yards (5,450—currently eighth) while tying for first in receiving touchdowns with 44 (currently tied for fourth). His yards-per-catch average for his Denver career was 18.0, which marks the second-highest career total in franchise history. He averaged more than 19 yards per catch in three consecutive seasons from 1976 to 1978.

Moses, who helped lead Denver to three playoff berths (1977–1979) and two division titles (1977 and 1978), was a key member of the first winning season in Broncos' history in 1973 (7-5-2) as he caught a career-high eight touchdown passes to earn Pro Bowl honors.

He teamed with quarterback Craig Morton to create what fans dubbed the "M&M Connection" during the glorious 1977 campaign in which Denver reached the national stage for good.

In the AFC Championship Game against Oakland during the 1977 season, Moses caught five passes for 168 yards and two touchdowns to propel Denver to its first Super Bowl appearance.

In 1979, he had career bests in receptions (54) and receiving yards (943). One of the most polished and sure-handed receivers in team history, he was known for making the big catch in key situations.

In college, Moses was a two-year letterman and an All-American as a wide receiver and defensive back at San Diego State University.

Moses' Denver Broncos Record

Games	Starts	Rec.	Yds.	Avg.	LG	TD
140	127	302	5,450	18.0	64t	44

Moses' NFL Career Record

Games	Starts	Rec.	Yds.	Avg.	LG	TD
199	N/A	448	8,091	18.1	76t	56

DISAPPOINTED BY DALLAS IN THE CRESCENT CITY

The Super Bowl seemed almost like an anticlimax to Bronco fans who never thought they would see a magical season like 1977. Sadly, the magic had to end sometime.

The Dallas Cowboys defeated the Broncos by a 27-10 score in Super Bowl XII, played at the Louisiana Superdome before the usual sellout crowd. Ninety million television viewers, the largest audience ever to watch a sporting event at the time, tuned in too.

Dallas converted two pass interceptions by safety Randy Hughes and cornerback Aaron Kyle into 10 points in the first quarter. Efren Herrera added a 43-yard field goal in the second quarter to give the Cowboys a 13-0 halftime advantage.

The Denver offense struggled in the first half. The Broncos lost three fumbles and had two interceptions

Jim Turner, shaking hands, is among a select group of NFL players to meet President Gerald Ford and first lady Betty Ford.

on their final five possessions of the first half, under fierce pressure from the Cowboy pass rush.

The Broncos came back momentarily at the outset of the third quarter. Craig Morton engineered a drive to the Cowboys' 30 yard line, where Jim Turner booted a 47-yard field goal to make the score 13-3. After an exchange of punts, Dallas wide receiver Butch Johnson made a spectacular diving catch in the end zone to complete a 45-yard pass from Roger Staubach, and put the Cowboys ahead 20-3 at 8:01 of the third quarter.

However, the momentum swung back to the Broncos as Rick Upchurch returned the kickoff 67 yards to the Dallas 26. On the second play of the series, Norris Weese relieved Morton at quarterback. Morton, who was intercepted an NFL-low eight times during the regular season, had thrown a Super Bowl record of four interceptions when he was replaced. Weese guided the Broncos to

a touchdown—a 1-yard run by Rob Lytle—to cut the Dallas lead to 20-10 with 5:39 left in the third.

Dallas clinched the victory when running back Robert Newhouse threw a 29-yard touchdown pass to Golden Richards on an option play at 7:56 of the fourth quarter. It was the first pass thrown by Newhouse since the 1975 regular season. The Cowboys' offense amassed 325 yards, while the defense limited the Broncos to 156 yards in a game that saw the Cowboys control the ball 38:34 to Denver's 21:26.

Staubach completed 17-of-25 passes (68 percent) for 183 yards while Harvey Martin and Randy White—who were named co-MVPs—led a Cowboys defense that recovered four fumbles and intercepted four passes.

In a fitting end to a dazzling season, Lyle Alzado, Randy Gradishar, Tom Jackson, Billy Thompson, and Louis Wright represented the Broncos in the Pro Bowl, the largest

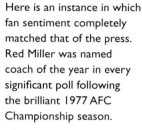

Here is an instance in which fan sentiment completely matched that of the press. Red Miller was named coach of the year in every significant poll following the brilliant 1977 AFC Championship season.

Denver contingent to date in the all-star game. Miller received numerous coach-of-the-year honors.

Morton, the collegiate golden-boy quarterback who resurrected his pro career in Denver, also received many postseason honors, including being named the AFC Offensive Player of the Year by *The Sporting News*. Frustrated in Dallas and New York, Morton had fulfilled all his potential in the Mile High City.

After that scintillating 1977 campaign, it was hard for the rest of the decade to be as exciting. Still, the franchise had embarked on a portion of its history that would be measured by an amazing percentage of winning seasons and a succession of playoff appearances that would redefine how the Denver Broncos were viewed in American sports.

DENVER STILL WARMED BY AFTERGLOW

The following season was one in which the defense played even better, but the offense sputtered just enough to turn some of those 1977 victories into 1978 losses. The team finished with a 10-6 record, winning a second consecutive division championship in the process.

Although a midseason legal ruling prevented the club from using the "Orange Crush" moniker, as the name and related logos belonged to the soft drink company, the name was still used for many years by the press to describe the Denver brand of defense.

The defense more than held its own, ranking second in the NFL in points allowed, fewest total yards allowed, and fewest passing yards allowed, while still being an almost impenetrable third in the league against the run. Randy Gradishar led the way with a credited 286 total tackles, a figure unbelievable to anyone except those who actually watched him play.

This was quite simply one of the best defenses in pro football history, putting up 31 interceptions to go along with those lofty statistical rankings. Tom Jackson had 6, another tremendous total from a linebacker, and Steve Foley played his safety position with the aplomb of a centerfielder, also posting 6 thefts to lead the defensive backs. Lyle Alzado rushed the passer with his usual intimidating passion and led the defensive line with 9 sacks.

The opponents reached the 20-point mark only three times all season. Oakland was held without a touchdown in both games against Denver, including a 14-6 win that began the season. Eight times, fully half the schedule, the opposition was held to single-digit point totals, including once in a loss, a wretched 7-6 defeat at Baltimore.

On December 3, the Broncos won with a 21-6 score at Oakland, the defense matching its no-TDs-allowed opening day win against the Raiders. With the win, Denver moved within one game of its second straight AFC West crown. The team clinched its division the following week at home against Kansas City, 24-3, as Morton

went 19-for-22 with 16 consecutive completions, both second-best all-time NFL marks.

The offense had the same philosophy and style as the year before but made fewer big plays and put greater pressure on the brilliant defense. Still, those defenders were more than up to the challenge all season long.

Denver's second foray in postseason play was on the road at Pittsburgh, against a Steelers team that eventually won four world championships in six years.

Without the Mile High Stadium crowd and with the playoff debut of Pittsburgh's Terrible Towels being waved by the rabid Steel City fans, the Broncos were defeated. Home quarterback Terry Bradshaw threw two fourth-quarter touchdown passes to carry the Steelers to a 33-10 victory at Three Rivers Stadium. Bradshaw's scoring tosses included a 45-yard bomb to John Stallworth

One of the game's fastest inside linebackers, Randy Gradishar had more than 2,000 tackles during his seven-time Pro Bowl career. Here, he draws a bead on an Oakland ball carrier.

Defensive end Barney Chavous chases down New England quarterback Steve Grogan in a November 1979 45-10 win. The game began under clear skies, but a heavy snowstorm engulfed the city by halftime.

Pittsburgh recorded 425 yards of total offense with Bradshaw accounting for 272 through the air. He completed 16-of-29 passes (55.2 percent) to go along with the two touchdowns. Stallworth led all receivers with 156 yards on 10 receptions, and Swann finished with 52 yards on just two catches.

The eventual world champion Steelers limited the Broncos' ground game to just 87 yards and held the offense to just 218 yards. Morton was knocked out of the game by the vaunted Pittsburgh pass rush, and Norris Weese finished the contest with 118 yards passing on 8-of-16 attempts and was sacked five times. Weese also was the team's leading rusher, accounting for 43 yards on four carries, while Preston was stifled for just 14 yards on four rushes.

The Broncos were represented by an all-time high of seven players in the NFL Pro Bowl, five on defense, including Alzado, Gradishar, Jackson, Thompson, and Wright, along with Odoms at tight end and the unbelievably talented Upchurch as the kick returner.

The day had long passed when Denver was lightly regarded by fans, press, or the opposition.

A MAGICAL DECADE CLOSES DOWN

In 1979, there was a spirited battle for the starting quarterback position during training camp. Fan favorite Weese was ultimately named as the starter instead of the aging Morton.

Although the team started off 2-1, the offense was sputtering. In game four at home against Seattle, the Seahawks were off to a 34-10 lead by the middle of the third quarter when Red Miller made the call to replace Weese with Morton, who received a huge ovation as his old legs ambled into the huddle.

Two minutes and 34 seconds later, Denver trailed by just three points. Morton threw a 2-yard touchdown pass to tackle Dave Studdard on a fourth-down, tackle-eligible play, and an 11-yard touchdown pass to Haven Moses, which closed out a drive set up by an Upchurch punt return. Morton also hit Upchurch with a 35-yard end zone strike following a Seattle turnover. With three touchdown passes in fewer than three minutes, Morton was back as the starter, when healthy, for the balance of the year. Denver shut down Seattle the rest of the way, and one final drive produced a 1-yard run by Rob Lytle and the greatest Denver comeback win of all time.

Denver was on its way to a 10-6 final mark, which the team moved toward with a sterling defensive performance against the superb San Diego offense on October 7. The Broncos posted a 7-0 win despite the Chargers' Dan Fouts passing for 305 yards on 27 completions.

Another fan favorite among the wins that year was a November 11 meeting with the Patriots that began on

and a 38-yarder to Lynn Swann, capping a brilliant performance by the Pittsburgh passer.

The Broncos took a 3-0 lead midway through the first quarter on a 37-yard Jim Turner field goal, but the Steelers were able to come right back and take control of the game.

Pittsburgh running back Franco Harris scored his first touchdown of the game on a 1-yard plunge, which capped a 66-yard, eight-play drive. After the extra-point try missed, the Steelers held a 6-3 lead at the 12:27 mark of the first quarter. The Steelers upped their margin on Harris' second touchdown of the game early in the second quarter. He scored on an 18-yard run that gave Pittsburgh a 13-3 advantage.

Denver was able to cut its deficit on a 3-yard Dave Preston touchdown run. But late in the first half, Pittsburgh's Roy Gerela kicked another field goal to make the halftime score 19-10.

Denver threatened to pull closer in the third quarter, but Turner's 29-yard field-goal attempt was blocked. Bradshaw's passing sealed Denver's fate early in the final stanza. His touchdown pass to Stallworth capped a 71-yard, four-play drive, and his last touchdown pass to Swann ended Denver's chances.

a warm fall afternoon. In the game, the Broncos racked up a 38-7 halftime lead before a tremendous snowstorm hit the Mile High City at the break. The field was completely covered by the early third quarter, and the concessions stands sold every piece of cold weather gear in a matter of minutes. Most of the audience of 74,379 scurried for home as Denver became blanketed by snow, and neither offense was able to handle the second half field conditions well, as the Broncos sledded into an easy 45-10 win.

In that game against New England, Rick Upchurch became the all-time pro football record holder in career punt return yardage, surpassing the late Emlen Tunnell's total of 2,209 yards. Upchurch later would be named to the 1970s all-decade team as pro football's finest return man that era.

The 1979 season came down to a final Monday night game at San Diego that would make the winner division champ and the loser a wild card. It was a tight defensive struggle tied 7-7 at the half, but Fouts threw a 32-yard third-quarter touchdown pass that held up for a final score of 17-7 in favor of the Chargers.

The Broncos had made the playoffs once again, but this time as the wild card team. Despite the team's improvement from the early 1970s, there was a definite sense that the club had reached a peak and was slipping from the two previous seasons.

In the wild card matchup, Houston kicker Toni Fritsch kicked two field goals to provide the six-point margin of victory as the Oilers played strong second-half defense and defeated the Broncos 13-7 at the Astrodome. Fritsch also opened the scoring with a 31-yard first-quarter field goal, which capped an 11-play, 64-yard drive.

Denver came back to take a 7-3 lead later in the first quarter on a 7-yard pass from Morton to Dave Preston on an 80-yard drive that took the Broncos 11 plays.

However, Houston went ahead to stay on a 3-yard burst by the great Earl Campbell at 14:14 of the second quarter. The drive amassed 74 yards in nine plays, but Campbell was injured on the scoring play and did not return to action in the second half. Still, Houston took the 10-7 lead into halftime.

Denver linebacker Bob Swenson intercepted a Gifford Nielsen pass at the Oilers' 26 yard line midway through the fourth period. However, two Morton sacks led to a 50-yard field-goal attempt by Fred Steinfort, which hit the upright. On the ensuing possession, the Oilers drove for a second field goal by Fritsch, this one from 20 yards, providing the final victory margin.

Denver drove to the Houston 27 yard line at the two-minute mark, but the Oilers' defense again rose to the occasion to stifle the threat and secure the win.

Oilers quarterback Dan Pastorini and wide receiver Ken Burrough left the contest due to injuries, both early

in the second half, putting a severe crimp in the Houston attack. Still, the Broncos were able to move the ball for only 216 yards, and the tenacious Houston defense sacked Morton six times for 40 yards on the afternoon. Denver also was limited to just 4-of-13 (31 percent) success on third down and was forced to punt six times in the contest.

Denver's defeat—despite the fact Houston's three main offensive weapons were out of the game for virtually the entire second half—left a bitter aftertaste for the Bronco organization.

Denver had Pro Bowl performances once again from Gradishar, Jackson, Upchurch, and Wright; however, a decade of passion and sellouts had made those individual awards nice but not quite enough for the team's fervent backers.

The Broncos' second decade ended with the frustration bred by their growing playoff success. The team had grown in the 1970s—to show it could compete at the highest level and thus the highest expectations were upon it.

1970s
DENVER BRONCOS
YEAR BY YEAR

1970	5-8-1
1971	4-9-1
1972	5-9
1973	7-5-2
1974	7-6-1
1975	6-8
1976	9-5
1977	12-2
1978	10-6
1979	10-6

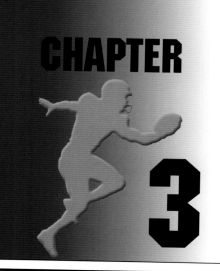
THE 1980S
THREE TIMES, WITHOUT A CHARM

Head coach Dan Reeves gives sideline instructions to running back Steve Sewell.

FAN FRENZY ACCOMPANIES TEAM GROWTH

The Denver Broncos franchise had grown and evolved as it began its third decade, and so had the team's fans. No longer was this a team happy to just exist, sell tickets, and compete for whatever the big guys left on the table. The 1978 Super Bowl appearance had changed all that. The team's stature also had grown on a national level, as Broncos games were now a fixture on national network coverage and the team was in the process of becoming a perennial contender.

Only 146 season tickets were not renewed for 1980, virtually assuring the club of its 11th consecutive sellout campaign. With each sellout came an increased demand from the fan base, who expected their NFL team to reach the championship game again and this time win.

In the two years since the Super Bowl, the team had seen its record dip each year, winning the division in 1978 and slipping into the playoffs as a wild card in 1979. Each year, the Broncos were eliminated in the first round of the playoffs. More was expected in 1980.

The Broncos had engineered a major offseason trade to bring quarterback Matt Robinson over from the Jets, with the hope that he could be the successor to the aging Craig Morton. However, Robinson proved erratic, completing less than 50 percent of his passes, holding an abysmal passer rating of 39.5. He eventually lost the starting job to Morton, whose creaky knees supported him enough to complete 60.8 percent of his throws for 12 touchdowns.

Still, the Broncos had seen their talent pool wane within the competitive AFC West, and Denver finished fourth with an 8-8 record in 1980. Fullback Jim Jensen was the leading rusher with just 476 yards and also led the team in catches with 49 for 377 yards; of course, watching a fullback lead all wide receivers in receptions was not what the team owners and fans had in mind.

On October 5 at Cleveland, Ohio, native Randy Gradishar returned an interception 93 yards for a touchdown to provide the impetus for a big road win over the Browns. That return still stands as the longest interception return in team history, and it was the NFL's longest for the 1980 season. The following week against Washington, placekicker Fred Steinfort booted a 57-yard field goal, tying the record for the third-longest kick in NFL history. Steinfort was named by *Pro Football Weekly* as the publication's recipient of the Golden Toe Award for the 1980 season, eventually leading the league with 26 field goals.

But overall, 1980's highlights were few and far between, and the Phipps brothers were getting older and a bit weary. They had invested in the team in its infancy and then a few years later saved it for Denver in the manner that had become commonplace for them— doing the best thing for the common good.

Denver had a place in pro football history entirely because of Gerry Phipps and his brother, Allan. Now they were looking to the future and thinking it might be time to sell the club into younger hands, putting a new generation of ownership in place.

NEW OWNER, NEW COACH, SAME FEVER

Numerous proposals to purchase the Broncos had been made and rebuffed over the years, but the feeling was that this was the time. So on February 25, 1981, Edgar F. Kaiser Jr. was introduced as the new owner of the Rocky Mountain region's proudest franchise, having purchased the club from principal owners Gerald H. Phipps and Allan R. Phipps. Negotiations had been conducted privately, and the news came suddenly to the fans.

Kaiser was chairman and chief executive officer of Kaiser Resources Ltd., which was a privately owned, diversified Canadian energy company. He also was vice chairman of the Henry J. Kaiser Family Foundation and was the grandson of the late construction industrialist Henry J. Kaiser.

He wasted little time putting his own stamp on the Broncos, making a decision to replace general manager Fred Gehrke and head coach Red Miller.

Grady Alderman was named the new general manager. He came to the Broncos after a long playing career and two years in the Minnesota Vikings front office. But the star of the show proved to be new head coach Dan Reeves, who came to Denver from the Dallas Cowboys at the age of 37, making him the youngest NFL head coach at that time.

Recognized as one of the most successful offensive coaches in the league, he had spent his entire pro career in Dallas, both as a player and a coach. He had been offensive coordinator for the Cowboys for the past three seasons, presiding over a multiple offensive attack

that had produced 454 points and 60 touchdowns in 1980, both tops in the NFL.

Fan shock over the suddenness of these front office moves quickly gave way to the excitement of what the Denver offense would look like under Reeves' command.

Reeves made several changes in the Denver coaching staff, as would be expected, but one coach who stayed put was the defensive coordinator. Joe Collier had become a local legend and was very popular, and the new head coach was determined to make his new offense a match for Collier's defense.

Randy Gradishar takes a breather while the offense is on the field. An annual Hall of Fame candidate, he led the team in tackles for nine straight years, accounted for 33 turnovers, and was voted the NFL Defensive Player of the Year in 1978.

Steve Foley was a quarterback at Tulane University but became a first-class safety for the Broncos. He remains the team's all-time interception leader, with 44.

An unheralded free agent from Temple, wide receiver Steve Watson had a breakout season in 1981. That year, the lithe target caught 60 passes for a 20.7-yard average and scored 13 touchdowns. With such a stellar effort, he earned a Pro Bowl berth.

When the 1981 campaign began, Bronco fans in the Mile High City had a rekindled excitement, which had extended into the club as well. Morton and Reeves had worked together in Dallas, and the veteran quarterback and young coach bonded quickly to lead the Broncos to a 10-6 record, which left the team eliminated from the playoffs by the slimmest of tiebreaker margins.

The new offense proved to be an elixir for Morton's big arm and sage skills. He had his best season as a Bronco with highs of 21 touchdowns, 3,195 passing yards, and a passer rating of 90.5. Marking a first in franchise history, Morton threw four touchdown passes in each of two consecutive September games, a 28-10 win over Baltimore and a 42-24 triumph over San Diego.

That contest against the Colts turned out to be the coming-out party for young wide receiver Steve Watson, who joined the club as a college free agent in 1979 and spent his first two years either on the bench or playing special teams. During that time, coaches realized he had big play ability as a receiver, and he moved into the starting lineup in 1981. He was not well known to Bronco fans going into the season, but that all changed when Morton threw touchdown strikes of 29, 18, and 48 yards to the smooth, young pass catcher. Watson went on to lead the team with 60 receptions for 1,244 yards and 13 scores during the season, becoming an all-time Denver fan favorite in his first year as a starter. His three receptions against the Colts were his first scores as a professional and tied Denver's single-game record.

The Chargers were still the reigning division powerhouse at that time, and when the Broncos jumped out to a 35-0 halftime lead, it signaled the arrival of a new offense and a new attitude in Denver. Denver shut out the Raiders at Oakland the following week, 17-0, and followed that up with a 27-21 victory over the Detroit Lions.

In the Detroit game, Morton threw three scoring passes, the first a spectacular 95-yarder to Watson in which the young wideout caught the ball over the middle, bounced off his defender, and set sail for the game's first score. He caught another touchdown, this one from 40 yards out, from Morton, and Denver ended the day with a record of 5-1.

The Broncos had a fine season in Reeves' rookie campaign as a head coach, with Morton rejuvenated under the tutelage of his old Dallas teammate and Watson earning a national reputation for his great hands and work ethic.

While Morton and Watson led the way on offense, the defense again was paced by Randy Gradishar. He led the team in tackles with what would be 258 total tackles by season's end. He also added four pass interceptions to his stats to tie Billy Thompson's total while Steve Foley led the Broncos with five. And Bob Swenson was having his finest season, returning from a severe 1980 leg injury to record 145 tackles, second only to Gradishar, while also intercepting three passes and forcing three fumbles.

At Cincinnati on November 22, Watson caught a touchdown pass to set a new Bronco single season record with 13 end-zone catches. However, the Bengals posted a 38-21 win, which was followed up with another Bronco loss, this one at San Diego by a 17-point margin, with a score of 34-17.

The team was better and the new offensive game was very popular, but the Broncos still had ground to make up in overall talent. They went into the season finale at Chicago with a 9-5 win/loss record, needing a win to capture the division and make the playoffs, while a loss would leave them out of the playoffs altogether.

It was a frigid 14 degrees in the Windy City when the Broncos and Bears took the field. Sideline personnel were wearing every piece of cold-weather gear they could find, but the temperature was no colder than the Broncos that day, as Chicago's pass rush was in Morton's face all day. Despite holding the Bears to just 281 yards of total offense, the Broncos watched as two Morton passes were intercepted and returned for Chicago scores in a disappointing 35-24 defeat that ended the Bronco season.

Nevertheless, Watson gained 82 yards on receptions at Chicago, establishing a new Bronco single season mark with 1,244 reception yards. Individually, Morton set single-season records for yards gained (3,213), yards passing (3,195), and average gain per play (8.37 yards), while Watson led the AFC in reception yardage and in touchdown receptions (13).

Watson was named to the Pro Bowl to cap off a magical first year in the starting lineup. He was joined by Gradishar, Thompson, and Swenson, with the latter making what would be his only Pro Bowl appearance in a career marred by injury.

As the 1982 season approached, again the Mile High City had a heavy dose of optimism about the Broncos' chances. In preparation, the Denver Broncos' player personnel department decided to clean out its résumé files early in 1982 by inviting every single player, prospect or not, to a Saturday morning free agent tryout camp.

The tryout had all the appearances of an NFL version of the *Star Wars* bar. It was a bizarre assortment of individuals, most of whom could be deemed to have no chance in the NFL just by one look at their physiques. Still, everyone got a chance to run a dash before being summarily sent home, and the kickers had a chance to kick. One player actually stood out enough to merit a contract and a chance to come to camp as a placekicker: Rich Karlis, who surely was making the most improbable entry into pro football imaginable. He was the survivor of a 478-player tryout camp.

Barefoot placekicker Rich Karlis kicks a field goal with Gary Kubiak holding. Karlis first made the team out of a 478-player tryout camp and went on to kick seven years for the Broncos, becoming one of the most popular players among fans.

Quarterback Steve DeBerg drops back to pass during a December 1982 game. A savvy vet, DeBerg transitioned the Broncos into the Elway era with his steady performance. Always-reliable tackle Ken Lanier holds off the rush.

That camp was just the beginning of a season that would shock the game and its fans.

The Broncos opened the season with two home games, a 23-3 defeat at the hands of the Chargers and an exciting 24-21 win against the San Francisco 49ers.

And then the players went home.

FOR AMERICA'S GAME, THE GAMES END

On September 21, the NFL Players Association began the first regular-season strike in NFL history, resulting in game cancellation for eight consecutive weeks.

It was one of the most surreal moments in Broncos' and pro football history. The strike created a tragedy of denial, shock, anger, blame, guilt, and, on top of that, no football for all those involved. The weeks dragged on with both sides initially far from agreeing. It appeared the season would resume numerous times, each one leading up to a cancelled game, neither side being able to settle upon an agreement.

Players tried to stay in shape during the long hiatus, but without structured workouts it was a losing battle for many, including the venerable Morton. His creaky knees made playing difficult under the best of circumstances.

When the strike was settled and the Broncos resumed play by hosting Seattle on November 21, it was obvious that the long layoff had taken its toll on Morton. His career was now effectively over.

Denver and its legendary legions of fans trudged through a grim half season of play, with the Broncos winning only once in the final seven games. That sole victory came in a 27-24 game over the Rams on the road in December.

The team with the best home record in pro football during the past decade did not have a home win after the September 19 pre-strike game with San Francisco. The most exciting home moment of the campaign came on December 19 when Rick Upchurch returned a punt 78 yards for a touchdown against Kansas City to tie the then-all-time pro football record of eight career touchdowns on punt returns.

Upchurch ended the year as the NFL's punt return leader with a 16.1-yard average and earned yet another Pro Bowl berth, along with Gradishar and punter Luke Prestridge. Prestridge had plenty of work due to the woeful campaign, finishing with a league-best 45-yard average.

The 1982 campaign ranked among the worst seasons the Broncos ever experienced, but it led up to the single most seminal moment in Denver sports history.

THE GREATEST TRADE IN DENVER SPORTS HISTORY

Sometimes in a franchise's history, a single event takes place that completely changes everything for the team, its city, its region, and its entire fandom. The acquisition of

Rulon Jones was a two-time Pro Bowler in the 1980s and a starting defensive end on the first two of the John Elway-quarterbacked Super Bowl teams. Jones had 73.5 career sacks as a fiery competitor and defensive leader.

Broncos fans—always present, vocal, and in orange at Mile High Stadium—were fired up for a new era in Denver with the arrival of John Elway in 1983.

Gary Kubiak came to the Broncos as a rookie along with Elway, and he was an exceptional backup quarterback throughout his nine-year Bronco career.

John Elway was that single event for the Broncos and for the city of Denver.

The most highly touted player to come into the NFL draft perhaps since Joe Namath two decades earlier, Elway was the superstar's superstar as a prospect, the obvious and only candidate to be the first pick in the 1983 NFL draft. But Baltimore held that first pick. However, Elway and his father, Jack, a longtime college coach who was very successful in his own right, preferred that John play his pro career in a system other than that of Colts coach Frank Kush.

Elway had previously been drafted by and signed a baseball contract with the New York Yankees. He had played a season for the Yankees' Oneonta farm club and was threatening to play baseball rather than football if selected by Baltimore. When the draft took place, Baltimore selected Elway against his wishes, and virtually every team in football made a pitch to trade for the unhappy college superstar.

While the other teams were making their calls to Baltimore general manager Ernie Accorsi and to head coach Frank Kush, Bronco owner Edgar Kaiser was cultivating his sales pitch directly with Colts owner Robert Irsay. The two had completed previous business deals, and both had fondness and respect for each other.

One week after the draft ended, Denver head coach Dan Reeves was on the golf course enjoying a spring round in the Mile High City when he got a call from

Pat Bowlen named John Beake as the Broncos' general manager in 1985, Beake's seventh season with the club. He worked directly with Bowlen directing the administrative and personnel dealings of the club for two decades, and he remains a consultant for NFL commissioner Roger Goodell to this day.

Kaiser informing him that the deal for Elway was virtually done. Reeves was shocked to find that to trade for one of the greatest quarterbacks ever to come into the NFL, all Denver would give up were its No. 1 draft choice Chris Hinton, the Broncos' 1984 No. 1 draft choice as well, and backup quarterback Mark Herrmann, who would become expendable with the addition of Elway to the roster. The Broncos also would host the Colts for two preseason games, after each the tidy game check would be handed over to Irsay.

With those terms, Reeves eagerly gave his blessings. Kaiser cemented the deal, and Elway and his legal party flew into Denver by private plane for a clandestine meeting on the aircraft. They concurred that if a contract agreement were reached, a press conference would immediately follow. If they could not agree, Elway and the plane would take off and the deal was off. The deal was made, and at 8:30 p.m. a hurried round of calls was made to a flabbergasted Denver press corps.

On May 2, in the biggest trade in franchise history and one of the most significant in the entire history of pro football, Denver acquired quarterback John Elway and signed him to a five-year contract. The deal was announced at a 10:30 p.m. press conference and set the stage for a level of sports reporting that, to this point, had not even been imagined in the Rocky Mountain region.

The trade first was discussed with the Broncos' PR department in Kaiser's suite at the San Diego Town and Country Hotel on November 28, 1982, more than five full months before the deal was consummated. At that time, Kaiser wanted to assess the public relations value of such a trade, which was monumental beyond any consideration. The owner greeted skepticism about it by noting that anything is for sale, if one is willing to pay the price. Kaiser made it very clear at that time that if the Broncos' operations people agreed upon what a quarterback of that ilk would mean to the team, then his intention was to make it happen.

And now on May 2, the path was set, as during Elway's career the Broncos would go to the Super Bowl five times, the legendary Baltimore Colts would eventually move to Indianapolis, and after three AFC Championship losses to the Broncos, Cleveland's beloved Browns would move to Baltimore, filling the void left by the Colts' departure.

ELWAY, ELWAY, ELWAY

But those were all things to come. The present was Elway, the team was the Broncos, and the city was Denver. The stars had aligned for the Broncos like never before.

It did not take long for the new quarterback to make his presence felt among the coaches and scouts at Denver's 1983 training camp. He was anointed as the Denver starter before the first regular-season game. However, the learning curve is great for all NFL rookies, and John Elway was replaced at halftime of the first regular-season game. Steve DeBerg led Denver in the second half to a 14-10 win against Pittsburgh.

The following week also saw a change at the half as Denver won 17-10 at Baltimore, with DeBerg again leading the second half win. The big story, however, was that Elway was making his first visit to Baltimore, home to

John Elway took his first regular-season snaps as Denver's quarterback in the 1983 season opener against the Pittsburgh Steelers at Three Rivers Stadium on September 4. Although Elway completed only one of eight pass attempts, the Broncos defeated the Steelers 14-10.
Photo by George Gojkovich/ Getty Images

Sammy Winder was a tough, working-class running back who started for the Broncos on all three Super Bowl teams during the 1980s. Winder's trademark touchdown celebration was known as the "Mississippi Mud Dance," a tribute to his home state.

some of football's most passionate fans and a community that felt totally spurned by the NFL rookie. The anticipation of an extraordinarily negative reception prompted the Broncos to bring their own security on the road for the first time.

Elway held onto the starting job for three more weeks, all Denver losses, before Dan Reeves made the decision to go with the veteran DeBerg and let his wunderkind quarterback take a breather and learn from the bench.

The Broncos proceeded to win four straight under journeyman DeBerg, but an injury to DeBerg put Elway back into the lineup for a road game at San Diego on November 27. Denver dropped that game to the Chargers, 31-7, and for one brief but long-remembered moment Elway lined up behind guard Tom Glassic and began to call the signals. Glassic eventually peered over his shoulder to alert the young signal caller to his gaffe.

Those looking for further embarrassing moments from Elway had to look hard because he was on the verge of his coming-out party as a pro quarterback. Denver had a record of 7-6 after the loss in San Diego and appeared to have a slim, outside chance at a playoff berth. Then the Stanford rookie with the great arm shuffled the wild card deck in the following two weeks.

Elway had his finest game as a pro against the Browns on the first weekend in December, passing for 284 yards and two touchdowns to lead the Broncos to a 27-6 victory. He connected on touchdown passes of 39 and

Whether in Baltimore or Indianapolis, Colts fans combined great respect with deep-rooted ill will for Elway.

Head coach Dan Reeves discusses strategy with backup quarterback Gary Kubiak during a December 1984 loss at Kansas City. Kubiak had a great mind for the game and gave early signs of his future career in coaching. After his playing days were over, he was Denver's offensive coordinator for years before becoming the head coach of the Houston Texans.

49 yards to wide receiver Clint Sampson in a 21-point Denver second quarter to pace the win.

The following week, Denver played its final home game of the season, and Elway made it memorable. The Broncos clinched their first playoff berth since 1979 with a 21-19 victory over the Colts, but there was nothing easy or routine about it. Baltimore built up a 19-0 lead after three periods, but Elway then threw three fourth-quarter touchdown passes to produce the winning margin. He threw to nine different receivers in the game, winding up with 348 yards and his first fourth-quarter comeback—a category that would ultimately be one of the many statistics to mark his entry into the Pro Football Hall of Fame.

In that first comeback win, Elway connected with Sampson for 21 yards and with rookie running back Jesse Myles for 26, but that still left Denver trailing with three minutes left and the ball at the Broncos' own 25 yard line. Elway drove the team to the Baltimore 26, where

LOUIS WRIGHT
CORNERBACK
1975–1986

Louis Wright was named to the Denver Broncos' Ring of Fame in 1993 following an electrifying 12-year career with the club as a cornerback.

Selected by the Broncos in the first round (17th overall) of the 1975 NFL Draft from San Jose State University, Wright was a five-time Pro Bowl selection (1977, 1978, 1979, 1983, 1985). He is one of only nine players in franchise history to be selected to at least five Pro Bowls. He was named All-NFL by *The Sporting News*, *Pro Football Weekly*, and the NEA in 1977, a year in which he was a key member of Denver's 12-2 team that reached Super Bowl XII.

During his career, Wright helped the Broncos earn six playoff berths (1977, 1978, 1979, 1983, 1984, 1986), four division titles (1977, 1978, 1984, 1986), and two Super Bowl appearances (XII in 1977 and XXI in 1986). He received All-AFC honors from UPI in 1985 after snagging five interceptions, while his teammates voted him Denver's MVP on defense following both the 1982 and 1984 seasons.

Wright played 166 career games as a Bronco, including 163 starts. That statistic ranked fourth in club history at the time of his retirement and currently stands eighth. The popular defensive back played every game in a season eight times, including the 1983 season in which he recorded a career- and team-high six interceptions. Many times, radio and television announcers of his era would remind viewers and listeners that Bronco fans were not booing, but they were just chanting "Louie."

Wright's 26 career interceptions rank seventh in club history and his 360 career interception return yards are eighth on Denver's all-time list. He recovered 11 fumbles for his career and scored touchdowns twice on fumble recoveries.

In addition, Wright had one of the most dramatic plays in team history on November 17, 1985, when he scored the fourth and final touchdown of his career on a 60-yard return of a blocked field goal in overtime. The play spurred Denver to a 30-24 win against San Diego.

At San Jose State, Wright was a two-time letter winner as a defensive back. He also won two letters in track and once ran the 100 in 9.6 seconds.

Wright's Denver Broncos Career Record

Games	Starts	Sacks	Int.	Yds.	Avg.	TD	Fum. Rec.	Fum TD	Tot. TD
166	163	3.0	26	360	13.8	1	11	2	4*

Includes a blocked field goal returned for a touchdown (versus San Diego on November 17, 1985)

Denver faced a fourth and two. He was blitzed hard up the middle when running back Gerald Willhite lost track of the defender he was supposed to block, so Elway adjusted on the run and hit the wide-open Willhite on the 16. Willhite scampered to the end zone for the winning score and one of his trademark back flips.

Randy Gradishar was in the midst of another great year with 224 tackles to pace Denver's defense. Steve Watson finished the year with 59 catches for a 19.2-yard average, and the Broncos were back in the playoffs again.

The fact that the team still had a lot of room for improvement was accented when Seattle easily handed the Broncos a 31-7 loss in the wild card playoff game. In the contest, Reeves opted to return DeBerg to the starting lineup, despite Elway's late-season heroics.

Three turnovers—interceptions by DeBerg and Elway, along with a fumble by Willhite—proved to be the difference in the game. Elway played the second half and completed 10-of-15 passes for 123 yards in his first career postseason appearance.

Gradishar and Louis Wright again were named to the Pro Bowl for their sterling defensive play, but the focus was turning toward Elway and the offense in Denver.

A GREAT DAWN IN DENVER

When Edgar Kaiser had the chance to sell the Broncos in the spring of 1984, the opportunity was too good to ignore. The team had seen home sellouts since the last game of 1969, the NFL had the most lucrative television contract in the history of professional sports, and the Broncos had become a very valuable property.

A new era in Denver sports history began on March 23 when Pat Bowlen was introduced as the new majority owner of the Broncos. A Wisconsin native with business and law degrees from the University of Oklahoma, Bowlen came to Denver as a successful businessman in both the United States and Canada. He had varied holdings in both real estate and natural resources. He immediately proved to be a dynamic chief executive who would take both winning and the expectation of winning to an unprecedented level in Denver during the next quarter century.

Bowlen quickly established a solid administration and created a positive atmosphere that was reflected both on and off the field. One of his first acts was to create an annual Bronco alumni reunion weekend and establish a Ring of Fame at Mile High Stadium, honoring the greatest

Quarterback Gary Kubiak scrambles for yards against the Raider defense during a stunning October 28, 1984, overtime win, 22-19, before 91,020 people at the Los Angeles Memorial Coliseum. Kubiak played the entire game in place of an injured Elway.

The Los Angeles Memorial Coliseum was the site of many classic Broncos-Raiders battles. The columns here make a striking background as Sammy Winder runs the ball.

players in what was becoming an illustrious history for this former ragtag franchise.

His drive and guidance proved to be vital elements as the Broncos posted a 13-3 record and won the AFC West Division in his first year as owner. During the 1984 season, Denver set franchise records for both victories (13) and consecutive wins (10) while once again leading the entire NFL in actual in-stadium attendance.

Denver opened the 1984 campaign with a 20-17 win over Cincinnati as Sammy Winder ran for 94 yards to go along with one scoring pass each from John Elway and backup Gary Kubiak. The next week at Chicago, the Broncos suffered a 27-0 thumping by a Bears team that was becoming world champion material. The following week, Denver started a winning streak that carried from September until Thanksgiving, reeling off 10 straight victories, five at home and five away, with the young Elway quickly making his mark as a winner in the NFL. Included in these triumphs was the team's first shutout of Kansas City, a 21-0 September win in which the Broncos ran for 210 yards while limiting the Chiefs to 50 yards.

The following week, Denver grabbed a share of first place against the defending world champion Raiders, winning a very physical 16-13 matchup. The Broncos scored two field goals by Rich Karlis and one touchdown on a four-yard run by Gerald Willhite. Defensive back Mike Harden added two interceptions to stifle Los Angeles drives.

Among the most notable of the wins in the 10-game streak was the game against Green Bay. Before a national television audience, the Broncos beat the Packers in a Monday night blizzard, unusual weather conditions considering the game took place on October 15. Only

37 seconds into the game, the Broncos led 14-0 after Green Bay fumbled on each of its first two offensive plays from scrimmage. First Steve Foley and then Louis Wright scooped up the errant balls and returned them for scores, Foley for 22 yards and Wright for 27. This remains the only game in pro football history in which the defense scored on fumble returns on the first two scrimmage plays of the game. The Broncos added a field goal from the barefooted Karlis in the second quarter and hung on throughout the second half, which was played in terrible field conditions.

Despite the horrific conditions—the snow came so quickly that the stands could not be cleared—Bronco fans again proved their mettle as 62,546 of them braved the season's first blast of winter. Not only did this win boost the Broncos to 6-1, but the nationally televised contest was a tremendous boon to the early season ski industry. Many ski resort phone lines were overwhelmed by out-of-state tourist interest.

The following weeks, the Broncos sailed past Buffalo, 37-7, and won a stirring 22-19 overtime game in the Los Angeles Coliseum before 91,020 silver-and-black-clad Raider fans. Karlis kicked his third field goal of the game to close out the win in the extra stanza.

On November 18, the Broncos beat Minnesota 42-21 for the club's record 10th consecutive victory, reminding the fan base of that glorious run in 1977. Elway tied a Denver record and established his personal high by throwing five touchdown passes against the overmatched Vikings.

A baby-faced rookie who kicked barefoot and beat veteran competition, Rich Karlis had become a household

KARL MECKLENBURG

LINEBACKER

1983–1994

Karl Mecklenburg joined the Denver Broncos' Ring of Fame in 2001 after establishing himself as one of the most outstanding defensive players in franchise history during his 12-year career from 1983 to 1994.

Mecklenburg overcame long odds to achieve greatness after being drafted by the Broncos in the 12th round—the 310th player chosen—in 1983.

After playing defensive end during his first professional season, Mecklenburg started playing linebacker in 1984. He became a starter by his third season in 1985 and went on to start 141 career games, a total that includes all 16 games in a year during five different campaigns.

His 180 career games played with Denver placed him fifth on the club's all-time list at the end of his tenure (currently ninth). Mecklenburg was voted to play in six Pro Bowls (1985, 1987, 1989, 1991, 1993), a total that ties for the fifth highest by a player in team history. He was named All-AFC and All-NFL four times (1985, 1986, 1987, 1989) and was tabbed the 1986 AFC Player of the Year by *Football News*.

Mecklenburg helped Denver to seven postseason appearances (1983, 1984, 1986, 1987, 1989, 1991, 1993), five division titles (1984, 1986, 1987, 1989, 1991), and three Super Bowls (XXI in 1986, XXII in 1987, XXIV in 1989). He finished his career with 1,145 tackles (787 solo), as well as a franchise-record 79.0 sacks.

Mecklenburg's career high of 13 sacks in a season came in 1985 and were a franchise record at the time (currently tied for the fifth most in a year). He had eight seasons with at least seven sacks. He recorded 11 multiple-sack games and is the only player in team annals to record four sacks in a game twice in his career.

Mecklenburg made 100 tackles in a season six times, including a career- and team-high 143 stops in 1989. Mecklenburg began his collegiate career at Augustana (San Diego) College before transferring to the University of Minnesota, where he earned second-team All-Big Ten honors as a senior in 1982.

Mecklenburg's Denver Broncos Career Record

Games	Starts	Solo	Assist	Total	Sacks	Int.	Yds.	Avg.	TD
180	141	787	358	1,145	79.0	5	128	25.6	0

name among Bronco fans during the first 12 weeks of a perfect season. He successfully made all of his field-goal attempts until November 25, when in a last-second field-goal attempt to send the contest into overtime, the ball hit the right-hand upright. The 27-24 defeat deadlocked Seattle and Denver atop the AFC West, setting up a rematch in Seattle to close out regular-season play.

Karlis was a consistent clutch kicker throughout his career with his barefoot, soccer-style approach, but the following week at Kansas City he again had a ball hit the upright in the final stages of the game. The Chiefs held on to win, 16-13.

Against San Diego the following week, Karlis' kick made it through the uprights to provide the victory, 16-13, with just 2:08 left on the clock. The looming trip to Seattle would determine the division crown.

The Broncos clinched that title with their 31-14 shellacking of the Seahawks. This was Denver's 13th win of the season, the most in team history, and was largely engineered by a phenomenal quarterback just a year and a half out of college. On the third play of the game, John Elway connected on a 73-yard pass play

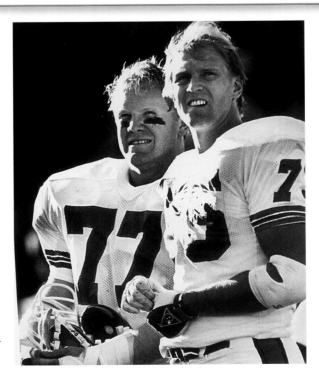

Ace defenders Karl Mecklenburg (No. 77) and Rulon Jones (No. 75) watch the game from the sideline. They were a superb pass-rush team in the 1980s, combining for more than 150 career sacks—Mecklenburg had 79 and Jones posted 73.5.

with Steve Watson, who carried the ball to the Seattle 1 yard line. Elway dove in for the score himself, and he later threw a touchdown pass to tight end James Wright at the start of the second half to make the score 17-7.

Midway through the third quarter, Steve Foley picked off a Dave Krieg pass and ran untouched 40 yards to the end zone. Denver put the game away in the fourth period as running back Rick Parros scored on a 4-yard run. Seattle's final hopes were dashed when Karl Mecklenburg—who had been Denver's unheralded 12th-round pick in the same 1983 draft Elway was in—intercepted Krieg and returned the ball 42 yards with less than two minutes remaining.

Sammy Winder finished the season with 1,153 yards rushing and Watson gained 1,170 yards receiving—the first time Denver ever had 1,000-yard performers in both categories in the same season.

The Broncos had finished 13-3 and were slated to host the 9-7 Pittsburgh Steelers in the playoffs. Denver's

fans and the entire Bronco organization were giddy with excitement over the chance of an easy first-round matchup, but the Steelers came prepared to play. Denver had two possessions in the final two minutes of the game but failed to score as Pittsburgh advanced to the AFC title game with a 24-17 win. Denver's opportunistic defense recovered two first-quarter fumbles and turned one into a Karlis field-goal attempt, but it sailed wide right. The other recovery became an Elway touchdown pass to James Wright. After a field goal of their own, the Steelers took the lead just before the half on a Frank Pollard run.

Watson was brilliant throughout the day, finishing with 11 receptions for 177 yards, including a 20-yard third-quarter score to give the Broncos their last lead. Pittsburgh scored the game's final two touchdowns and held on for the win, amassing 25 first downs to Denver's 15 and holding the ball for nearly 33 minutes. The Broncos could not move the ball on their final two possessions, as time ran out on the season.

Running back Steve Sewell talks with general manager John Beake in the locker room before a game. Sewell was one of the Broncos' most popular and versatile players, and Beake had a vital role in building the championship teams of this era.

THE SEEDS OF LOSS BRING NEW GROWTH

Early in 1985, owner Pat Bowlen named longtime administrator John Beake to the position of general manager. The promotion capped a rise in football that began while Beake was coaching with Joe Paterno at Penn State in 1961. Beake had steadily moved through the ranks and was a veteran NFL personnel man who brought a savvy acumen to the position.

Bowlen, Reeves, and Beake now were the major decision makers for the Broncos, and much was expected on the heels of the successful 1984 campaign. The franchise now had strong management and stability, and one of Reeves' first moves was to name a new offensive coordinator—Mike Shanahan. Shanahan had joined the team as a young receivers' coach the year before and had shown a dynamic knowledge of the passing game, as well as a good rapport with the young Elway. Shanahan's entry into pro football was not noticeably trumpeted, and few would have guessed that in his first 24 years in the NFL he would coach in an AFC or NFC championship game 10 times.

The future was brilliant, but Denver would not cash in on that potential in the season at hand. The Broncos had an excellent 1985, finishing 11-5, but in second place in the AFC West. Unfortunately, the NFL tie-breaking procedures made Denver the first team to ever go 11-5 and miss the playoffs entirely. The Broncos set season records with total yards (5,496) and total points (380). Elway threw for 432 yards in the season's closing game against Seattle, winning 27-24. He set Denver records in total offense (4,144 yards) and passing yards (3,891) for the season. Mecklenburg's 13 quarterback sacks also set a new Bronco standard.

A new generation of Denver defense was represented in the Pro Bowl with the selection of Mecklenburg, defensive end Rulon Jones, and safety Dennis Smith, joined by perennial all-star Louis Wright at his customary cornerback spot.

After the shocking home loss to the Steelers at the end of the 1984 year—followed by a nonplayoff year despite 11 wins—there was talk that Elway, who had not played in a bowl game while at Stanford, just was not made up to win the big ones. However, Elway had an unusual blend of unimaginable physical skills and a quiet but absolute passion to win, and he was about to put his footprint on NFL history in a big way.

Denver jumped out of the starting blocks in the 1986 season opener with a 38-36 win over the Los Angeles Raiders as Elway connected a seven-yard touchdown pass to running back Gene Lang with five minutes remaining, putting Denver ahead for good. He also hit Watson with a 35-yard scoring pass, but the Mile High Stadium crowd was electrified in the second quarter when, after driving the Broncos 77 yards, Elway scored

himself on a 23-yard pass from running back Steve Sewell. Elway became the first and only quarterback in Denver history to score via passing, rushing, and receiving attempts, which still stands today.

The Broncos had consecutive East Coast road games the next two weeks, posting relatively easy wins in Pittsburgh and Philadelphia, 21-10 over the Steelers on Monday Night Football and overwhelming the Eagles 33-7 on the following Sunday.

Center Keith Bishop watches from the sideline during a 1985 win over Atlanta. Bishop combined dirt and grime with leadership by example on Denver's offensive line.

Running back Gerald Willhite (No. 47) celebrates a touchdown during a December 1984 game at Mile High Stadium. Willhite sometimes would punctuate a score by doing a back flip in the end zone.

AFC rival New England jumped out to a 13-3 half-time lead in Denver the following week, but the Broncos roared back to roll over the Patriots in the second half and win 27-20, increasing their record to 4-0. Elway's offense put up 19 first downs to the Patriots' five in the second half, with the "Orange Crush" defense registering five sacks. Steve Foley caught an interception to total 44 for his excellent and underrated career, the most in Bronco history.

Dan Reeves grabbed his 50th victory as Denver's head coach the following week in his first matchup against Dallas, the team he had spent 15 years with as player and coach. The Broncos exploded for 22 second-quarter points and never looked back. The Denver defense held Dallas to 41 rushing yards in the game and helped propel the team's record to 5-0. The offense was paced by Gerald Willhite, who scored on passes of 9 and

15 yards from Elway and added a third touchdown on a 1-yard run.

On October 12, the Broncos posted a 31-14 win against San Diego to equal the best start in team history with a 6-0 record. Willhite scored twice more in that game, and Winder ran for a score as well. Denver completely dominated with 38:47 minutes of possession in the lopsided game.

All winning streaks must end, though, and this one passed away meekly in New York as an inspired Jets team routed Denver, 22-10. The Broncos increased their AFC West lead to two games with a win over Seattle in their next game, but the prosperity did not last as Denver dropped two straight, to the Raiders in Los Angeles and then by a 9-3 score against San Diego at home. The San Diego loss was the first time in team history that the Broncos lost in Mile High Stadium

Left: Broncos fans raise their hands in celebration after a touchdown. The 1980s gave them plenty of reason to cheer—they watched arguably the greatest quarterback of all time lead the only AFC team that decade to three Super Bowl appearances.

Right: Dave Studdard was a solid tackle for the Broncos from 1978 through 1988, including on two AFC Championship teams.

without surrendering a touchdown to the opposition. The Chargers kicked three field goals and had the ball for almost 36 minutes in their win.

The special teams scored two touchdowns and the defense one as the Broncos bounced back to lace the Kansas City Chiefs, 38-17, making Denver's record 9-2. The game's first score came when punter Chris Norman connected with Steve Watson on a 43-yard touchdown pass. Defensive end Andre Townsend returned a fumble seven yards for a score, and Willhite took a punt back 70 yards to the end zone, too.

After a loss to the Giants and a win over Cincinnati, the Broncos traveled to Kansas City, where the Chiefs took out their rancor over its earlier loss. The bitter division rivals pasted Denver by a 27-point margin, the final score being 37-10. Kansas City intercepted the Broncos five times and scored 20 fourth-quarter points in a cold, rainy Arrowhead Stadium.

On December 13, Denver clinched the AFC West Division title by virtue of a Seattle win over Los Angeles the previous Monday. The team won home field advantage for first playoff game by defeating Washington, 31-30. In that game, Elway completed 20 passes for 282 yards. However, the following week, the Seahawks rolled over Denver, 41-16, in the Kingdome. Seattle running back Curt Warner spanked the Broncos for 192

Steve Watson awaits the snap. During his career, he caught 353 passes for 6,112 yards and 36 touchdowns.

yards rushing, and Denver concluded regular-season play with a second consecutive 11-5 record. Thirty-five individual and team records were set by the Broncos in 1986. Defensive end Rulon Jones was named the AFC Defensive Player of the Year by UPI, and linebacker Karl

Mecklenburg was named the AFC Player of the Year by the *Football News*.

The Broncos posted a 22-17 playoff win over New England on January 4 before 76,105 people, the largest crowd ever to watch a Denver home game. Rich Karlis

Quarterback John Elway is introduced at Mile High Stadium before a win over the Cardinals.

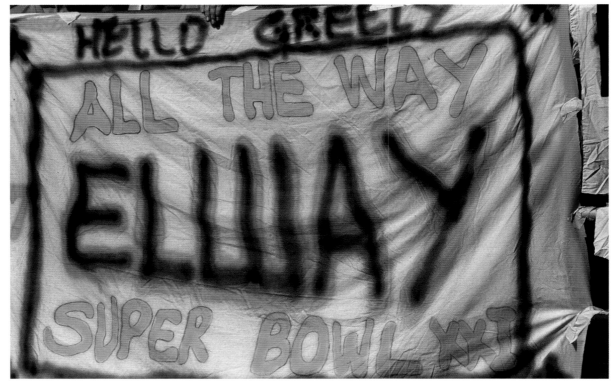

Fans hold up a sign in October 1986 imploring John Elway to take the team to Super Bowl XXI. No one had any inkling it would be such a wild ride, or that this would be just the first of five Super Bowls for the fourth-year quarterback.

kicked two field goals, and John Elway accounted for two scores—the first on a 22-yard run and the second on a 48-yard pass to Vance Johnson, which put the Broncos ahead 20-17 as the third quarter ended. The two teams both punted three times in the fourth quarter, and the last one, by Denver's Mike Horan, backed the Pats to their own 10 yard line. On first down, New England quarterback Tony Eason dropped back to pass but was sacked for a safety by the fiery Rulon Jones, making the final score 22-17. The crowd serenaded Jones with the familiar chant of "Ruuuuulon," knowing that his sack had set up a trip to Cleveland.

"THE DRIVE"

The Broncos were playing for the conference title, but no one had any idea this trip to Cleveland would be another step toward immortality for John Elway.

The title game was played before a crowd of nearly 80,000 fans who braved a wind-chill factor of minus 5 degrees Fahrenheit at Cleveland Stadium, which had hosted many Browns championships in the 1940s and 1950s. Despite wildly exhorting the Browns and pelting the Broncos with hundreds of dog bones, the Cleveland fans went home crushed. In a game that will forever be remembered for "The Drive," Rich Karlis kicked a 33-yard field goal 5:48 into overtime to give the Broncos a 23-20 win over the Cleveland Browns in the 1986 AFC Championship Game.

While Karlis eventually put the final points on the board, it was the right arm, legs, head, and heart of John Elway that thrust this game onto pro football's list of the 25 greatest games ever played.

Cleveland took a 7-0 lead when Bernie Kosar threw a 6-yard pass to Herman Fontenot in the first quarter. The

Running back Sammy Winder follows his lead blocker Dave Studdard during a January 4, 1987, playoff win (22-17) against the New England Patriots. This victory set up a date in Cleveland for the game that would become known for "The Drive."

John Elway loved the shotgun, a formation from which he was particularly dangerous. Here, Keith Bishop protects Elway in the shotgun against the Chargers.

Running back Sammy Winder grinds out some tough yards during the January 11, 1987, AFC Championship Game, which ended in an overtime win at Cleveland.

Wide receiver Mark Jackson makes a catch with fellow receiver Ricky Nattiel looking on. Together with Vance Johnson, the trio was collectively known as "The Three Amigos."

The Broncos are going to the Super Bowl! Holder Gary Kubiak (left) celebrates after Rich Karlis' January 11, 1987, game-winning field goal at Cleveland, which crushed the Browns and sent the Broncos back to the Super Bowl.

Broncos stopped the next two drives with interceptions, the second by linebacker Jim Ryan, whose return set up a 19-yard field goal by Karlis. Linebacker Ken Woodard recovered a fumble on Cleveland's next drive, putting the Broncos in position for Gerald Willhite's 1-yard run

TOM JACKSON
LINEBACKER
1973–1986

Tom Jackson was the only player inducted into the Denver Broncos' Ring of Fame in 1992. "TJ" was always one of the most popular players among his teammates, who voted him most inspirational player six consecutive seasons (1981–1986).

Selected by the Broncos in the fourth round (88th overall) of the 1973 NFL Draft, Jackson finished his 14-year career having played the most games in Broncos' history at 191, and he currently stands fourth in that category. He also finished his career tied for second in games started by a Bronco with 177 (currently tied for fifth) and is one of only five Broncos to wear the Denver uniform for at least 14 seasons.

Jackson, who started every possible game in a season seven times in his career, made three consecutive Pro Bowl appearances from 1977 through 1979 and was named first-team All-Pro twice (1977-1978).

He also was named by his teammates as Denver's defensive MVP in 1974, 1976, and 1977. The linebacker helped the Broncos to six playoff berths (1977, 1978, 1979, 1983, 1984, 1986), four division titles (1977, 1978, 1984, 1986), and two Super Bowls (XII in 1977 and XXI in 1986).

He was a key member of the 1977 squad that posted a 12-2 regular season and advanced to Super Bowl XII against the Cowboys.

Jackson is tied with fellow Ring of Famer Randy Gradishar for the most interceptions in Broncos' history by a linebacker with 20, a career total that currently ties for the 10th highest by any player in club annals. His seven interceptions in 1976 mark the highest single-season total by a linebacker in Broncos' history.

Jackson finished among Denver's top five tacklers during 11 consecutive seasons from 1974 to 1984 and recorded a career-high 169 stops in 1980. Upon his retirement after the 1986 season, he was fifth on the Broncos' all-time sack list with 44 and currently remains eighth on that chart. Jackson joined the Broncos after a standout career at the University of Louisville, where he was a three-time all-conference selection.

Today's era of fans know Jackson as one of the most recognizable and respected NFL analysts on television as a result of his work for ESPN, where he is the co-host of its award-winning *Sunday NFL Countdown* and *NFL PrimeTime* shows.

Jackson's Denver Broncos Career Record

Games	Starts	Sacks	Int.	Yds.	Avg.	TD
191	177	44.0	20	340	17.0	3

at 4:24 of the second quarter, giving Denver a 10-7 lead. The Browns tied the score with a 29-yard Mark Moseley field goal 20 seconds before halftime.

Karlis and Moseley exchanged second-half field goals to leave the score knotted at 13. After two Denver punts, Kosar's 48-yard pass to wide receiver Brian Brennan put Cleveland ahead by seven with just 5:43 remaining in the game.

The kickoff rolled to the 2 yard line, where Denver return man Ken Bell recovered and gave the Broncos a first down, forever to go, 98 yards away from a tie with Browns' faithful screaming at the top of their lungs. The Broncos huddled up deep in the end zone, and guard Keith Bishop said to no one in particular, "We've got 'em right where we want 'em." And thus Elway began "The Drive."

On the fifth play of the possession, Elway scrambled for 15 yards and a first down. He then connected with Steve Sewell for a 22-yard gain followed by a 12-yard strike to Steve Watson, giving Denver a first down on the Cleveland 40 yard line. The next pass was incomplete, and then Elway got sacked for an 8-yard loss, sending the Browns fans into a complete euphoria. In conference on the sideline, Dan Reeves reminded Elway that he had two downs to get the 18 yards, so he did not have to get it all in one play.

Of course, gunslingers never back down. Elway was in the shotgun with Watson in motion, and as the ball was snapped, it deflected off the receiver's rear end. In what seemed like one eternal second of time, Elway caught the ball in one hand, saw a flash of opening to wide receiver Mark Jackson, and rifled a bullet to him for 20 yards and a first down at the Cleveland 28. The crowd cheered and groaned almost simultaneously.

An Elway-to-Sewell pass gave the Broncos a first down at the Browns' 14 yard line with 57 seconds left. After an incomplete pass, Elway seemed trapped but took off for a nine-yard run to the Cleveland five. On the next play, he hit Jackson for a touchdown, and Karlis calmly tied the score at 20 with 37 seconds left.

The Browns won the coin toss for overtime and elected to receive, but the Broncos stifled Cleveland on three plays. Willhite returned the punt to the Denver 25. Elway took the field again, now accompanied by fate and destiny. He passed 22 yards to tight end Orson Mobley and three plays later rolled out and tossed a 28-yard pass to Watson. From the Cleveland 22, the Broncos rushed three times to get to the 15, and Ohio native Karlis—who in a pensive moment before the game said, "I just have a feeling it is going to come down to a field goal"—made the biggest 33-yard kick in Bronco history.

The Broncos were going to Pasadena for Super Bowl XXI, but first there was one unfinished detail to take care of before leaving Cleveland. A radio station had promoted where the Broncos were staying and asked that fans annoy the team by driving around the hotel honking their horns during the night before the game. Of course, the giddy Ohio populace was delighted to comply with this suggestion. Now, as the buses departed the stadium parking lot for the joyous ride home, line-backer and inspirational leader Tom Jackson, riding in the lead bus and sitting in a front seat that marked his status, leaned forward and told the driver to take the caravan of buses past Cleveland's Stouffer's Hotel. The five buses took a couple of trips around the hotel block, honking their horns the entire time. Sometimes vengeance can come in the small things, but feel very large.

The plane left Cleveland with Gary Glitter's "Rock and Roll Part II"—the theme song popularized by the Broncos at Mile High Stadium—blaring over the aircraft sound system as the wheels lifted. Broncos travel coordinator Bill Harpole had planned for this moment and brought a copy of the tune with him, giving it to the flight attendants as the team boarded.

The celebration began immediately in Denver and seemed to go on unabated. Throngs of fans, a makeshift stage, and the Broncos Band greeted the team plane at its private runway back upon return.

RETURNING TO SUPER STATUS

On January 18, the team flew out to Pasadena for game week, but first stopped at Mile High Stadium for a rally. It was attended by a crowd of more than 63,000. Bronco love had never been greater or more freely expressed.

In the Super Bowl, the New York Giants broke open a close game with 24 unanswered points to begin the second half, capturing a 39-20 win over the Broncos in Pasadena. Quickly, the Mile High City mood had turned from electric orange to somber blue.

The Broncos drove to the Giants' 31 yard line on their opening drive and took a 3-0 lead when Karlis booted a Super Bowl record-tying 48-yard field goal. New York answered with a 78-yard scoring drive that culminated with a 6-yard touchdown pass from Phil Simms to Zeke Mowatt.

Midway through the first quarter, Elway scored the team's first touchdown from four yards out on a quarterback draw, giving Denver a 10-7 lead. The Giants' next drive stalled, and the Broncos got the ball back at the 14-minute mark of the second quarter. On the third play of the drive, third-and-18, Elway unleashed a 54-yard bomb to Vance Johnson, giving the Broncos a first down at the Giants' 28 yard line. Seven plays later, Denver had a first-and-goal at the New York 1 yard line, but failed to score in three plays. Karlis was wide right on the subsequent 23-yard field-goal attempt.

Denver's defense stifled the next Giants drive at the New York 47, and after a punt, the Broncos got the ball back on their own 15. Controversy entered the game

when, on second-and-12, Elway threw an apparent completion to tight end Clarence Kay for a first down. The pass was ruled incomplete, a call that was upheld after review of the replay. On the next play, Giants defensive end George Martin sacked Elway in the end zone for a safety to pull New York within a point of Denver, 10-9. The Denver defense held again, giving it the ball at its own 37. The Broncos drove down to New York's 16 yard line, but Karlis was wide right on a 34-yard field-goal attempt with 13 seconds left in the half.

Fans line the streets of Denver during a parade to celebrate the 1987 AFC Championship.

Vance Johnson spikes the ball after scoring a touchdown. Given to colorful and often outlandish comments and onfield celebrations, Johnson had a natural gift for showmanship, but he was also a fine receiver and one of Elway's favorite targets.

Clarence Kay was one of the best blocking tight ends in the NFL during the 1980s.

The failure to score on those two possessions, intended to create some breathing room, proved devastating. New York scored on all three of its third-quarter drives and posted 163 yards to Denver's 2 in the quarter. With the score 26-10, the Giants mounted a scoring drive on their first possession of the fourth quarter. They pulled ahead 33-10 after Phil McConkey caught a deflected pass in the end zone, for Simms' third touchdown strike of the day. Denver got the ball back at its own 16, and Elway moved the squad to the New York 10. Karlis then kicked a 28-yard field goal to make the score 33-13. The Giants took only five plays to move 46 yards for their next touchdown, a 2-yard run by Otis Anderson that brought the score to 39-13. Elway took Denver down the field again and hit Johnson for a 47-yard touchdown pass for the game's final points at 12:54.

The game was watched by 101,063 in the legendary Rose Bowl and by a television audience of 127 million, in addition to being shown live in 53 other nations.

UNABATED LOVE AND ANOTHER CHAMPIONSHIP RIDE

It had been a decade since the Broncos' first Super Bowl appearance. Bronco fans were proud and beaming just to have returned to the NFL championship game, especially with a team that boasted the kind of future that guys like John Elway could provide. More than 100,000 fans welcomed the Broncos home in a parade through downtown Denver, unheard of for a team returning from a defeat. But such was the unconditional love Bronco fans felt toward their team.

The Broncos started off the 1987 season 1-1 before the NFL Players Association went on strike again, resulting in the game cancellation for the weekend of September 28. The NFL made a decision to go with replacement players while fighting the union, and Denver went 2-1 with the substitutes, including a Monday night 30-14 home win against the Raiders. The game was played

before 61,230 at Mile High Stadium—Bronco fans again proving that their loyalty trumped any other conditions.

The veterans came back within a month, and Denver continued its march through the schedule. On November 29, the team grabbed a 31-17 win over San Diego in the 400th game for both franchises. That contest also marked Dan Reeves' 100th game as the Broncos' head coach.

Denver clinched its third AFC West title in four years after shutting out San Diego 24-0 in a blizzard, finishing with a 10-4-1 record that made the Broncos the NFL's only team to post eight 10-win seasons since 1977.

Elway followed up that immortal drive of 1986 with a 1987 campaign that resulted in being named the NFL Most Valuable Player by the Associated Press. His glittering stats included 19 touchdown passes and four more rushing, but he was becoming just as respected for his toughness, leadership, and the ability to excel in clutch situations.

Quarterback John Elway talks with his father, Jack Elway, Broncos director of pro scouting.

Stalwart defenders Simon Fletcher and Greg Kragen celebrate a defensive stand with Karl Mecklenburg (center).

As the playoffs began, Denver had the challenge of trying to be the first AFC team to win consecutive conference titles since the Steelers of 1978–1979. The Broncos advanced to the AFC Championship Game after beating the Houston Oilers 34-10 in front of 75,968 fans at Mile High Stadium. Denver's 24-point win was the largest margin in a postseason victory.

The Broncos were led on defense by cornerback Mark Haynes and by Karl Mecklenburg, who both picked up key interceptions. Offensively, John Elway was 14-of-25 for 259 yards with two touchdowns, Vance Johnson had four catches for 105 yards, and Clarence Kay—a devastating blocker for the running game—had three catches for 57 yards with two touchdowns.

Punter Mike Horan put the Oilers in a hole after the Broncos' first drive stalled, sending a punt to the Houston 5 yard line, where two plays later, Mike Rozier fumbled a lateral pass from Warren Moon.

Veteran corner Steve Wilson recovered for Denver on the 1 yard line. Gene Lang scored two plays later to give the Broncos an early 7-0 lead. Houston's next drive reached the Broncos' 20 yard line before Mecklenburg intercepted a pass and returned it to the Denver 28. Elway hit Kay for 29 yards to move into Houston territory, and five plays later the same connection was made for a 27-yard touchdown pass, giving the Broncos a 14-0 lead.

Both teams added field goals on their first drive of the second quarter to make the score 17-3 in Denver's favor, and the legendary steel stands rocked with Bronco faithful jumping up and down in full force.

After the Houston field goal, Elway threw a 55-yard bomb to Johnson, moving the ball to the Oilers' 11 yard line. Five plays later, Elway hit Kay again for a touchdown on a 1-yard pass, upping the score to 24-3 with less than two minutes left in the half.

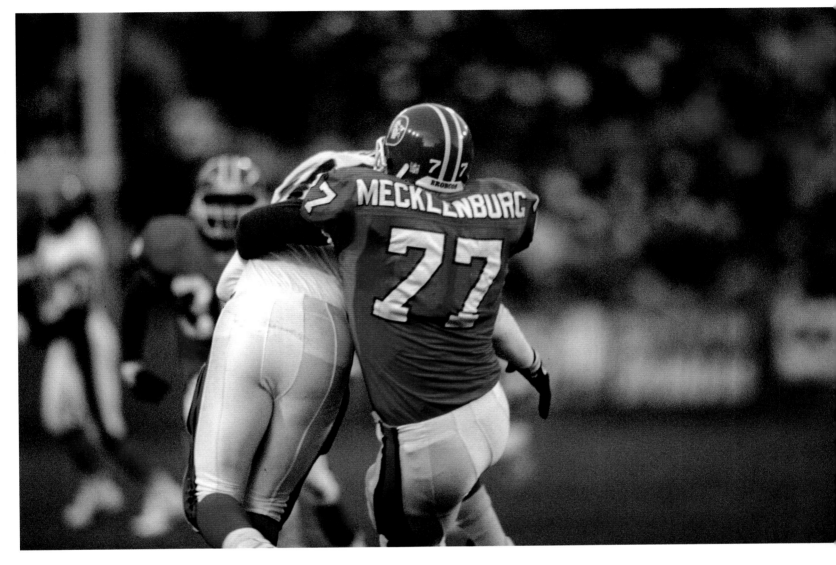

Denver's first possession of the second half resulted in a Rich Karlis field goal. Houston then took 10 plays to reach the Denver 7, but Haynes picked off a Moon pass in the end zone and returned it 57 yards to set a Bronco playoff record.

Houston's next drive reached the Broncos' 11, but a pass on fourth down fell incomplete. The Oilers got the ball back three plays later on an interception, and that led to a 19-yard touchdown pass by Moon, cutting Denver's lead to 27-10. The Broncos recovered the onside kick that followed, and Denver moved 52 yards in seven plays to score the final points of the game on a 3-yard run by Elway.

THE FUMBLE

Cleveland came to Mile High Stadium for the AFC title game to avenge the previous year's bitter loss. The classic struggle played out, with more shock and disappointment added to the Browns' history with Denver.

Defensive end Freddie Gilbert's interception set up the Broncos' first score of the afternoon. Elway found wide receiver Ricky Nattiel for an eight-yard touchdown about three minutes into the first quarter, putting Denver ahead 7-0.

Next, Lang took off on a 42-yard run, setting a franchise record for longest postseason rush. Later, Denver faced third-and-goal from the Cleveland three yard line late in the first quarter. Elway threw an incomplete into the end zone, but the Browns were penalized for holding, giving the Broncos new life at the one yard line. Steve Sewell scored on first down to give Denver a 14-0 lead 11:06 into the first quarter.

However, the Browns roared back, scoring their first points of the game on a 24-yard Matt Bahr field goal at 1:41 of the second quarter. Denver answered at 6:59 with a 1-yard Lang touchdown run that upped its lead to 21-3.

Linebacker Karl Mecklenburg wrestles a Bengal down during a 1994 win over Cincinnati at Mile High Stadium. Mecklenburg's great play earned him a spot in the Broncos' Ring of Fame.

Denver seemed to be in control, but after Elway was intercepted by Felix Wright four plays into the second half, Cleveland needed just three plays to go 35 yards and score on Kosar's 18-yard pass to Reggie Langhorne. The Broncos answered when Elway scrambled right and threw to Mark Jackson, who caught the ball at the Broncos' 25, evaded two tacklers, and sprinted for an 80-yard touchdown, giving the Broncos a 28-10 lead at 5:03 of the third quarter. Cleveland moved the score to 28-17 when Kosar found running back Earnest Byner for a 32-yard touchdown at 8:10 of the third quarter.

Cleveland narrowed the Broncos' lead to 28-24 on a Byner four-yard run at 11:15 of the third quarter. Just before the end of the third period, Karlis capped off a Denver possession with a 38-yard field goal.

The Browns tied the score at 31 on Kosar's four-yard pass to wide receiver Webster Slaughter at 4:12 of the final period. After an exchange of punts, Denver began a drive at its own 25 yard line with 5:14 left in the game. A pair of 26-yard pass plays to Nattiel put Denver at the Cleveland 20 and set up a 20-yard Elway-to-Winder pass for a touchdown that put the Broncos up 38-31 with just over four minutes left.

However, Cleveland was determined to claim the title it felt it deserved the year before. Kosar and the Browns advanced to the Bronco eight yard line with 1:12 remaining, when this game got a name of its own in Bronco lore. Byner took a handoff and ran to the three yard line, and as he broke free to the end zone, reserve defensive back Jeremiah Castille stripped and recovered the ball. Just as the previous year's game was known as "The Drive,"

John Elway fades back to make yet another pass.

Right: Wide receiver Mark Jackson celebrates a touchdown with tight end Orson Mobley.

the 1987 Broncos-Browns matchup became known for "The Fumble."

Denver took an intentional safety and time ran out for the Browns. Denver won its second AFC Championship Game in a 38-33 victory to become the first AFC team to repeat the feat in the decade and advance to the Super Bowl for the third time.

BACK-TO-BACK DISAPPOINTMENT IN ROMAN NUMERALS

This time Denver was favored and expected to win the Super Bowl, not just by national pundits, but by a fan base that had raised its expectations for the beloved Broncos.

Yet, it was not to be. At the Jack Murphy Stadium in San Diego, in front of 73,202 fans, the Washington Redskins scored 35 points in the second quarter to power their way to a 42-10 victory against the Broncos in Super Bowl XXII.

Super Bowl MVP Doug Williams of Washington completed 18-of-29 passes for 340 yards with four touchdowns, while running back Timmy Smith gained 204 yards on 22 carries, scoring twice. Wide receiver Ricky Sanders caught nine passes for 193 yards and two touchdowns.

The Broncos took the early lead on their first play from scrimmage, a 56-yard bomb from John Elway to Ricky Nattiel, with 1:57 gone in the game. Denver's next possession stalled at the Redskins' 7 yard line, but Rich Karlis put the Broncos up 10-0 with a 24-yard field goal.

In the second quarter, however, Denver's dreams of a world championship were blown apart by the Redskins. On Washington's first play of the quarter, Williams and Sanders combined for an 80-yard touchdown to bring the score to 10-7. The Redskins took the lead for good on the fifth play of their next possession when Williams hit Gary Clark for 27 yards and a score.

Denver got as far as the Washington 26 on its next drive, but Karlis had his 43-yard field-goal attempt sail

Center Keith Bishop blocks a Redskin lineman as Elway drops back during the Super Bowl loss to Washington at Jack Murphy Stadium in San Diego on January 31, 1988.

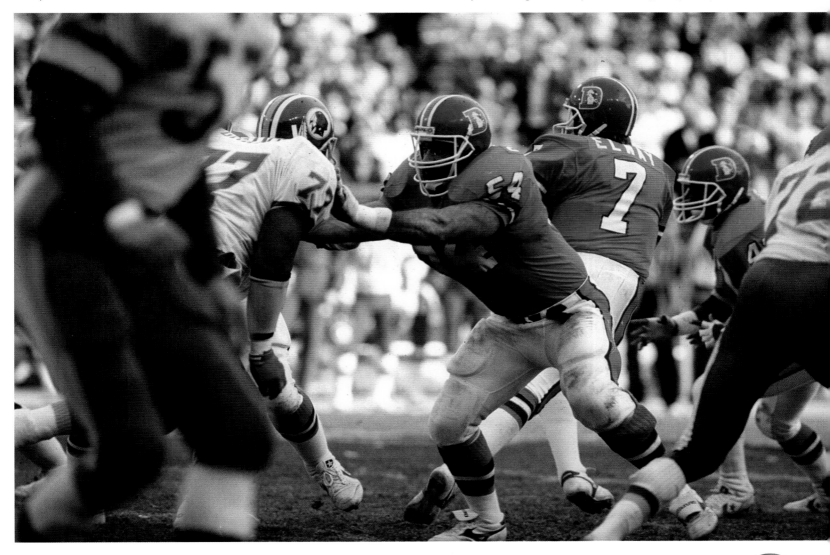

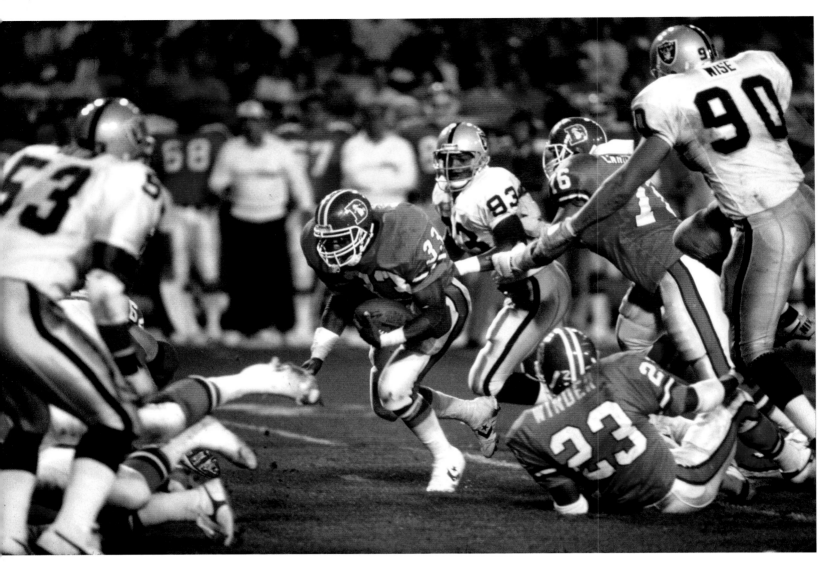

Hall of Fame running back Tony Dorsett ended his fabled career with two seasons in Denver. Here he picks up some yardage in traffic against the Raiders.

wide left of the upright. Two plays later, Smith scored on a 58-yard run to increase the Washington lead to 21-10. The Redskins' next possession ended with a 50-yard Williams-to-Sanders touchdown pass. Minutes later, Williams and Clint Didier combined for an 8-yard touchdown pass to give the Redskins a 35-10 lead at halftime. It was the most astonishing negative quarter in Bronco history.

The Broncos could move only as far as the Redskins' 48 yard line in the second half, and Washington closed out the scoring late in the game on a 4-yard run by Smith.

Not regarded as an outstanding offensive team, the Redskins finished with 602 total yards, including the 340 passing yards from Williams. Their defense limited Denver to 327 total yards while holding Elway to just 14-of-38 passes for 257 yards and intercepting him three times. The Broncos were only able to muster 97 rushing yards in the game and were held to a miserable two-of-12 (16.7 percent) success on third down by Washington.

This was one of the worst moments in Bronco history. The team had lost its third Super Bowl, but this one was not like the first two. The first time everyone was just delighted to be there, the second time happy to return. This one carried with it the expectation of victory, and so this defeat bore the greatest shame for the Broncos and their fans.

The aftereffect was felt throughout 1988. Because of consecutive Super Bowl losses, the Broncos made an attempt to add a veteran spark to their offense in the offseason, acquiring future Hall of Fame running back Tony Dorsett from the Dallas Cowboys, in exchange for a future draft choice. The 1988 campaign was Dorsett's 12th in pro football. While he was able to show glimpses of the greatness that marked his career, overall he could only rush for a 3.9 average on 703 yards, scoring five touchdowns. On September 26 against the Raiders, Dorsett eclipsed Jim Brown to become

Running back Gerald Willhite slashes through the hole during an October 9, 1988, overtime win (16-13) over the 49ers in San Francisco.

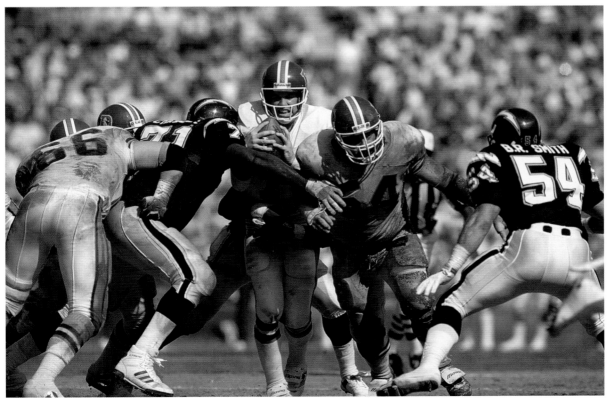

Quarterback John Elway gets sacked as center Keith Bishop blocks Charger Billy Ray Smith during a 12-0 shutout win at San Diego in 1988.

the second leading rusher in pro football history, trailing only Walter Payton.

Denver found the challenge of winning three straight conference titles very difficult. The Broncos closed out the season with a 21-10 win over New England, but ended with a disappointing 8-8 record; this marked the end of Denver's two-year reign as AFC champions. The Broncos' record was only 2-6 away from Mile High that year, including a blowout loss of 55-23 in a Monday night game at Indianapolis on Halloween.

A portrait of Vance Johnson standing in an open locker room doorway prior to kickoff. From 1985 to 1995, Johnson had 415 career receptions, 37 of which went for scores.

Still, Elway ended the season with 3,309 yards passing and 234 rushing to become the first player in football history to have four consecutive years with more than 3,000 passing yards combined with more than 200 rushing yards. Dorsett finished the year second to Payton among football's all-time rushing leaders with 12,739 yards. The only Bronco to be named to the Pro Bowl was punter Mike Horan, a symbol of the disappointing campaign.

THREE-TIME CHAMPS IN FOUR YEARS

The sour taste of 1988 did not linger, and the Broncos closed out their third decade with a 20th consecutive sellout campaign and a return to the winners' circle.

Running back Bobby Humphrey led the ground game in 1989 with 1,151 yards and seven scores, while Vance Johnson had a great year in receptions with 76 for 1,095 yards and seven touchdowns as well. The Broncos started off 3-0 and never looked back, moving out to a 10-3 record before coasting home with their third AFC West title in four seasons. They clinched that crown with a 41-14 win over Seattle in a November 26 contest at home.

Often winning the division so early can lead to a December letdown, and Denver had one. The team dropped two straight before finally wrapping up home field advantage for the AFC playoffs with a 37-0 win at Phoenix in the next-to-last game of the season. That game once again demonstrated Denver's emotional ownership of the Rocky Mountain time zone, as the Phoenix crowd of 56,071 was almost entirely in favor of the road team. Players and the press all commented on how surreal it seemed for the visiting team to be cheered at a road venue.

The first playoff game was against a familiar adversary, the Pittsburgh Steelers, who Denver respected. With a come-from-behind 24-23 victory in front of 75,868 fans at Mile High, the Broncos advanced to their third AFC Championship Game in four years. Although Pittsburgh had the upper hand in total yards (404 to 364) and time of possession (34:14 to 25:46), Denver was able to mount a late fourth-quarter drive and score the winning touchdown with just more than two minutes remaining.

The Steelers took the opening kickoff and drove 65 yards in 13 plays, scoring on a 32-yard field goal by Gary Anderson. Late in the opening quarter, Pittsburgh took possession at its own 7 yard line. After a 45-yard run by Merril Hoge and a 33-yard Bubby Brister–to–Tim Worley pass play, the Steelers quickly were knocking on the door. They scored three plays later on Hoge's 7-yard run to pull ahead 10-0.

The Broncos took their first possession of the second quarter and drove 75 yards in 12 plays to score on a

1-yard plunge by fullback Mel Bratton on third and goal. The Steelers roared back, traveling 77 yards in 12 plays to score on Brister's 9-yard pass to wide receiver Louis Lipps. The Broncos got the ball back on their own 33 with 20 seconds left in the half. Two Elway passes put Denver at the Pittsburgh 26 with two seconds left, which set up David Treadwell's 43-yard field goal that pulled Denver within seven points at the half. The Broncos were staying close, but the fans were nervous about the way this matchup was playing out.

Early in the third quarter, Denver nose tackle Greg Kragen forced a Tim Worley fumble, and cornerback Tyrone Braxton recovered for the Broncos on the Steelers' 37. On first down, Elway hit Johnson for a touchdown to tie the score at 17. Pittsburgh's next two possessions ended in Anderson field goals, and the tough, physical Steelers still held a six-point lead in the early stages of the fourth quarter.

After an exchange of punts, the Broncos took possession on their own 29 yard line with 7:06 left in the game. It was again time for the Broncos quarterback to show the way. John Elway hit Mark Jackson for 18 yards and then handed off to Bobby Humphrey, who pitched the ball back to Elway. The legendary quarterback then threw a 36-yard strike to Vance Johnson, giving Denver a first down on the Steelers' 26. The crowd was electrified as Humphrey ran on the next four plays, gaining 24 yards and taking the ball to the two. On third-and-goal from the one, Bratton scored again and Treadwell's extra point gave Denver its first lead of the game with 2:27 left.

Pittsburgh got the ball back on its own 20, but on third down Brister's signals were drowned out by the crowd and he mishandled the snap. Defensive back Randy Robbins recovered for Denver on the Pittsburgh 18, and the Broncos were able to run out the clock and set up yet another title game versus the Cleveland Browns.

Team leaders Steve Atwater and John Elway enjoy another victory.

Coach Dan Reeves prays with his players before the January 14, 1990, AFC Championship win against the Cleveland Browns.

Dennis Smith (No. 49) celebrates one of his two interceptions in the 1990 AFC Championship Game.

This time, a different air surrounded the game. The series had seen "The Drive" and "The Fumble," but this time Denver was a proven champ widely regarded as the better team. On top of that, Cleveland quarterback Bernie Kosar was nursing an injury to this throwing hand as he led his squad into the hostile ground of Mile High Stadium.

In a game that was not ever very close, the Broncos won their third AFC Championship in four years with a dynamic 37-21 victory against Cleveland before 76,005 screaming faithful. Elway threw for 385 yards and three touchdowns, Sammy Winder tied a Denver postseason record with two touchdowns, and strong safety Dennis Smith nabbed two of the Broncos' three interceptions. Denver also totaled 497 yards of total offense.

The Broncos took the opening kickoff and drove to the Cleveland one yard line, but on third down Elway's pitch to Humphrey was fumbled and the Browns recovered on the eight. With five minutes left in the first quarter, Smith picked off a Kosar pass and returned it to the Cleveland 32. Denver moved to the Cleveland 12 but had to settle for a 29-yard field goal by Treadwell.

Ring of Famer Dennis Smith, a silhouette in the snow.

DENNIS SMITH

SAFETY

1981–1994

Dennis Smith was inducted into the Denver Broncos' Ring of Fame in 2001, reflective of his stellar 14-year career with the club. During his tenure, he established himself as one of the most feared safeties in the NFL.

A ferocious hitter, Smith was voted to six Pro Bowls (1985, 1986, 1989, 1991, 1993), which ties for the fifth most by a player in Broncos' history. A four-time All-NFL choice (1985, 1986, 1989, 1993), Smith was a key part of seven playoff teams (1983, 1984, 1986, 1987, 1989, 1991, 1993), five division champions (1984, 1986, 1987, 1989, 1991), and three Super Bowl teams (XXI in 1986, XXII in 1987, and XXIV in 1989). He received the Bob Peck Award in 1992 as the Broncos' most inspirational player, and he was named the club's MVP on defense in 1989 and 1991.

Selected by the Broncos in the first round (15th overall) of the 1981 NFL Draft, Smith finished his career ranked third all time in games played by a Bronco (184) and fifth in games started (170). He currently ranks sixth in club annals in both categories. He also is one of just four Bronco players to play at least 14 seasons with the club.

Smith's 30 career interceptions and 431 career interception return yards both were the fifth-highest totals at the time of his retirement (currently both sixth). In addition, his 14.4-yard career average on interception returns currently stands as the 10th best in club history.

Smith's career totals also include 1,171 tackles (794 solo) and 15 sacks. He posted a career-high five sacks in 1983, a career-high five interceptions in 1991, and a career-high 120 tackles in 1992. For his career, Smith recorded five seasons with at least 100 tackles.

He was a consensus All-America choice in 1980 as a senior at the University of Southern California, where he lettered four times in football and three times in track. He posted 205 career tackles and 16 interceptions at USC and appeared in two Rose Bowls as a Trojan.

Smith's Denver Broncos Career Record

Games	Starts	Solo	Assist	Total	Sacks	Int.	Yds.	Avg.	TD	Def. TD
184	170	794	377	1,171	15.0	30	431	14.4	0	1 (Fumble return)

Bobby Humphrey cuts up the field during Super Bowl XXIV. This was just not the Broncos' day, but it nevertheless marked the team's third Super Bowl appearance in four years.

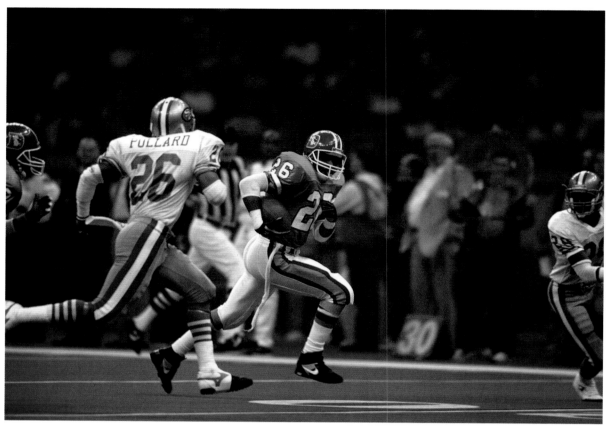

Vance Johnson picks up extra yardage after making a reception.

Neither team mounted more scoring drives until the Broncos took possession on their own 18 with 6:54 left in the half. On first down, Elway hit Jackson for 12 yards, and three plays later he connected with wide receiver Michael Young for a 70-yard touchdown play. The Browns took the opening kickoff of the second half and drove 70 yards in eight plays, scoring on a 27-yard pass from Kosar to Brian Brennan. Denver roared right back on its next possession. The Broncos went 80 yards in six plays and scored on a 5-yard pass from Elway to tight end Orson Mobley, who always bedeviled Cleveland in postseason. The key play on that drive was a 53-yard pass from Elway to Young.

Cleveland was unable to move the ball in its next drive and punted back to Denver. The Broncos moved from their own 40 yard line, and buoyed by a stunning 25-yard run by Elway, the team covered 60 yards in six plays. It scored on a 7-yard jaunt by Winder, bringing the score 24-7 and energizing the crowd.

The Browns needed just six plays to go 72 yards and score on a 10-yard Kosar-to-Brennan pass. Two plays into Denver's next drive, Cleveland's Felix Wright recovered a Denver fumble and returned it to the Broncos' one, making a considerable amount of orange-clad stomachs very nervous. On second down, the Browns scored, cutting Denver's lead to 24-21 with one second left in the third quarter.

The Broncos shut out the Browns in the final quarter while posting 13 points. Their initial drive of the quarter covered 80 yards in six plays and ended with a beautiful 39-yard touchdown pass from Elway to Winder. Denver reserve safety Kip Corrington intercepted Kosar to set the Broncos up on the Cleveland 39. Denver got as far as the 17 but had to settle for a 34-yard Treadwell field goal. Smith then grabbed his second interception to end the Browns' next drive, leading to a 31-yard field goal and putting the Broncos in the Super Bowl for the third time in four years.

GREAT MEETS GREATER IN NEW ORLEANS

For Super Bowl XXIV at the Louisiana Superdome, the Broncos were pitted against a San Francisco team with the talent and determination to make its mark on the ages. Heavily favored, the 49ers captured their fourth world championship in front of 72,919 fans. San Francisco quarterback Joe Montana completed 22-of-29 passes for 297 yards and five touchdowns—three to wide receiver Jerry Rice, who ran amok in the Denver secondary.

The 49ers scored two touchdowns in every quarter and outgained the Broncos 461 yards to 167 in a merciless pummeling. After stopping Denver on the game's initial possession, San Francisco drove 66 yards in 10 plays, scoring on a 20-yard pass from Montana to Rice. The Broncos' next possession covered 49 yards in 10 plays and resulted in a 42-yard field goal by David Treadwell.

After limiting the 49ers to four yards on their next drive, Denver took possession on its own 49. However, on first down Bobby Humphrey fumbled and defensive end Kevin Fagan recovered for San Francisco on its 46. That turnover led to Montana's seven-yard touchdown pass to tight end Brent Jones. After a failed extra point attempt, San Francisco led 13-3 with three seconds remaining in the first quarter.

The Broncos failed to cross midfield in the second period, while the 49ers scored on a 1-yard run by running back Tom Rathman and a 38-yard pass from Montana to Rice.

San Francisco was unable to move the ball on the initial drive of the second half, but Elway was intercepted on the first play of Denver's next drive to give the 49ers possession on the Broncos' 28 yard line. Giving the ball back to Montana was not what the Broncos had in mind. On first down, two future Hall of Famers connected again as Montana threw a touchdown pass to Rice, putting the 49ers up 34-3 with just 2:12 gone in the third quarter. The next Denver drive also ended with an interception, leading to a 35-yard scoring pass from Montana to John Taylor.

On their next drive, the Broncos, spurred by a 34-yard run by Humphrey, moved 61 yards in five plays and a

penalty, scoring on a 3-yard run by Elway that seemed like a mere footnote to the day's events. San Francisco roared back with an 11-play, 75-yard drive that ended with a 3-yard touchdown push by Rathman. Following yet another Broncos fumble, running back Roger Craig plowed into the end zone from one yard out to round out the scoring early in the fourth quarter and give the 49ers a 55-10 victory.

While the afternoon could not have gone worse, the Denver Broncos had ended the decade of the 1980s as the only AFC team to win three conference titles.

Greg Kragen and David Treadwell joined annual participants Karl Mecklenburg and Dennis Smith at the Pro Bowl.

While the franchise had now reached a height of success once considered unimaginable, there was a pall over the city, the team, and the quarterback for having lost the ultimate game three times in four years. Observers were quick to dismiss the obvious fact that Denver never would have gotten there without John Elway at quarterback, instead attaching any number of adjectives to the brilliant superstar for coming so close, without success, to the greatest prize of all.

1980s
DENVER BRONCOS
YEAR BY YEAR

1980	8-8
1981	10-6
1982	2-7
1983	9-7
1984	13-3
1985	11-5
1986	11-5
1987	10-4
1988	8-8
1989	11-5

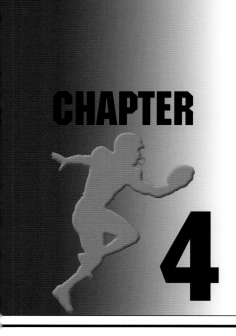

CHAPTER 4

THE 1990S
MANIFEST DESTINY IN ORANGE AND BLUE

GROWTH TO MATCH SUCCESS FOR THE BRONCOS

The new decade began with the Denver Broncos fully entrenched within the NFL hierarchy, perennial contenders that sold out all their games to some of the most rabid fans in America.

Team loyalists, national sports fans, and the press had a deep respect for what the Broncos had become, yet

The classic pose of an all-time great quarterback.

the disappointment of losing three Super Bowls seemed like it would never go away. Observers were unsure if the team, despite getting close repeatedly, would ever win it all.

The early 1990s were marked by physical changes for the franchise, with the whiff of greater change wafting through the air. The physical changes were prompted by the need for an expansion and modernization of the team's facilities that would be on a par with the best in the league and befitting the franchise's status. There also was a sense that time was starting to run out on the Dan Reeves era, which had seen the team through three Super Bowls while at the same time watching the development of a dominant coach and superstar quarterback who did not always see eye to eye.

The team headquarters in Adams County had been getting progressively more crowded and outdated as staffs and assignments expanded since its opening in the late 1960s, and on March 5, 1990, the Broncos moved into the Paul D. Bowlen Memorial Broncos Centre, a new state-of-the-art headquarters. The complex was named for the Bronco owner Pat Bowlen's late father and was the culmination of Bowlen's desire to maximize a positive working environment for his team. The new Broncos facility, situated on 13.5 acres in the rapidly expanding Dove Valley Business Park in south Arapahoe County, was more than three times the size of the team's previous complex and included a huge administrative building, a conditioning center, and three full-size practice fields.

Denver and its extraordinary quarterback had become a favorite of the NFL for its overseas American Bowl games, and in 1990 the Broncos defeated the Seattle Seahawks by a score of 10-7 in the American Bowl in the Toyko Dome. The game was played before a sellout audience in Japan and marked Denver's

114

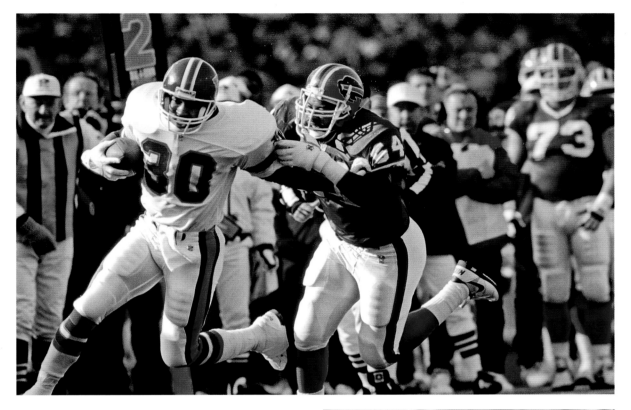

Steve Sewell gains some yards here during the 1991 AFC title game at Buffalo, but his fumble in the closing minutes was a key turning point. Heavy underdogs heading into the game, Denver put up a valiant effort before losing to the Bills by a 10-7 score.

second appearance in an international game, having played the Los Angeles Rams in London in the 1987 American Bowl. Before the decade ended, Denver had played in seven American Bowl games at international sites such as Berlin, Barcelona, Mexico City, Sydney, and a second time in Tokyo.

The Broncos had become one of the most popular teams in American's most popular sport. Yet as a result of that popularity, the coaches and players had ever increasing pressure to win, especially Dan Reeves and John Elway.

After three Super Bowl appearances in four years, it was perhaps natural to expect a letdown; however, the team's 5-11 record in 1990 was extremely unpopular with fans who wanted more.

Bobby Humphrey finished the season with 1,202 rushing yards, becoming one of just 10 backs to rush more than 1,000 yards in each of his first two NFL seasons. Mike Horan led the entire NFL in punting (44.4) and in net punting average (38.9). Individual honors aside, there was still a lot of grumbling in the Mile High City.

Due to finishing last in the AFC West in 1990, the Broncos had a somewhat softer schedule in 1991, which was like a balm to their wounds. The team rebounded for an outstanding 12-4 record, good enough to win the division. It was the Broncos' fifth such title in eight years and entitled them to serve as a playoff host in the divisional round again. This time, Denver faced the Houston Oilers and Warren Moon.

Linebacker Mike Croel wraps up a Chargers receiver. The Broncos' No. 1 draft choice in 1991, Croel was named the NFL Defensive Rookie of the Year for a first-year performance that included 10 quarterback sacks and four forced fumbles.

Reggie Rivers made the team as a free agent running back in 1991 and played six seasons for the Broncos, primarily on special teams. Articulate and engaging, Rivers quickly became one of the most popular players in the community and forged a journalism career. He currently is the weekend sports anchor for CBS Channel 4 in Denver and is the color commentator for the Broncos' preseason telecasts.

ELWAY OUTSHINES HOUSTON MOONBEAMS

The game was a classic shootout between two future Hall of Fame quarterbacks and did not disappoint from start to finish.

With the crowd barely settled into their seats, Moon drove his team 70 yards in four plays for a touchdown to put Houston up by seven points just 1:46 into the game. A nervous flutter raced through the stands— it was apparent that Houston was well prepared and determined to get a major win on the road. After a Denver punt, Moon again drove the Oilers down the field and threw his second touchdown pass, this one for 9 yards to wide receiver Drew Hill. Just like that it was 14-0, Oilers.

The Broncos started their next possession on the 35 and covered 65 yards in eight plays to score on a 10-yard pass from John Elway to Vance Johnson, but a fumbled snap on the conversion attempt left the score 14-6. On the sixth play of the ensuing Oilers' drive, free safety Steve Atwater intercepted a pass from Warren Moon, but a roughing-the-passer call nullified the effort and crushed the crowd. Three plays later, Houston compounded the locals' misery, scoring again on Moon's 6-yard pass to wide receiver Curtis Duncan.

The next Oilers' possession ended when Atwater, always a tremendous physical presence at safety, intercepted a pass again, this time giving Denver the ball on its own 12 with 6:03 left in the half. In a drive that saw Elway complete all six passes for 64 yards and the versatile Steve Sewell complete one to Johnson for 10, the Broncos covered 88 yards in 12 plays to score on a

1-yard run by running back Greg Lewis. They now had cut the Houston lead to eight points; the score was 21-13 at the half.

After a missed Houston field-goal attempt in the third quarter, the Broncos drove from their 20 to Houston's 31. Then David Treadwell nailed a 49-yard kick, the longest in Denver postseason history. Now up by only five at 21-16, the Oilers reached the Broncos' 7 yard line on their next drive but had to settle for a 25-yard field goal. It was less than they wanted, but still enough to retain control as the opponents entered the final period.

Denver started on its 20 and nine plays later faced a fourth-and-four from the Houston 41. Elway threw a short pass to wide receiver Michael Young, who broke two tackles and was finally brought down on Houston's 15 for a gain of 26 yards. Three plays later, Lewis scored on a 1-yard plunge for his second touchdown of the day, making the score 24-23.

The defense held Houston on the next drive, but the Oilers got a beautiful punt that pinned the Broncos down at their own 2 yard line with just 2:07 remaining in the game. With shades of "The Drive" in the minds of the Bronco faithful, everyone wondered if the team could pull off another stunning comeback victory. Elway immediately answered that, connecting with wide receiver Michael Young for a 22-yard gain on first down. However, three incomplete passes later, the Broncos had a fourth-and-six on the 28 yard line. Elway dropped back, then scrambled left upfield and ran out of bounds a yard past the first-down marker. Again, after three consecutive incomplete passes, Denver faced a do-or-die fourth-down situation. Elway again dropped back and scrambled left, stepping forward just in time to avoid a sack from behind. As he headed upfield, he tossed a pass sideways to an open Vance Johnson, who ran to the Houston 21 for a 44-yard gain. Steve Sewell ran for 10 yards on first down, and two plays later David Treadwell came on for the winning 28-yard field goal, getting an excellent hold from Gary Kubiak on a high snap.

Before 75,301 fans in their aging but legendary venue, the Broncos advanced to their fourth AFC Championship Game in six years in one of the most exciting games, defeating Houston 26-24. But the team was denied its fifth AFC Championship, losing 10-7 to the Bills in front of 80,272 fans at Rich Stadium. Denver's defense shut down the high-powered Buffalo offense, limiting it to just 213 total yards and only 12 first downs, but the Broncos' offense failed to capitalize on several first-half opportunities.

Both teams struggled to find their offenses in the first half, and the game was scoreless at halftime. Buffalo punted on its first two drives after a total net of minus two yards and had its third drive end when nose tackle Greg Kragen tipped and then intercepted a pass on

Buffalo's 29 yard line. Denver could not take advantage of the turnover, though. David Treadwell's ensuing 47-yard field-goal attempt sailed wide left. After the Broncos halted another Buffalo drive, Treadwell missed a 42-yard field-goal attempt.

Once again, the Bills punted after failing to get a first down, and a 10-yard punt return by Johnson set Denver up on the 50 yard line. On first down, Elway threw a middle screen to Sewell, who gained 26 yards to Buffalo's 24 yard line. The Broncos could move no closer than the 20, and Treadwell's 37-yard attempt was wide right to end the last scoring threat of the first half. The field goal miss was devastating, as the Broncos had held their highly favored opponent scoreless in the first half on the Bills' home turf.

The Bills' second drive of the third quarter began at their 20, and 11 plays later, they faced a third-and-seven on Denver's 26. Quarterback Jim Kelly's pass to James Lofton was intercepted by cornerback Tyrone Braxton and returned to the Denver 19. On second-and-10, Elway attempted another middle screen to Sewell, but linebacker Carlton Bailey picked off the pass and ran 11 yards for a touchdown and a 7-0 Buffalo lead.

The Broncos' first possession of the fourth quarter began with Kubiak at quarterback. Elway left the game with an injured thigh muscle. Kubiak drove Denver from its own 21 yard line to the Buffalo 23, but the Broncos failed to convert a fourth-down attempt. The Bills then drove 50 yards in nine plays to score on a 44-yard field goal by Scott Norwood. Now down 10-0, Kubiak engineered a frantic drive in which Denver covered 85 yards in eight plays. On the final play of the drive, Kubiak scored on a three-yard quarterback draw to pull Denver within three points, with a score of 10-7.

The ensuing onside kick was recovered by the Broncos' Atwater, and Denver began its last-chance drive on its 49 with 1:43 left on the clock and two timeouts. On first down, Kubiak hit Sewell for seven yards, but cornerback Kirby Jackson stripped the ball away and recovered it on the Buffalo 44. The Broncos' defense forced the Bills to punt, but Denver could only reach the 50 as time and the season ran out.

It seemed like not just the end of a season but the end of an era as well, as the Broncos had followed up their three Super Bowl appearances with a subpar year and then the loss at Buffalo.

Change was in the air as the popular Kubiak retired in the offseason. The 1992 Broncos went into the new campaign with Reeves in the final year of his contract. While he had enjoyed well-documented success, there was also the growing feeling within the community that these Broncos had gone as far as they could and that complete championship success would always elude the proud franchise and its passionate followers.

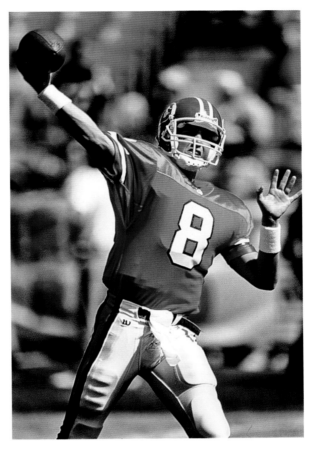

Rookies Tommy Maddox (left) and Shawn Moore (below) shared quarterbacking duties during a four-game stretch in 1992 when John Elway was injured. Dan Reeves literally alternated the two quarterbacks on a play-by-play basis, in one of the most unusual playing combinations. Reeves' explanation for the strategy was that since he was sending in every play for the inexperienced signal callers, each player would get the play directly from him on the sidelines and go in for that one play, back and forth through the course of the game. Although Maddox, the team's No. 1 draft choice in 1992, threw five touchdown passes in the four games, the Broncos did not fare well in Elway's absence, losing all four games with the two rookie quarterbacks at the helm.

Denver was shut out twice on the road, once in a 30-0 shellacking at Philadelphia and later in the year by a 24-0 defeat at the hands of the hated Raiders. A 42-20 thumping at the hands of the Chiefs in Kansas City continued the season-long pall.

The season finale in Kansas City was on December 27, and the plane ride home had a surreal quality about it. No one really talked to each other, least of all Pat Bowlen and Dan Reeves, with Bowlen contemplating the future of his beloved team.

The next day Bowlen informed Reeves that his contract as head coach would not be renewed, and Reeves left Denver with the solid accomplishment of a 116-78-1 record.

NECESSARY CHANGES IN THE MILE HIGH CITY

A new era was beginning for the Broncos, but the full ramifications of this move would not be completely felt for two more years. Often in an earthquake, the aftershock is felt more strongly, and such would be the case as Pat Bowlen filled his coaching post for the first time in his ownership.

Two candidates quickly emerged as the frontrunners for the job: the brilliant Mike Shanahan, now offensive coordinator of the San Francisco 49ers, and the

Coach Wade Phillips watches from the sideline. Phillips had some of the NFL's best defenses as defensive coordinator from 1989 to 1992 and was head coach in 1993 and 1994, producing a .500 record in his two-year tenure.

extremely popular Wade Phillips, the Broncos' current defensive coordinator. Bowlen had extensive interviews with both men. After careful soul searching, Shanahan opted to remain in his post with the 49ers. Under Shanahan's three-season stewardship, San Francisco played in the NFC Championship Game against Dallas three times, winning once and going on to win a Super Bowl.

Phillips was hired as the 10th head coach in Bronco history, signing a three-year contract after four seasons as the Broncos' defensive coordinator. Under Phillips' leadership, the defense led the AFC in fewest points allowed twice in four years (1989 and 1991), and the 1991 club was paced by a defensive unit that led the AFC in 12 separate categories. In 1989, Phillips had been the mastermind of a unit that led the NFL in fewest points allowed and was the conference's stingiest unit against the run. The son of legendary NFL coach Bum Phillips, he put his stamp on the Broncos with a staff that included seven members who previously had been head coaches at the college or pro level.

The offensive coordinator was Jim Fassel, who had known Elway since he coached him in college. Freed from the offensive constraints of the Reeves system and boosted by Fassel's dynamic offense, Elway responded with his best season statistically as a pro. He was named the AFC's most valuable player (selected by UPI, the Kansas City 101 Club, and the *Football News*) for a season in which he led the AFC in quarterback rating (92.8), attempts (551), completions (348), completion percentage (63.2), touchdowns (25), and yards (4,030).

With Elway, the Broncos returned to the playoffs as a wild card team in 1993, dropping a 42-24 first round game to the Los Angeles Raiders at the Los Angeles Memorial Coliseum. Phillips was well liked by his players and the media and Elway was among the game's all-time greats, but the loss at Los Angeles pointed out that the Broncos' talent had slipped within the conference.

In 1994, the Broncos got off to a dismal 0-4 start. One of the losses included an at-home 48-16 debacle to the Raiders in the third game of the season, which was Pat Bowlen's annual alumni reunion weekend. The loss to the team's archrival in front of former Bronco greats was embarrassing, and the day ended with despair and resignation regarding the future.

After a routine 16-9 win at Seattle, Denver returned home for a Monday night national television contest against Kansas City, which pitted Elway against Joe Montana in a game for the ages. Montana passed for 393 yards and Elway for 263. The Broncos' star also carried the ball six times for 38 more yards and scored on a 4-yard quarterback draw that gave Denver the lead with just 1:29 remaining in the game. However, Montana staged his own comeback, driving the Chiefs on an incredible nine-play, 75-yard drive in just over a minute. He completed seven passes and capped the drive with a game-winning 5-yard touchdown pass with just eight seconds remaining. The game was everything that the national audience could have asked for and more, with the two quarterbacks accounting for 700 yards of total offense and each leading a final touchdown drive. Still, only one team could ultimately win, and with the loss to Kansas City, Denver dropped to a 1-5 record. With that kind of performance, it seemed inevitable that the Wade Phillips era would conclude at the end of the season.

The Broncos fought the good fight the rest of the way, winning 6 of their last 10. But the 7-9 final tally ended Phillips' tenure and gave every indication of a franchise that was drifting listlessly on the turbulent seas of the NFL.

Yet with Bowlen's next head coach hiring, this franchise would drift no more.

MIKE SHANAHAN RETURNS TO DENVER

The only coach seriously considered by Bowlen this time around was Mike Shanahan, who since joining the Broncos as a young assistant in 1984 had parlayed intelligence, experience, drive, and passion into a rise that most recently included a three-year stint with the 49ers. There, he deftly coordinated a San Francisco offense that set a plethora of NFL and team records on its way to the 1994 world championship. Over his career, Shanahan had displayed brilliance in matching team success with the individual talent of quarterbacks like Joe Montana, Steve Young, and John Elway.

Now Elway was older, possessing the same talent and greater experience, but carrying the baggage of critics who kept pointing to those three Super Bowl losses. With Mike Shanahan calling the plays, Elway would take the team and the city to a place only dreamed about thus far. The new coach signed a seven-year contract on January 31, 1995, and immediately set out to improve the Denver roster to the level with which he had thrived in San Francisco.

Shanahan had a clear picture of the type of player he needed, one with the talent, intelligence, work ethic, and ability to put team before individual. The Broncos hit the free agent market immediately, signing wide receiver Ed McCaffrey, who had been with the 49ers, and guard Mark Schlereth, who had been a Super Bowl champion at Washington. Schlereth joined holdovers Tom Nalen and future Hall of Famer Gary Zimmerman to form the foundation of a great offensive line in Denver.

In the draft, Shanahan found a young running back who he and the coaches liked in the sixth round: Terrell Davis of the University of Georgia. The coaches could tell as soon as the 1995 training camp began that they had something special in Davis. By the second preseason

Mike Shanahan's arrival as head coach signaled a new era in Denver Broncos' history, measured by the greatest level of championship success.

Below: Hands, toes, eyes, focus: Fan favorite Ed McCaffrey makes a touchdown reception in the back of the end zone against San Diego.

Left: Mark Schlereth gets out of his stance to pass block in the playoff win over Jacksonville. Schlereth was a two-time world champion with Denver, after having already won one ring with Washington.

Right: Offensive tackle Gary Zimmerman blocks Chiefs linebacker Derrick Thomas during a September 22, 1996, game at Kansas City.

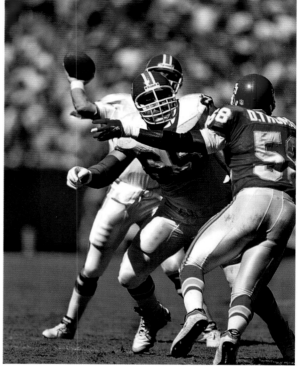

Five-time Pro Bowl center Tom Nalen leads the pass protection for John Elway against Green Bay.

game, a 24-10 win over the 49ers in an American Bowl game played in Tokyo, the rookie began to make his mark. His devastating special teams tackle in that game put him on every fan's radar. He quickly earned greater playing time and more carries, and his rise to the starting lineup was immediate and dramatic. Finally, the Broncos had a running back to play with Elway.

While the Broncos posted just an 8-8 mark in 1995, Elway was finding the comfort zone that he had with Shanahan when Shanahan was an assistant. In a 38-6 pasting of the Cardinals in November, the Denver quarterback passed for 256 yards to exceed the 40,000-yard mark. He was just the seventh player in history to accomplish that feat.

Another individual accomplishment of the season came in the last home game against Seattle, when running back/kick returner Glyn Milburn tallied an NFL-record 404 all-purpose yards in a 31-27 loss to the Seahawks. He surpassed Billy Cannon's previous record of 373 yards, set 35 years prior on December 10, 1961. Milburn racked up 131 rushing yards, 45 receiving yards, 133 yards on kickoff returns, and 95 yards on punt returns.

The season was not special, but was a sign of things to come. The Broncos established franchise single-season records in seven different offensive categories: points scored (388), total yards (6,040), average gain per play (5.70), average gain per rush (4.53), touchdown passes (27, tie), passing yards (4,045), and first downs gained by passes (205).

Top: Dominating Terrell Davis is the only player in history to win both the league and Super Bowl MVP awards and have a 2,000-yard rushing season.

Bottom: Elusive all-purpose back Glyn Milburn accounted for 2,080 combined yards (rushing, receiving, and returns) in 1995 and set the NFL single-game record with 404 combined yards (131 rushing, 45 receiving, and 228 on kick returns) against Seattle at Mile High Stadium on December 10, 1995.

A GREAT SEASON ENDS WITH A BITTER DEFEAT

With the dawn of the 1996 season, Bronco fans were going to see their team rise again to glory.

In the 1996 draft, the Broncos picked linebacker John Mobley in the first round, after having signed defenders that included linebacker Bill Romanowski and defensive end Alfred Williams as free agents. The remodeling of the roster paid immediate dividends as the new season began.

TERRELL DAVIS
RUNNING BACK
1995–2002

Terrell Davis was inducted as the 21st member of the Ring of Fame in 2007 after establishing himself as the Denver Broncos' all-time leading rusher in a magnificent eight-year career. Selected by the Broncos in the sixth round (196th overall) of the 1995 NFL Draft, Davis rushed for at least 1,000 yards in each of his four full seasons. This includes the 1998 campaign in which he totaled the fourth-most rushing yards (2,008) in a season in NFL history and earned league MVP honors. That year Davis also set a club record with 21 rushing scores.

The three-time Pro Bowl and first-team All-Pro selection (1996–1998) finished his career with a franchise-record 7,607 rushing yards and 60 rushing touchdowns on 1,655 carries (4.6-yard average) in 78 regular-season games (77 starts). He was a key member of the Broncos' back-to-back Super Bowl championship teams in 1997 and 1998. The brilliant Davis, who spent his entire career playing in Denver, had a career 97.5-yard per game rushing average in the regular season, which is the third best in NFL history (minimum of 75 games). That statistic only trails Pro Football Hall of Fame members Jim Brown and Barry Sanders. A semifinalist for the Pro Football Hall of Fame Class of 2008, Davis owns three of the top-five single-season rushing outputs in Broncos' annals, as well as the club's single-season scoring record (138 points in 1998).

In the postseason, Davis was equally as impressive, totaling at least 100 rushing yards in seven of his eight career playoff appearances. One of these games included his 157-yard, three-rushing touchdown performance against Green Bay in Super Bowl XXXII, in which he earned MVP honors. Those seven 100-yard games were consecutive and all Bronco wins—the only time in NFL history a back has accomplished that feat in postseason play.

Davis averaged an NFL-record 142.5 rushing yards per game in the postseason (minimum of five games) for his career, totaling a playoff club-record 1,140 total rushing yards on 204 carries (5.6-yard average) with 12 touchdowns.

Davis, who played his first collegiate season at Long Beach State before transferring to the University of Georgia, ranks first in Bronco history in career 100-yard rushing games (41), first in rushing touchdowns (62), second in overall touchdowns (65), and second in yards from scrimmage (8,887). His Hall of Fame credentials are buoyed by the fact that he is the only back in NFL history to have done all four of the following, which will be almost impossible to equal: being the regular-season MVP, the Super Bowl MVP, posting a 2,000-yard rushing season, and having seven consecutive postseason 100-yard games, all of which were victories.

He remains close to the game as an analyst for NFL Network.

Davis' Denver Broncos Career Record

		RUSHING					RECEIVING			
Games	Starts	No.	Yds.	Avg.	LG	TD	No.	Yds.	Avg.	LG	TD
78	77	1,655	7,607	4.6	71t	60	169	1,280	7.6	35	5

Bill Romanowski (No. 53) listens to the postgame talk in the locker room. Romanowski was an intense competitor on defense during the Denver title run.

The Broncos started the 1996 regular season on the right foot with an impressive 31-6 victory over the visiting New York Jets before a sellout crowd of 70,595. Denver wasted no time in taking control of this contest, scoring touchdowns on three of its first four possessions. One of these strikes was a 13-yard John Elway–to–Shannon Sharpe touchdown toss on Denver's initial possession. Early in the second quarter, Elway hooked up with Ed McCaffrey from 39 yards out to open up a 14-0 advantage for the home team. An interception set up Terrell Davis' 1-yard plunge to make the score 21-0.

Later in the quarter, Alfred Williams and Michael Dean Perry combined to force a fumble that Perry recovered. On the next play, Anthony Miller scored on a 26-yard end around to widen the margin to 28-0. A Jason Elam 28-yard field goal ended the Broncos' scoring for the day as they went to the locker room with a 31-0 advantage. The 24 second-quarter points were the second-most in team history and marked the seventh time in franchise history that the Broncos scored that many points in a quarter.

The defense recorded nine sacks—second most in team history—by a team-record eight different players and held the Jets to 188 total yards (just 72 yards coming through the air).

The next week, the Broncos improved to 2-0 for the first time since 1993 with a convincing 30-20 road victory against the Seattle Seahawks at the Kingdome. It

was another excellent day for the Bronco defense, but it was a record-setting day for Elway. He surpassed Tom Jackson on the team's all-time games-played list with his 192nd appearance in a Denver uniform. He also broke his own team record by throwing a touchdown pass for the 14th consecutive game.

Elway needed only 2:47 to take the offense 84 yards in five plays, capping the drive with a 39-yard touchdown toss on a dump pass to fullback Aaron Craver. It gave Denver a 10-6 advantage. Another Elam field goal right before the half was set up when Romanowski recovered a fumble that resulted from blitzing cornerback Ray Crockett's sack of Seahawks quarterback Rick Mirer. Romanowski also had an interception in the second quarter.

Denver's ground game—which totaled more than 175 yards for the second consecutive week—gave the Broncos control, while the defense held Seattle to one rushing first down and only 211 total yards for the game. The Denver defense also totaled three sacks, giving the team 12 sacks after two games, the most in the NFL. The Broncos were rolling.

Next up, the Broncos lifted their record to 3-0 for the first time since the 1989 season, showing resolve and determination in defeating the winless Tampa Bay Buccaneers, 27-23. Defensive back Tyrone Braxton—thought of as undersized, but who always seemed to come up big—returned an interception 69 yards for

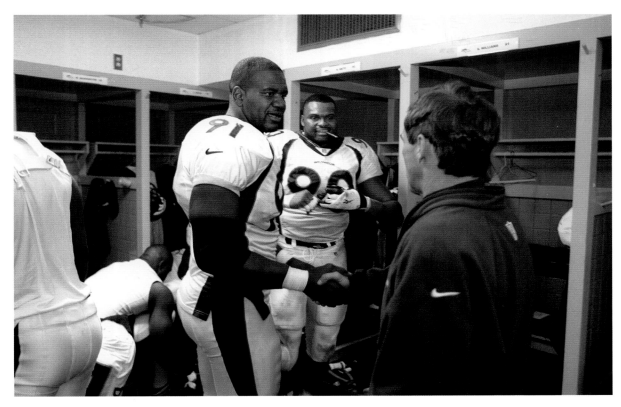

Defensive end Alfred Williams receives congratulations from Mike Shanahan on a job well done. Neil Smith looks on in the background.

a touchdown, the longest return of his career. The Broncos put the game away when Elway led the Broncos on a methodical 14-play, 80-yard drive that culminated with a 3-yard touchdown run by Davis with 3:32 remaining. The run gave Denver a 27-23 lead the team never relinquished, thanks to a timely sack, a forced fumble, and a fumble recovery by Williams on Tampa Bay's next possession.

The fourth-quarter game-winning drive was the 38th of Elway's career, the most in NFL history. He also surpassed the 45,000-yard mark in total offense in the game, as well as 6,000 pass attempts. Davis finished the game with 137 yards on 22 carries and a touchdown despite missing a quarter and a half due to a migraine headache, a condition that plagued him throughout his pro career. The following year it would be a big part of the story in the greatest game of his life.

The Broncos suffered their first loss of the 1996 season in a 17-14 defensive struggle at Kansas City. The loss dropped Denver out of a first-place tie with the Chiefs and into a second-place tie with the San Diego Chargers in the AFC West. Even in defeat, Davis was brilliant, racking up his third consecutive 100-yard rushing performance, the first time since 1990 that a Bronco runner (Bobby Humphrey) had accomplished this feat.

This was not a team that would stay down for long.

The Broncos overcame offensive and special teams mistakes to secure their fourth win of the season at

Ray Crockett crushes a Seattle receiver, recording a tackle. Crockett was a sure-handed defender and did not shy away from contact.

Safety Tyrone Braxton heads for the end zone after picking off a pass. A sure-handed ballhawk, Braxton had 34 interceptions as a Bronco and earned a big-play reputation during his 12 years in Denver.

Cincinnati, vaulting back into a tie for first place. It was a defensive struggle that continued into the second half, when Denver finally forged ahead on a John Elway–to–Anthony Miller 23-yard touchdown connection with 2:18 remaining in the third quarter. It proved to be the final score of the day by either team, as Denver's defense held the Bengals scoreless for the entire second half. The biggest play of the game probably occurred on Cincinnati's final possession, as a long pass was tipped away at the last second by Ray Crockett to prevent what would have been the go-ahead score.

October began at Mile High Stadium with a game against San Diego. After the Chargers took a 17-0 second-quarter lead, the Broncos got their act together and proceeded to run off 28 unanswered points, en route to a 28-17 victory. Heading into their bye week, the Broncos had sole possession of first place in the AFC West.

John Elway and Shannon Sharpe repeatedly burned the Charger secondary, helping Denver overcome the loss of Davis, who suffered a migraine during the game. Things didn't start well for the Broncos, as San Diego put back-to-back touchdown drives together in the second quarter. Then the Denver offense, led by Sharpe and Elway, woke up. The two connected for the first of three touchdowns on the day with 1:25 left in the first half to bring the Broncos within 10 at the intermission. In the third quarter, Elway hooked up with Sharpe on another 20-yard score and then followed that with another touchdown to Sharpe—a 3-yard hookup—to put Denver ahead 21-17. In that quarter, the Denver defense held San Diego to just two first downs and 26 total yards.

The Broncos dominance continued in the fourth quarter, as Elway closed out the scoring by hitting fan favorite Ed McCaffrey from nine yards out, giving Denver a 5-1 start.

Sharpe's 13-catch day tied a team record and set a personal high, as did his three touchdown receptions. After arriving in Denver, Shanahan had challenged Sharpe to take his game to another level as a blocker as well as a receiver, and the tight end responded brilliantly to Shanahan's guidance and focus.

Left: Shannon Sharpe makes a reception and takes off for more yardage. He won two Super Bowl rings with Denver and another with the Baltimore Ravens. He was football's finest tight end of the 1990s.

Right: Running back Terrell Davis congratulates tight end Shannon Sharpe after a touchdown during a big win over the Kansas City Chiefs.

In the October 20, 1996, game against the Ravens, the Broncos offense had another record-setting day. The Broncos' 45-34 come-from-behind victory over the Baltimore Ravens was the first meeting between the two franchises, as 70,453 watched the Broncos maintain a one-game lead in the AFC's western division.

Of the various stellar performances of the day, the most impressive was that of second-year running back Terrell Davis, who rushed for a career- and franchise-high 194 yards on 28 carries with two touchdowns. One of the scores came via a career-best 71-yard scamper to give Denver a 14-0 first-quarter advantage.

The lead grew to 21-3 in the second quarter on Davis' second touchdown run, this one from four yards out. The Ravens outscored Denver 10-7 for the rest of the half as Denver went to the locker room with a 28-13 advantage.

In the third quarter, Baltimore rallied for 21 points to turn an 18-point deficit into a 34-31 lead at the start of the fourth quarter. At that point, the Elway magic took over, as the legendary comeback quarterback led Denver on two touchdown drives. The first ended with him throwing his third touchdown pass of the day to McCaffrey. With that catch, McCaffrey tied a team record for most touchdowns in a game and most receiving touchdowns in a game. Elway, who led Denver on

A great blocking fullback and team leader, Howard Griffith was a key component of the running game that helped pave the way to consecutive world championships.

Guard Dan Neil protects John Elway from the New England pass rush.

his 39th fourth-quarter game-winning drive, capped the scoring on a nine-yard touchdown run of his own.

For the game, Elway threw for 326 yards—his third consecutive 300-yard passing day—and three touchdowns and ran for a score. During the contest, he passed Warren Moon and moved into third place all-time in both completions and passing yardage, behind Dan Marino and Fran Tarkenton. It was also the 32nd regular-season 300-yard passing game of his career, second among active quarterbacks behind Marino.

The 548 yards of total offense rolled up by Denver broke the franchise record of 543 set on September 19, 1976, against the New York Jets. The win gave Denver its first 6-1 start since 1989, when the franchise last appeared in a Super Bowl.

The Broncos' most resounding victory of the season came the following week versus one of their key AFC West rivals, the Kansas City Chiefs. After the 34-7 win, Denver had a two-game lead in the AFC West at the season's halfway point. The game was never in doubt after Denver jumped out to a 17-7 lead at the end of the first quarter. Denver held the Chiefs to only 22 rushing yards for the game and zero rushing first downs.

During the game, Elway—who had a career-high 62 yards rushing—exceeded the 3,000-yard rushing mark for his career, making him the second player in NFL

history to rush for more than 3,000 yards and pass for more than 40,000 yards in his career. Davis, who ran for 77 yards, became the fastest Bronco in team history to reach the 2,000-yard rushing mark, doing it in his 22nd professional game. With the win, Denver opened the season 7-1 for the first time since 1986, and fans were getting that Super Bowl feeling.

The Broncos upped their record to 8-1 with a thrilling 22-21 comeback victory over archenemy Oakland. The game was played in front of not only the 61,179 at the Oakland-Alameda County Coliseum, but also a national Monday Night audience. It was Denver's only Monday Night Football appearance in 1996. Oakland ran off 14 consecutive fourth-quarter points in just over two minutes to take a 21-16 advantage, but that set the stage for Elway to work his magic once again. Elway used only 47 seconds of the game clock to drive Denver 73 yards in six plays. The last 49 yards came on a hitch-and-go touchdown hookup with Rod Smith to put the Broncos in the lead for the rest of the game. Elway had his NFL-record 40th game-winning or game-saving drive, and the Broncos marched on.

Bronco fans watched one of the wildest finishes in franchise history the following week, as the Broncos survived a valiant effort from the 4-5 Chicago Bears, escaping with a 17-12 victory. The home victory pushed their Mile High record to 6-0 as Davis, in just the 10th game of the season, surpassed the 1,000-yard rushing mark, faster than any Bronco running back in team annals. He also became the 14th player in NFL history to rush for more than 1,000 yards in each of his first two seasons in the league.

Denver then went on the road to win back-to-back games at New England and Minnesota, staging one of the most miraculous endings in team history in the Minneapolis Metrodome. The winning score came with just 19 seconds remaining in the game. Elway, who led Denver down the field 84 yards in just over five minutes, tossed a pass over the middle that was intended for Sharpe, but was deflected three times before finally being cradled by McCaffrey for the winning score. Elway's 41st career game-saving drive was one of his most spectacular, and the Broncos truly had the look of destiny's darlings. The win improved Denver's record to 11-1 and gave the Broncos a three-game lead in the division with four weeks to go.

The next week, the Broncos clinched their first AFC West Division title since 1991 with a 34-7 victory over the Seattle Seahawks. They also were able to secure home-field advantage throughout the AFC playoffs by virtue of losses earlier in the day by Buffalo and Pittsburgh.

With milestones becoming routine, the team reached a few more during the game. At the end of the second quarter, Elway threw his 250th career touchdown pass, and on the Broncos' first play of the second half, he connected with Sharpe for a 7-yard gain that put Elway over the 3,000-yard mark in passing yards in a season for the 11th time in his career. He was now tied with Miami's Dan Marino for the most 3,000-yard seasons in league annals.

With the victory, the Broncos improved their all-time record to 268-267-10, putting the franchise on the winning side of the ledger for the first time since November 6, 1960. The win also improved their home record since 1974 to 138-46-1 (130-45-1 in regular-season play), best in the NFL in this period.

With all their regular-season goals complete, the Broncos saw their nine-game winning streak come to a screeching halt in front of 60,712 people at Lambeau Field. The Green Bay Packers took advantage of various Bronco mistakes and the absence of three Broncos' starters—most notably quarterback John Elway—to cruise to a 41-6 victory. Denver bounced back the following week to beat the Raiders and in the process improved the team's record to 13-2—its best mark after 15 games in franchise history. The Broncos also finished undefeated at home for only the second time in the franchise's 37-year history (1981 was the other year).

The Raider win was also a day when Denver set many records. Elway earned his 126th victory as a starter, breaking the NFL record previously held by Fran Tarkenton. He also became just the third player in NFL history to pass for more than 45,000 yards in a career. Davis won the AFC rushing crown with a then franchise-record 1,538 yards while also posting franchise bests in carries (345), rushing touchdowns (13), and total touchdowns (15). The team tied for the NFL's best record and ranked first in the league in total offense and rushing offense. In addition, the defense finished with the number one mark against the run. The Broncos also set a franchise record for points scored with 391, and the supremely gifted Davis was named NFL Offensive Player of the Year by the Associated Press.

The Broncos closed out the 1996 regular season resting most of the key players as they prepared for the postseason, dropping a 16-10 decision to the San Diego Chargers at Jack Murphy Stadium.

Two veteran anchors of the Bronco offense, quarterback John Elway and center Tom Nalen, discuss strategy before taking the field.

JACKSONVILLE TAKES ITS PLACE IN BRONCO LORE

At the time of his retirement, Shannon Sharpe was the all-time leader among tight ends in receptions, yardage, and touchdowns. There's little doubt that Sharpe earned his credentials for future induction into the Pro Football Hall of Fame.

Not only were the Broncos feeling on top of the world as the playoffs began, but they felt confident they could beat their first playoff opponent. The expansion Jacksonville team had been 2-7 before a late-season winning streak propelled the new franchise into the post-season. The Broncos were gigantic favorites, but no one told the Jaguars.

Denver's most successful season since 1991 came to a surprising end at the hands of Jacksonville in an AFC

divisional playoff game in front of 75,678 stunned fans at Mile High Stadium. The underdog Jaguars won by a final score of 30-27. The loss was Denver's first of the season at home and only its second loss at home in postseason competition.

The contest began on a promising note for the Broncos, as they scored on two of their first three possessions to take a 12-0 lead into the second quarter. First, running back Vaughn Hebron scored his first postseason touchdown on a 1-yard plunge on fourth down. During that drive, Terrell Davis set a franchise record for the longest postseason run with a 47-yard scamper. On Denver's next possession, Shannon Sharpe hauled in an 18-yard pass from John Elway to produce the 12-point margin.

The Jaguars then proceeded to score on their next six possessions, with the first five unanswered by the Broncos. When Jacksonville went up by a score of 23-12, orange-clad loyalists went into an emotional tizzy. The Broncos responded with a nine-play, 57-yard drive, capped by a 2-yard touchdown run by Davis, who then tacked on the two-point conversion himself to cut the deficit to three. But Jacksonville's Mark Brunell, who threw for 245 yards and two touchdowns on the day, completed a scoring pass on a critical third-and-five play from the Broncos' 16 yard line with 3:39 remaining in the game to restore a 10-point advantage.

Denver again pulled to within three points when Elway found McCaffrey in the end zone for a 15-yard touchdown with 1:50 left, but the Mile High magic ran out as the Jaguars held on for their shocking 30-27 win.

This was arguably the most depressing home loss in franchise history, so dramatic that Sharpe suggested it would take the franchise 10 years to overcome the emotional letdown.

NEW UNIFORMS, SAME GOALS FOR 1997

The stunning loss was deeply felt by every member of the organization and the entire Rocky Mountain region. However, no one counted on the brilliant leadership of Mike Shanahan, who, in the following year, forged an absolute focus on the future and what could be done, not allowing anyone to dwell on what might have been. No one would have guessed that the enormous disappointment of 1996 would be the beginning of the best three-year run by any NFL team to date.

The blockbuster event of the offseason came on February 4 when the Broncos unveiled new uniforms, featuring traditional Bronco orange with a navy blue jersey. The helmet became a darker, navy blue, with a new powerful, dynamic Bronco head done in white with orange highlights.

When Shanahan met with the team to set its goals for 1997, he emphasized that the team was good enough to win the Super Bowl and that was the prize—regardless of regular-season record, regardless of whether the club won its division.

Yet when the Broncos made their sixth American Bowl appearance—this time on August 4 against the Dolphins in Mexico City before 104,629 fans—the season took what appeared to be a disastrous turn when Elway suffered a complete tear of his upper right biceps tendon. To make matters worse, the brilliant superstar had been playing with joint soreness in his right shoulder for some time.

For the next week, Bronco fans held their collective breath until trainer Steve Antonopulos pronounced his optimism. As it turned out, this tear had actually freed up the joint and relieved the pain that Elway had been experiencing. His biceps tendon rolled down his upper arm like a window shade, but for the first time in a long time, the arm was pain free. The city exhaled, and the season began.

The Broncos kicked off the 1997 campaign with a 19-3 victory over the Chiefs. After settling for three field goals from Jason Elam through the first three quarters of play, the Broncos finally scored their first touchdown in the fourth quarter on a 10-yard run by Terrell Davis. During the game, he rushed for 101 yards on 26 carries, the 11th 100-yard rushing performance of his career.

The third of Elam's four field goals was set up by Elway's 78-yard connection with wide receiver Rod

A united team: The Broncos put their hands together in a huddle.

The Denver Broncos cheerleaders perform during a timeout. In addition to performing at home games, they have represented the Broncos at each Super Bowl and American Bowl contest.

Smith, the third longest nonscoring pass play in franchise history and the longest reception of Smith's career. In the third quarter, the Broncos defense put up a goal-line stand that kept Denver up by a touchdown, and the home team held on for the win over a solid division rival.

The Broncos improved to 2-0 on the season with a 35-14 victory against the Seattle Seahawks (their largest margin of victory ever at the Kingdome). Denver's defense took over a close game in the third quarter, holding Seattle to 131 total yards in the second half and actually outscoring the Seahawks offense 6-0, thanks to a 32-yard interception return for a touchdown by cornerback Darrien Gordon. Denver already had taken a 21-14 lead on Jason Elam's second field goal of the game to end the first half, coupled with McCaffrey's second touchdown catch of the game. Elam moved past the 500-point mark for his career with that kick.

The next game was a day of record-setting as the Broncos ran their record to 3-0, the first back-to-back 3-0 start in franchise history. Showing that his shoulder had no lingering problems, Elway threw four touchdown passes to beat the St. Louis Rams. Gordon became the first Bronco to return a punt for a touchdown in 10 years, taking one back 94 yards in the third quarter, the longest return in team history.

Alfred Williams was on the University of Colorado national championship team in college prior to winning two Super Bowl rings with Denver. Williams led the Broncos with 13 sacks in 1996 and then shared the team lead, with Neil Smith and Maa Tanuvasa, in 1997 with 8.5 sacks.

During the contest that Denver won 35-14, Elway passed Dan Fouts, Sonny Jurgensen, and Warren Moon in career touchdown passes, moving into sixth place all time, and also passed Fran Tarkenton in pass attempts, moving into second place all time. Tight end Shannon Sharpe went over the 5,000-yard receiving mark for his career, and Terrell Davis was becoming the best back of his era in the NFL. He rushed for 100 yards again, the 13th time in his career and the third straight time this season (one off his own team record for consecutive 100-yard performances). The win improved Denver's home mark since 1974 (regular and postseason) to 141-47-1, best in the NFL over that time period. It was also Denver's 10th straight regular-season home win, the second-longest streak in franchise history.

The team's dominance continued with a 38-20 come-from-behind victory against the Bengals at Mile High. With the victory, the Broncos had started their season with four straight wins for only the third time in franchise history (the others being 1977 and 1986, both Super Bowl seasons). The triumph also was Denver's fourth straight win by 10 or more points, a mark topped only by five straight double-digit wins in 1977.

The fourth quarter became the Terrell Davis show, as he ran for 98 yards in the quarter and 130 in the second half, including a 50-yard touchdown dash that gave Denver a 28-20 lead. The Broncos capped the scoring with a 51-yard fumble return by Alfred Williams after a sack by fellow defensive end Neil Smith. Davis' dominating 215-yard effort was not only a career high, but also a franchise high, as were his 228 total yards from scrimmage.

Denver finished with a perfect September for the first time since 1989 when it took a 29-21 win from the Falcons in Atlanta. The Broncos roared out of the gate to a 23-0 advantage, thanks to a 65-yard touchdown reception by tight end Shannon Sharpe on the fourth play from scrimmage, a 10-yard touchdown pass to Willie Green on the Broncos' second series, and a 13-yard scoring run by Davis. Sharpe, returning to his native Georgia, produced his first 100-yard receiving game of the season. He caught six passes for 119 yards and a score, moving both he and his brother Sterling to more than 1,000 receptions as a brother tandem, an NFL first. On an offense that featured two future Hall of Famers in John Elway and Gary Zimmerman, Sharpe was fashioning Canton credentials of his own.

Battles of unbeatens always excite football fans and the networks, and in an October 6 matchup against the previously unbeaten Patriots, Denver came away with another win. It was the team's 10th in a row over the New England Patriots and improved its record to 6-0. It was the latest point in the season two unbeaten teams faced off on Monday Night Football. The final score was 34-13.

Denver jumped all over the Pats early in the first quarter, using an 11-play, 75-yard drive capped by a 2-yard run by Davis to take a 7-0 lead. Later in the opening quarter, linebacker John Mobley returned his second career interception 13 yards for a score to boost Denver's margin to 14-0.

The second half was all Denver as the Broncos put up 20 points. Davis put the punctuation mark on the Monday night performance in becoming the fastest player in franchise history to reach 4,000 total yards from scrimmage.

The Broncos suffered their first loss of the 1997 season at the hands of the Raiders, 28-25, and then faced one of the most unusual situations in franchise history, one which tested their mettle as a potential championship club.

NEITHER SNOW NOR JET LAG SLOWS THE BRONCO EXPRESS

Before 78,458 rain-drenched fans at Buffalo's Rich Stadium, the Broncos overcame one of the most trying weekends in team annals to defeat the Bills 23-20 in overtime. After a severe Denver snowstorm delayed the flight to Buffalo by 10 hours, the team finally arrived in Buffalo after midnight, barely 12 hours before the game's 1 p.m. kickoff.

After a scoreless first quarter, the Broncos broke on top first with a 23-yard Elam field goal. Davis, who had another career day, then capped an 11-play, 74-yard drive with a 9-yard touchdown run, sending Denver to the locker room with a 10-0 lead. Amazingly, the Broncos showed no ill effects of their grueling past 24 hours. When Buffalo fumbled away the kickoff to open the second half, Denver turned the miscue into another field goal and a 13-0 advantage. The team's lead increased to 20-0 when defensive tackle Keith Traylor recorded his first career interception, picking off a pass and rumbling 62 yards for a touchdown.

The Bills, however, staged a fourth-quarter comeback, scoring 20 unanswered points, including a 55-yard field goal by Steve Christie with two seconds remaining in regulation.

After winning the coin toss to start overtime, the tiring Broncos elected to kick and take the wind, only the seventh time in NFL history that a team has done so. The strategy paid off when Elam connected on a 33-yarder with just 1:56 remaining in overtime.

At the end of the grueling game, Davis had rushed for 207 yards on a franchise-record 42 carries. In addition, he had five receptions for 29 yards, giving him a new team mark of 236 total yards from scrimmage. His numbers also made him the eighth back in NFL history to rush for 1,000 in each of his first three seasons in the league (the first Bronco to ever do it) and the first Bronco to have three 1,000-yard rushing seasons in his career.

The Broncos kept rolling with a 30-27 win over Seattle and a 34-0 shutout of the Carolina Panthers, extending their record home winning streak to 14 games.

The first quarter of the Carolina game was a showcase of Darrien Gordon's skills, as the Broncos' starting right cornerback and punt returner took back two punts for touchdowns (82 and 75 yards) to take the home team to a 14-0 advantage. It marked only the ninth time in NFL history that a player had run back two punts for touchdowns in the same game and only the third time in NFL annals that a player had done so in the same

Pro Bowl defensive end Neil Smith was one of the key players on the Denver defense after coming over from Kansas City in 1997.

quarter. Gordon's 168 yards in punt returns set a new team record and produced his third and fourth scores on returns for the season, tying the franchise record set by Rick Upchurch in 1976.

The game, for all intents and purposes, was over at this point, as the Broncos' defense held Carolina to just 147 yards of total offense and just seven total first downs. Lost among Gordon's accomplishments was the franchise-record eighth 100-yard performance of the season by Terrell Davis and an eight-catch, 174-yard performance by tight end Shannon Sharpe, the second-highest yardage total of his blossoming career.

Each season comes with its twists and turns and one of those for the 1997 Broncos came during its next matchup, against the Kansas City Chiefs. At Arrowhead, Denver suffered a heartbreaking 24-22 defeat when Pete Stoyanovich connected on a 54-yard field goal as time expired. The loss shrunk Denver's lead in the AFC West to just one game over the Chiefs. It was the team's third straight loss at Kansas City and its fifth in the past six years.

Denver bounced back, though, to maintain its lead in the AFC West by avenging one of the team's two earlier defeats with a 31-3 mauling of the Oakland Raiders before a raucous home crowd. Davis took control of

the game by scoring three touchdowns, establishing a personal high and tying the team record. He also went over 5,000 total yards from scrimmage for his career that night. In reaching that plateau in his 42nd game, Davis did so faster than anyone in team history and became only the eighth player in league history to accomplish this feat in his first three NFL seasons.

Still, the Broncos were focusing on going beyond a playoff berth. The previous year's loss to Jacksonville was still very much in their minds when they clinched a playoff spot and a chance at redemption with a 38-28 win against the Chargers in San Diego. Denver maintained its slim one-game lead over division-rival Kansas City in the AFC West standings, and the team felt good heading into cross-country road games at Pittsburgh and San Francisco.

However, hitting the road was unkind to Denver. The Broncos got spanked in both games, 35-24 at Pittsburgh and 34-17 at the hands of the 49ers. The loss to the 49ers ended Denver's hopes of winning back-to-back AFC West Division titles and virtually eliminated any home-field advantage for the Broncos in the playoffs. To accomplish the goals laid out by Shanahan at the start of the year, the Broncos were going to have to be road warriors in January.

Terrell Davis outruns the Cowboy defense for one of his 60 career rushing touchdowns. Always brilliant, Davis excelled in the postseason for Denver. He set the NFL record with seven consecutive 100-yard rushing performances, all in victories, a mark that will be very difficult to break.

They returned home to close out the regular season on a positive note, defeating San Diego 38-3 and assuring a home wild card game the following weekend against the same Jacksonville team that handed them a stunning loss the year prior. The Broncos also wrapped up their second straight undefeated regular season at home, a franchise first. No matter what the playoffs held, the fans were brimming with pride as the Broncos became only the third team since the 16-game schedule was instituted in 1978 to accomplish that goal. (The others were Dallas in 1980-1981 and Green Bay in 1996-1997). The team also had produced the first back-to-back seasons with 12 or more wins in franchise history.

Sharpe had a stellar day against the Chargers, finishing with eight receptions for 162 yards and a career best 1,107 for the season. His performance put him over the 1,000-yard mark for the third time in his career (tied for most among tight ends) and for the second consecutive season. It also enabled Denver to become one of only three teams in history (Detroit in 1995 and 1997) to have a 3,000-yard passer, a 1,500-yard rusher, and two 1,000-yard receivers. Denver also finished tops in the NFL in both points scored for the first time and in total offense for the second straight season. Elway's four touchdowns gave him 27 for the season, a career and franchise high. Bronco fans took great solace in these stats, as they knew the long odds that faced their wild card team on the road to the Super Bowl.

TEAM ON A MISSION

One overwhelming fact was yet to be proven—that the Denver Broncos were simply the best team in the NFL, one on a mission of redemption as the playoffs began.

The Broncos advanced to the AFC divisional playoffs by running the Jacksonville Jaguars out of town, as they piled up a club postseason-record 310 rushing yards en route to a 42-17 victory. They scored touchdowns on each of their first three possessions, racking up a 21-0 lead on 32 offensive plays, during which time the Jaguars ran only six. Davis capped Denver's opening drive with a 2-yard touchdown run, and Rod Smith punctuated the next when he reeled in a 43-yard touchdown pass. The lead increased to 21-0 when Davis—who set franchise postseason records for rushing attempts (31), rushing yards (184), and longest run from scrimmage (59) before leaving in the third quarter with bruised ribs—tied franchise records for rushing touchdowns and total touchdowns in a postseason game with his second TD of the day. This one was from 5 yards out.

Left: Defensive end Trevor Pryce celebrates after sacking Mark Brunell in the playoff win against the Jaguars in 1997.

Right: Tom Nalen prepares to block during the playoff win over Jacksonville in 1997. The offensive line paved the way for 310 rushing yards against the Jaguars and was collectively named Player of the Week by the NFL.

The Jaguars answered by scoring the game's next 17 points, but the Broncos dominated from there. Derek Loville took over for the injured Davis and slashed his way to 103 yards (second most by a Bronco in postseason) on 11 attempts and scored two fourth-quarter touchdowns on runs of 25 and 8 yards to tie the club touchdown record already achieved in the game by Davis. Vaughn Hebron then got into the act himself, scoring Denver's fifth rushing touchdown of the day on a 6-yard run with 1:11 remaining and pushing the lead to its final margin of 42-17. With Davis' 184 rushing yards and Loville's 103, Denver became just the third team in NFL postseason history to boast two 100-yard rushers in the same game. Additionally, Denver's 40:59 minutes of possession time and their 310 rushing yards both were the fifth-highest recorded in an NFL playoff game.

Denver had redeemed itself for that Jacksonville defeat one year earlier, but the Broncos were far from finished.

The next week in Kansas City, the Broncos posted their first road playoff win in 11 years—and only the second in franchise history—with a 14-10 victory at Arrowhead Stadium. Denver advanced to its first AFC Championship Game since the 1991 season on the strength of two Terrell Davis touchdowns—tying the franchise postseason record for the second week in a row—and a defensive effort that limited the Chiefs to just 10 points (that mark tied for the fewest points in club playoff history).

Playing through the pain of bruised ribs suffered in the previous game, Davis broke a scoreless tie late in the second quarter, plowing into the end zone from 1 yard out to give Denver a 7-0 lead. The touchdown capped an eight-play, 65-yard drive that covered 4:51 on the clock. Key to the drive was a 17-yard John Elway completion to Rod Smith on a third-and-seven play that gave the Broncos a first down at the Kansas City 4 yard line.

The Chiefs, limited to 58 yards total offense in the first half, came out strong after the break, moving the ball to the Denver six before settling for a 20-yard Pete Stoyanovich field goal. Kansas City struck again late in the quarter when Elvis Grbac found tight end Tony Gonzalez in the back of the end zone for a 12-yard score, the Chiefs' only touchdown of the day.

The Broncos, however, answered on their ensuing possession, driving 49 yards in six plays for what proved to be the game-winning touchdown. The key play of the drive was a 43-yard Ed McCaffrey reception, which gave Denver a first down at the Chiefs' 1 yard line. After two unsuccessful attempts from close range, Davis muscled his way through the middle of the determined Chiefs' line for his second touchdown of the day and the fifth of his career in the postseason.

Kansas City had possession three more times in the game but was turned back each time by the furious Broncos' defense. The Chiefs reached Denver's 31 and their own 36 before having to punt and finally drove to the Broncos' 20 with 19 seconds left. The final play was a fourth-down pass to the end zone that was knocked down by Darrien Gordon, ending the Chiefs' hopes and propelling Denver to the AFC title game.

The Broncos advanced to their fifth Super Bowl and their first since 1989 with a 24-21 victory at Pittsburgh in the AFC Championship Game at Three Rivers Stadium. They beat the odds to become just the fifth wild card team to date to advance to the Super Bowl since the current playoff format was established in 1970.

Elway's passing game and Davis' running, along with a defensive effort that included big play after big play, combined to propel Denver to a 24-14 halftime lead that the team rode to a 24-21 win.

Elway was intercepted on the game's second play, but the Steelers failed to answer when Norm Johnson's 38-yard field-goal attempt sailed wide to the left. Denver then got on the board when Davis—who rushed for 139 yards and became the club's all-time postseason rushing leader in the contest—capped a six-play, 72-yard drive with an 8-yard touchdown run on the Broncos' second possession.

Pittsburgh evened the score on its next possession, as quarterback and University of Colorado alumnus Kordell Stewart rushed 33 yards for a touchdown to punctuate a six-play, 65-yard drive that covered 3:02 on

Tom Nalen walks down the hallway toward the field at Arrowhead Stadium before the second-round playoff game against the Chiefs in 1997.

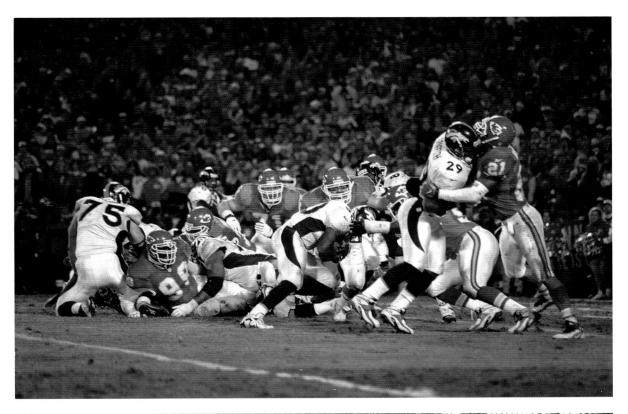

Terrell Davis lowers his head and rushes for the deciding touchdown of the 1997 playoff win at Kansas City. The final score was 14-10.

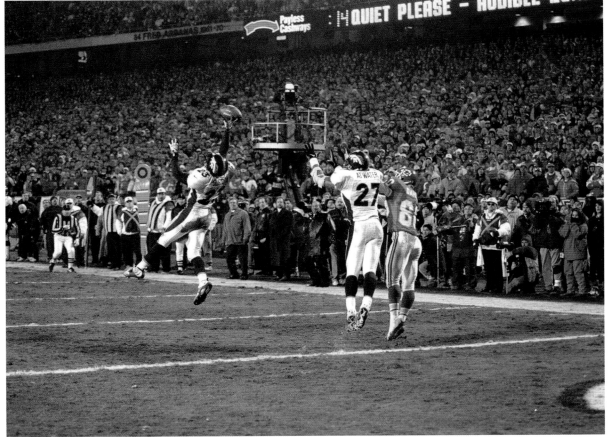

Cornerback Darrien Gordon sealed the fate of the Chiefs with his last-second pass deflection near the end zone on fourth down. Eleven seconds remained when Gordon clinched the Broncos' win.

the clock. The Steelers then broke the deadlock early in the second quarter when Jerome Bettis powered his way into the end zone from a yard out to put the finishing touches on an 11-play, 68-yard drive.

However, the partisan Pittsburgh crowd was shocked as the Broncos scored the game's next 17 points and, in effect, put the game away as the defense held up its end of the bargain down the stretch. The Broncos' scoring began with a 43-yard Elam field goal with 8:20 remaining in the half. After each team punted on its next possession, Denver got the ball back when Ray Crockett intercepted a Stewart bomb in the end zone. The pick set up a 14-point assault that sent Denver to the locker room ahead, 24-14. Elway hit fullback Howard Griffith for a 15-yard touchdown with 1:47 remaining. Then Denver forced a Pittsburgh punt and found the end zone when Elway connected with McCaffrey for a 1-yard touchdown. These were not the same Broncos that Pittsburgh had thumped just five weeks ago, and

STEVE ATWATER
SAFETY
1989–1998

Steve Atwater was inducted as the 20th member of the Broncos' Ring of Fame in 2005 after a brilliant 10-year career with the club. Regarded as one of the toughest safeties in the NFL during his playing days, Atwater was voted to a franchise-record seven consecutive Pro Bowls from 1990 to 1996. His eight career Pro Bowl selections are the second most by a player in Broncos' history.

Selected by the Broncos in the first round (20th overall) of the 1989 NFL Draft, Atwater was named NFL Defensive Rookie of the Year by *Football Digest* on a club that advanced to Super Bowl XXIV. He also served as a key leader on the Broncos' back-to-back Super Bowl championship teams from 1997 and 1998, and he was voted an All-Pro by the Associated Press in 1991, 1992, and 1996. He started all 155 regular-season games he played with Denver, a total that ranks 10th in franchise history.

One of the hardest hitters in team history, Atwater also recorded 24 interceptions that tie for eighth in Denver annals. He had 408 interception return yards, which rank seventh in the club record book. He led the Broncos in tackles during two seasons (1993 and 1995) and finished second in that category five times during his career.

His performance against Green Bay in Super Bowl XXXII—a game in which he totaled six tackles, one sack, one forced fumble, and two pass breakups—was instrumental in Denver winning its first world championship. The safety ranks second to only John Elway in career postseason starts (14) by a Bronco. He played in three Super Bowls and four AFC championship games.

Atwater, who was a three-time All-Southwest Conference selection and a two-time All-American at the University of Arkansas, played one season with the New York Jets in 1999 following his Bronco career.

Atwater's Denver Broncos Career Record

Games	Starts	Solo	Assist	Total	Sacks	Int.	Yds.	Avg.	TD
155	155	818	483	1,301	5.0	24	408	17.0	1

Atwater's NFL Career Record

Games	Starts	Solo	Assist	Total	Sacks	Int.	Yds.	Avg.	TD
167	166	854	502	1,356	5.0	24	408	17.0	1

Denver rode that 24-14 lead into the fourth quarter before the Steelers scored the only points of the second half on a Stewart pass with 2:46 remaining. The Broncos succeeded in running out the clock on their final possession, using Davis' legs and a key first-down pass to Sharpe to maintain possession and advance to Super Bowl XXXII in San Diego.

TRIUMPH AND REDEMPTION

Denver was ecstatic about a return to the Super Bowl, but the Broncos were going in as double-digit underdogs to the defending champion Green Bay Packers. In pregame commentary, John Elway was always mentioned as a quarterback who had lost this game three times.

But any doubts about the team's chances existed only outside the locker room, for within it the Broncos were supremely confident that this was the year, this was the time, and they were the team. Elway's passion to win a championship had never abated, and as he prepared to become the first quarterback in NFL history to start five Super Bowl games, he just wanted to win. In fact, he was more than willing to share the stage with his great young running back if he could get a victory.

Mike Shanahan had the team prepared like a well-oiled machine, and his pregame speech was short but succinct: "Let's go show the world what this team is all about."

To the pure elation of long-suffering fans, the Denver Broncos won that game, capturing their first Super Bowl title and becoming the first representative from the AFC in 14 years to claim the Vince Lombardi Trophy. They used a powerful running game and a solid defensive performance to dethrone the Packers, 31-24, in front of what became a highly partisan Bronco crowd.

Playing in his hometown, Terrell Davis was named the game's most valuable player (MVP) in recognition of his 157-yard rushing effort on 30 carries. His rushing attempts included a Super Bowl–record three rushing touchdowns,

Opposite: Steve Atwater (right) unwinds after a win at Kansas City. Along with Ray Crockett (center) and Tyrone Braxton (seated, lower left), this trio helped bring championship success to the Mile High City.

Below: John Mobley pressures the Packers' Brett Favre in Super Bowl XXXII.

Left: In a pivotal moment of Super Bowl XXXII, John Elway was spun 180 degrees by the defense as he went for the first down on third-and-six in the third quarter. The play gave the Broncos momentum and showed Elway's desire to risk everything for the win.

Right: Defenders Bill Romanowski and Mike Lodish stop Dorsey Levins during the Packers' first drive of the fourth quarter.

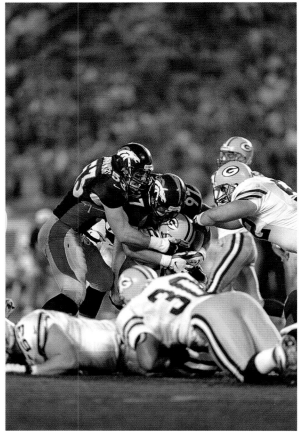

Ed McCaffrey catches a pass from John Elway and advances it to the Green Bay 25 yard line in the third quarter as part of a 13-play, 92-yard scoring drive.

each from 1 yard out. Davis' touchdowns and statistics were even more remarkable in that he missed almost the entire second quarter while he was sidelined by the onset of a migraine.

Both offenses displayed their talents immediately, as Super Bowl XXXII became the first in which each team scored a touchdown on its opening possession. The Packers struck first when Brett Favre connected with Antonio Freeman on a 22-yard scoring pass to cap a 76-yard, eight-play drive. The Broncos answered by driving 58 yards in 10 plays the first time they touched the ball, culminating in the first Davis touchdown with 5:39 remaining in the first quarter.

The Broncos turned two Packers turnovers into 10 more points to take a 17-7 lead early in the second quarter, making them the fourth team in Super Bowl history to score on each of its first three possessions. One of the team's opportunities was created when strong safety Tyrone Braxton intercepted a Favre pass, and eight plays later John Elway rushed for a 1-yard score. Free safety Steve Atwater sacked Favre on the next Green Bay possession, forcing a fumble that was recovered by defensive end Neil Smith. Four plays later, Jason Elam converted a 51-yard field goal, the second-longest in Super Bowl history.

Green Bay pulled to within 17-14 with a touchdown just before halftime and tied the score early in the third quarter when Ryan Longwell connected on a 27-yard field goal. Denver broke the tie late in the third quarter on the second Davis touchdown run and looked to

increase the lead after recovering a Green Bay fumble on the ensuing kickoff. However, Elway was intercepted by the Packers' Eugene Robinson in the end zone on the first play of the drive. Green Bay then moved 85 yards in four plays to tie the game at 24, setting the stage for Davis' late-game heroics.

By this point, it was evident to all that the Broncos were being driven every step by a passionate quarterback who refused to lose as long as he had the ball in his hands. Elway never demonstrated his will to win more clearly than in a dash for a pivotal first down in which he declined the traditional slide in favor of a dive. He flipped his body sideways to get more yardage. The entire stadium was electrified by Elway's determination. From that moment on, the sense was that the Broncos could not be denied in this championship showdown.

The Denver defense turned back the Packers on their next two possessions—including one advance to the Denver 39 yard line that was thwarted when Steve Atwater, having perhaps the best game of his great career, broke up a potential first-down pass to Robert Brooks. After getting the ball back at the Packers' 49 yard line, the offense was set up for a game-winning drive and Elway's biggest comeback.

Five plays later, Davis scored his third touchdown of the day, from one yard out, giving Denver a 31-24 lead that held up over the final 1:45.

When time expired, the feeling was surreal. Finally! The Broncos were world champions. "This one's for John,"

Victory in San Diego: Bill Romanowski holds his hands in triumph as the defense stops Green Bay for the last time on a fourth-and-six.

Redemption! John Elway holds the Vince Lombardi Trophy for the first time in his career during the awards presentation after Super Bowl XXXII.

Bronco owner Pat Bowlen shows off the Vince Lombardi Trophy as he enters the locker room during the postgame celebration in San Diego. Media Relations Director Jim Saccomano, author of this book, applauds him.

An estimated 650,000 fans turned out along 17th Street and Broadway and in Civic Center Park to cheer on the Broncos during their championship parade, the day after returning from the Super Bowl.

Broncos owner Pat Bowlen proclaimed from the stage set up on the playing field. The world celebrated with the Denver quarterback and the entire Mile High City that, at long last, he had become the ultimate champion.

An estimated 650,000 fans gathered in downtown Denver for a victory parade and rally to honor the new Super Bowl champs. The parade followed a route along 17th Street, from Wynkoop to Broadway, and then along Broadway for several blocks before working its way to the steps of the Denver City and County Building, where the rally was held. Pat Bowlen, Mike Shanahan, John Elway, and Terrell Davis were joined by Colorado Governor Roy Romer and Denver Mayor Wellington Webb, each addressing the sea of Broncos fans who packed the grounds in front of the stage. Not surprisingly, the fans were jubilant, and the thrill of victory was enough that they were ready to support a push for a new stadium.

The capacity of the fabled Mile High Stadium now stood at 76,082, making it one of the largest facilities in the NFL. Unfortunately, at more than 50 years of age, it also was the oldest. In order for the Broncos to draw more dollars from premium seating and entertainment venues, the team needed an updated playing arena. So in April, after years of discussions and negotiations, Governor Romer signed into law SB 171, a bill authorizing voters to decide whether to appropriate tax money to partially fund a new football stadium in Denver. The new stadium would assure the Broncos of the type of

revenue needed to be competitive at a championship level as professional football prepared to move into the twenty-first century.

The offseason was a whirlwind, as players and coaches received their Super Bowl rings in a private ceremony at team headquarters in early June and then later that month traveled to Washington, D.C., for a special ceremony in which they were honored by President Bill Clinton at the White House.

THE BEST TEAM PLAYS LIKE IT

The Broncos went into the new campaign in the unusual position of being recognized by all as the best team in pro football, unanimous favorites to win the Super Bowl again. They were expected to be great, but no one thought they would make a run at actually being undefeated.

The Broncos opened defense of their world championship with a bang, earning a 27-21 victory over New England in front of a national television audience on Monday Night Football. Mile High's 74,745 screaming fans forced the Patriots to use all three of their second-half timeouts by the midpoint of the third quarter.

Elway completed a 44-yard bomb to Ed McCaffrey on the game's first play from scrimmage, leading to a 53-yard field goal by Jason Elam. The Broncos ended the first quarter with a seven-play, 49-yard drive, culminating in a 12-yard touchdown hookup between Elway and

Bill Romanowski stands on the sideline and surveys the situation. He was an emotional leader on the Denver defense in the late 1990s.

Shannon Sharpe. The all-pro tight end surpassed the 6,000-yard receiving plateau during the contest, becoming just the third Bronco to reach that lofty total and the fourth tight end in NFL history to do so.

Three sacks from the Denver defense—two of which came from Bill Romanowski—kept the Pats from getting any closer than six points behind as the Broncos rambled to their 17th consecutive victory at home in the regular season (a franchise record). The victory also was the team's fourth straight on opening day, another franchise record.

In their next game, the Broncos improved to 2-0 for the third straight year—and the 12th time in history—with an impressive 42-23 victory over the Dallas Cowboys in front of 75,013 fans at Mile High Stadium. The Broncos' offense dominated the day, scoring 21 points in the first quarter and 35 points in the first half, en route to 515 yards of total offense.

Pummeling the proud Dallas team, Denver scored on five straight first-half possessions, starting with a 38-yard touchdown from Elway to Sharpe. Davis then took over, scoring from 63 and 59 yards out on consecutive plays to produce the seventh 100-yard half of his career (154 yards total) and the second 100-yard quarter of his career (138 total). Another Sharpe touchdown and an Elway 1-yard touchdown run gave the Broncos a 35-17 halftime cushion in a devastating offensive show.

Denver truly was a juggernaut as it rolled through the 1998 campaign. Favored every week, the Broncos did not disappoint. They pounded out a 34-17 victory over the Raiders in Oakland, improving their record against the Raiders to 6-1 since Mike Shanahan took over as head coach, their most successful stretch in the history of the storied rivalry.

Next up was Washington at Jack Kent Cooke Stadium, where Denver went to 4-0 with a methodical 38-16 victory over the Redskins without starting Elway, who sat out with a strained right hamstring. Popular backup Bubby Brister ran the offensive machine as the Broncos posted their first victory in a game that Elway did not start since November 20, 1989—coincidentally also a win at Washington. After taking a 17-7 advantage to the locker room at halftime, the Broncos put the game away in the third quarter when Davis scored from 42 yards out and fullback Howard Griffith caught a 14-yard touchdown to give Denver a 31-7 lead. Davis reeled off his third straight—and 23rd career—100-yard regular-season rushing game while Brister threw for two touchdowns. For just the second time in team history, five different players scored touchdowns.

It was more of the same the following week when Philadelphia was the victim in a 41-16 thumping at the hands of pro football's best team. Denver's 5-0 start was

Howard Griffith runs the ball downfield against the Giants, who ended the Broncos' 18-game winning streak in 1998.

the best by a defending Super Bowl champion since the 10-0 start by the 1990 San Francisco 49ers.

Although Denver was without Elway for the second consecutive week, the Broncos managed to set a team record by scoring 28 points in the first quarter, essentially ending the game shortly after it started. Davis rambled for 168 yards and scored two touchdowns all in the first half; he sat out the entire second half with his team comfortably ahead. In another record-setting day for the Broncos' tailback, he passed Jim Brown for the sixth-most rushing yards in the first four years of a career. His most impressive feat of the day was becoming the seventh player in NFL history to rush for 5,000 yards in his first four NFL seasons. Davis reached that total in his 50th NFL game, faster than any other Bronco and fourth-fastest in NFL history. Only Eric Dickerson (45), Earl Campbell (46), and Jim Brown (48) did so faster. The fans never stopped cheering, nor were the Broncos giving them any reason to.

The Broncos improved to 6-0 and recorded their 300th regular or postseason win in franchise history with a 21-16 victory over a stubborn Seattle team at the Kingdome. Denver opened up an 11-point advantage on the strength of the running game as football's best back scored his franchise-record 44th career rushing touchdown. The score gave Denver a 21-10 lead that looked safe until the Seahawks answered on their next drive with a touchdown. The victory wasn't sealed until Terrell

Davis turned a third-and-three play at the Denver 25 into a 70-yard gain with 1:37 to play.

Davis added another stellar performance to his coffers with his third career 200-yard rushing effort, finishing the day with 208 yards and a touchdown on 30 carries. The 208 yards represented the second-highest rushing total of his career and the second-highest in franchise history. His fourth-quarter touchdown moved him into first place in Broncos' history for rushing TDs.

The next week, the Broncos ran their record to 7-0 for the first time with a 37-24 victory over Jacksonville at home, using a balanced offense (465 total yards), an aggressive defense (seven sacks), and a special teams effort that will never be forgotten. The triumph was the team's 20th consecutive regular-season home win, its eighth straight regular-season win, and its 12th consecutive victory (regular and postseason) overall.

The highlight of the day was an NFL-record-tying 63-yard field goal by Jason Elam, equaling the 28-year-old standard set by New Orleans' Tom Dempsey (set on November 8, 1970). Davis finished the day with 136 yards to put him at a staggering 1,001 yards after seven games. The win was the 40th in the regular season for Mike Shanahan as Broncos' head coach. He reached this total in just 55 games, another team record.

Denver was rolling, and the big question was becoming not if the Broncos would repeat as Super Bowl

Jason Elam celebrates after tying the record for the longest field goal in NFL history with a 63-yarder against Jacksonville in 1998.

champions, but whether they might be undefeated in doing so.

In the game before voters approved construction of the team's new stadium, the Broncos won a 33-26 nail-biter over the Bengals in Cincinnati. The Broncos then beat the Chargers by a relatively easy 27-10 margin to set up a Monday night game at Kansas City in what appeared to be one of the largest remaining hurdles to the unlikely goal of an undefeated season.

Arrowhead Stadium has always been a tough play, and the Broncos odds at winning were more in doubt when Elway sat out with a rib injury. Again, backup Bubby Brister was called upon to lead the team, and he was up to the task. The Broncos ran their record to 10-0 and won their franchise-record 11th consecutive regular-season game (15 including the 1997 postseason) with a 30-7 triumph at Kansas City.

The Broncos blew the contest wide open in the first quarter, scoring long touchdowns on their first two drives. First, Brister shocked the crowd by ending the opening drive with a career-best 38-yard bootleg run for a 7-0 lead. Davis followed that with a 41-yard touchdown run on Denver's next possession, capping a 79-yard drive that took just three plays and 1:05 off the clock. The rout was on. That win made the Broncos the first team in NFL history to start three consecutive seasons winning nine of their first 10 games, as Shanahan's club had begun 9-1 in both 1996 and 1997.

The entire nation's sporting press now was gripped by the Broncos' season and their quest for the perfect record. In their next matchup, Denver crushed Oakland by a 40-14 margin, the highlight of which came on a routine 5-yard completion by John Elway to Willie Green. The pass lifted Elway over the 50,000-yard passing mark for his career, just the second player to do so. Elway thus became the only player in NFL history to rush for more than 3,000 yards and throw for more than 50,000 yards in a career. Davis also moved past the 7,000-yard career mark in total yards from scrimmage, the second-highest total for a player in the first four years of his career. Only he and Hall of Famer Eric Dickerson had been able to reach this staggering number so quickly.

The Broncos then wrapped up their ninth AFC West crown and improved to 12-0 on the season with a 31-16 victory at San Diego. The win stretched Denver's overall win streak to 17, just one away from the all-time NFL record.

Fans were having every dream come true. The Broncos were defending Super Bowl champions and were just one week away from not having lost a game for an entire calendar year. In their next contest, the Broncos triumphed again in 35-31 come-from-behind victory over the Chiefs in front of a celebratory Mile High Stadium crowd, moving to a 13-0 record. The game went back and forth until the Broncos took the lead for good on Shannon Sharpe's only catch of the day, a 24-yard score from John Elway on a third-and-inches play. Elway notched his NFL-record 47th career game-saving drive and posted the second-highest passing-yardage total of his brilliant 16-year career with 400. During the contest, Davis became just the third NFL player to compile 6,000 rushing yards in the first four years of a career and passed Marcus Allen for the most touchdowns scored by a player in his first four seasons.

REACHING THE RECORD BOOKS

The win also was Denver's 18th straight to tie the NFL record, 14th straight in the regular season, and 23rd straight at home in the regular season. It seemed like every week brought a previously unimagined new height, and the city was reveling in it. The Broncos were making their mark as one of the greatest teams in NFL history, and the undefeated season seemed a reality.

Then, in a flash, Denver's NFL-record-tying string of 18 consecutive victories came to a surprising halt at the hands of the New York Giants. The 20-16 loss was the first for Denver in 363 days, covering 14 regular-season games and four postseason contests.

The Broncos' offense was sluggish the entire day, producing only 329 total yards—nearly 60 yards below their season average—and was held without a touchdown until just 4:08 remained in the game. That touchdown, which came on a 27-yard Terrell Davis scamper around the left corner, gave Denver a 16-13 lead and looked as though it would be enough to send the Broncos home victorious. Denver's Tyrone Braxton forced a fumble that was recovered by Bill Romanowski to end the Giants' next possession. The Broncos took over the ball—and seemingly game—at their own 29 yard line with just 3:36 to play.

However, the Broncos could not generate a first down and were forced to punt, giving the Giants possession at their own 14 yard line with just 1:49 remaining. The Giants promptly drove 86 yards in six plays in just 1:01 and took the lead on a 37-yard touchdown hookup from Kent Graham to Amani Toomer to go on top 20-16. The Broncos had one more chance, reaching the Giants' 30 before a Hail Mary pass by Elway fell incomplete in the back of the end zone.

Davis, who played despite a bad chest cold that bothered him throughout the game, eclipsed his own franchise record of 1,750 rushing yards in a season, finishing the day at 1,801. He also tied his own team record of 10 regular-season 100-yard games in a year and had now notched 30 100-yard games in the regular season. He also passed Earl Campbell (55) and Eric Dickerson (55) for first place all time in rushing touchdowns during the first four years of a career.

Rod Smith went over the 1,000-yard mark during the contest for the second straight year, and Denver set a

Terrell Davis reaches the 2,000-yard rushing mark against the Seahawks on December 27, 1998.

The scoreboard tells the tale: Terrell Davis joins the exclusive club of backs who rushed for 2,000 yards in a single season.

new team record for touchdowns in a season with 56. The team surpassed the 55 it scored in 1997 with two games still to play.

With the chances of an undefeated season now gone, Denver dropped its second straight decision. This time the team came up on the short end of a 31-21 score at Miami in the second meeting between John Elway and Dan Marino. Of note in the loss was the fact that Vaughn Hebron ended a 26-year drought by returning a kickoff 95 yards for a touchdown, the first Broncos' kickoff return for a score since Randy Montgomery reached the end zone on a 94-yarder at San Diego on September 24, 1972. The night belonged to the Dolphins. With the win, Miami earned a trip to the postseason, setting up another potential meeting with the Broncos, but this time in Mile High Stadium.

The Broncos closed the 1998 regular season with a 28-21 victory over Seattle in a game that saw more record-making than Motown. The win was Denver's 14th of the season, establishing a new team mark, and the team's 24th in a row at home in the regular season. The victory set an NFL record, as the Broncos were the first team since the 16-game schedule began in 1978 to claim three consecutive undefeated regular seasons at home.

After falling behind 7-0, Denver reeled off the game's next 28 points, with all four touchdowns coming on touchdown passes from Elway. He connected twice with Sharpe and once each with Smith and Davis. Davis was the man who stole the show on this day, becoming the fourth player in NFL history to rush for 2,000 yards in a season with a 15-yard gain on a second-and-six play from the Seahawks' 48 yard line midway through the fourth quarter. His season total of 2,008 yards ranked third all time behind Eric Dickerson and Barry Sanders. With his efforts, the magnificent Terrell Davis claimed his first NFL rushing title and the second ever by a Bronco with his

third carry of the game (a 9-yard gain) and also claimed his third straight AFC rushing crown. He also became the Broncos' all-time leading rusher, passing Floyd Little in the third quarter, and set four new single-season franchise records: in scoring, with 138 points, passing Gene Mingo (137); in 100-yard games, notching his 11th of the year; in total yards from scrimmage, breaking his own record of 2,037 set in 1997; and in rushing attempts, breaking his own team mark of 369 from 1997.

Shannon Sharpe got in on the act too, with his two touchdown catches tying him with Ring of Famers Lionel Taylor and Haven Moses for first place on the Broncos' all-time list for touchdown receptions. Elway's four scoring passes gave him 300 for his career, a feat that had been accomplished by only Marino and Tarkenton.

Denver's 501 points scored on the season made the Broncos just the sixth team in NFL history to top the 500-point mark in a campaign. Regardless, all the team cared about was that it was headed for the postseason, and this time the Broncos were America's favorite to go all the way.

DENVER JUGGERNAUT ROLLS TO MIAMI

The Broncos won their fifth straight postseason contest and advanced to the AFC Championship Game for the second year in a row after a record-setting 38-3 win over Miami in the AFC divisional playoff game, played before 75,729 raucous fans at Mile High Stadium. Miami was no match for a motivated Broncos team, which was unlike the one that had lost in Miami just a few weeks earlier.

The 35-point differential represented Denver's largest margin of victory in a postseason game and was punctuated by a defensive effort that limited Miami to just 14 yards on 13 carries for an average of 1.1 yards per rush, all of which set new franchise records. The three points allowed were also the fewest allowed by Denver in a postseason game.

The offense was just as sharp, putting points on the board in all four quarters, including 14 in both the first and fourth quarters. Denver's two first-quarter TDs both came courtesy of T. D.—Terrell Davis—himself. He scored on runs of 1 and 20 yards, the latter of which would qualify for any highlight film as he juked past two Dolphins defenders with separate moves and dashed to the end zone. Again, Davis was unequivocally the offensive star, posting a franchise-record 199 yards on 21 carries, the fourth-highest single-game total in NFL postseason history. Davis, who moved into eighth place all time in NFL postseason rushing in just his sixth game, had rushed for 129 yards by halftime to notch his first 100-yard half in the postseason, to go along with 10 in the regular season.

Miami closed the gap to 14-3 in the second quarter, scoring its only points of the game on a field goal.

Howard Griffith breaks a tackle and dives into the end zone in the Broncos' 1998 AFC Championship Game win over the New York Jets.

Denver answered with an 11-play, 87-yard drive capped by Derek Loville's 11-yard run to increase the lead to 21-3 at halftime. The Broncos pushed the margin to 24-3 early in the third quarter with a Jason Elam field goal. Elway put the game far out of reach early in the fourth quarter when he hooked up with the underrated, but brilliant, Smith for a 28-yard touchdown play; this was Elway's 25th career postseason touchdown. The icing on the cake came when Neil Smith picked up a fumble and ran it back 79 yards for his first career postseason score.

The Broncos clinched their AFC-record sixth berth in a Super Bowl by defeating the New York Jets 23-10 in the AFC Championship Game. After not scoring in the first half, the Broncos scored 20 third-quarter points and reached the title game for the second consecutive season to match the back-to-back AFC Championships of the 1986 and 1987 Broncos.

The Jets took a 10-0 lead on a field goal and a 1-yard Curtis Martin touchdown run that was set up by a blocked punt at the Broncos' 1 yard line. That touchdown proved to be just the wake-up call Denver needed to ignite its offense, as well as the unusually quiet Mile High crowd. On first down from the Denver 36 yard line, Elway connected with Ed McCaffrey on a 47-yard pass play. Two plays later,

he found Howard Griffith for an 11-yard pass to score, putting Denver on the board and narrowing the Jets' lead to 10-7.

Then, a wind-stifled kickoff was recovered by special teams ace Keith Burns. The play eventually turned into a 44-yard Elam field goal. Another Elam kick of 48 yards gave Denver the lead. A 31-yard dash by Davis for a touchdown gave the Broncos a 10-point cushion they never relinquished.

The Broncos defense, which deserved credit for keeping the Broncos in the game in the first half while the offense sputtered, held the Jets to 14 yards rushing on 13 carries and forced six turnovers. Two of those came on interceptions by Darrien Gordon. The four fumbles Denver recovered set a franchise postseason record.

Now arguably the best running back in pro football and one of two Broncos who could legitimately be called the best overall player in the game, Terrell Davis set numerous records during the contest. He passed his own NFL-record total of 2,331 yards rushing in an entire season (regular and postseason combined) set in 1997 and rushing for 100 yards for the sixth straight postseason game, tying John Riggins for the most all time.

The Broncos were established as heavy Super Bowl favorites before they even hit the showers.

A typically passionate Broncos crowd shows its support during one of the team's Mile High Stadium Super Bowl rallies.

Right: Bill Romanowski sacks Falcons' quarterback Chris Chandler in one of the pivotal defensive plays of Super Bowl XXXIII. The Falcons never mounted a serious offensive threat after this, as the Broncos pulled away for their second straight title.

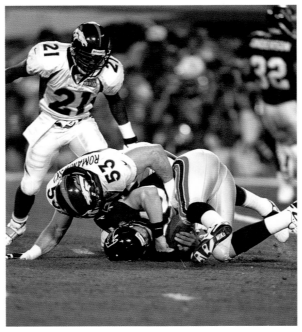

Below: Mike Shanahan and John Elway confer on the sideline before Elway connects with Rod Smith for an 80-yard touchdown that put the Broncos well ahead of Atlanta in Super Bowl XXXIII.

WORLD CHAMPIONS, BACK TO BACK

The Denver Broncos went to Miami as the pride of the Rocky Mountain West and clinched their second straight world championship with a 34-19 victory over the Atlanta Falcons in Super Bowl XXXIII at Pro Player Stadium. With the win, Denver joined just five other franchises who to date had won back-to-back Super Bowl titles. The win also gave Denver 33 wins in the past two seasons and 46 wins in the past three, both NFL records, and hence the best three-year mark in pro football history at that time.

John Elway claimed the game's most valuable player (MVP) award by completing 18-of-29 passes for 336 yards. One of his completions included an 80-yard touchdown toss to Rod Smith in the second quarter that tied for the second-longest touchdown pass in Super Bowl history. Elway also ran for a 3-yard score in the fourth quarter, making him, at age 38, the oldest player to score a touchdown in the Super Bowl, eclipsing the record he set a year earlier by scoring in Super Bowl XXXII.

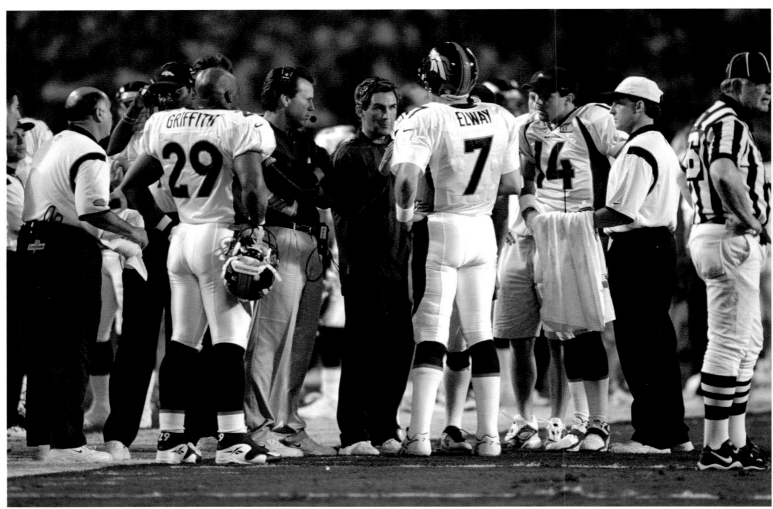

Atlanta focused on stopping the superb Bronco running game and forcing Elway to beat them, and he was more than willing to accommodate the Falcons. The Broncos' defense chipped in, as well, with two sacks and four forced turnovers. Two of those were interceptions by Gordon, who set a Super Bowl record for most interception-return yards in a game with 108.

Atlanta took the opening kickoff and capped its drive with a 32-yard Morten Andersen field goal before Denver answered convincingly with the game's next 17 points. The first score came on a 1-yard run by fullback Howard Griffith. It ended a 10-play, 80-yard opening drive by the Broncos, and their lead increased to 10-3 on a third-possession Jason Elam field goal. After Andersen missed a 26-yard field-goal attempt, the Broncos' answered with the Elway-to-Smith 80-yard score on the next play to stun the Falcons and push the lead to 17-3. The Falcons narrowed the margin to 17-6 at halftime with a 28-yard Andersen field goal, but observers rightly felt that this one was over.

After a scoreless third quarter, Denver took advantage of Gordon's first interception by capping a short drive with another Griffith run early in the fourth quarter. Gordon's second pickoff set up Elway's 3-yard score that put Denver ahead 31-6 with 11:20 remaining. Two late touchdowns by Atlanta, sandwiched around a 37-yard Elam field goal, produced the final margin.

Davis set an NFL record with his seventh-straight 100-yard game in the postseason, defensive tackle Mike Lodish set a record by playing in his sixth Super Bowl, and Bill Romanowski became the second player to win back-to-back titles with two different teams.

The Broncos returned triumphant to Denver and were greeted by an estimated 375,000 fans lining the parade route. From the steps of the Denver city and county building, Broncos players and coaches joined the civic dignitaries in thanking the fans for their support.

John Elway and Mark Schlereth (No. 69) celebrate while prone in the end zone after a quarterback draw against the Falcons. This was the final score of Elway's career, cementing the Broncos' consecutive world championships.

To the victors go the spoils, and the Broncos were represented in the Pro Bowl by a franchise-record 10 players: Steve Atwater, Terrell Davis, Jason Elam, John Elway, tackle Tony Jones, Ed McCaffrey, Tom Nalen, Bill Romanowski, Mark Schlereth, and Shannon Sharpe. Davis was named the NFL's most valuable player by the Associated Press, on the heels of earning the Super Bowl MVP one year earlier. He was a unanimous All-NFL selection, along with tight end Shannon Sharpe.

The Broncos were big, even international. On April 10, 1999, Chinese Premier Zhu Rongji visited the team headquarters as part of a nine-day U.S. tour to promote

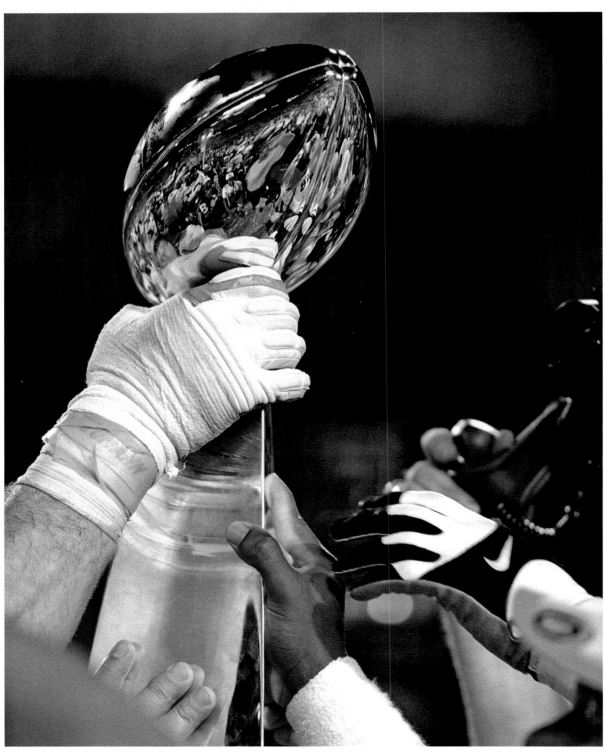

One more time: Several Broncos join in holding a piece of the Vince Lombardi Trophy after winning their second Super Bowl.

1990s
DENVER BRONCOS
YEAR BY YEAR

1990	5-11
1991	12-4
1992	8-8
1993	9-7
1994	7-9
1995	8-8
1996	13-3
1997	12-4
1998	14-2
1999	6-10

Running back Terrell Davis sprints to the end zone en route to another touchdown. Despite injury, Davis amassed Hall of Fame credentials in his brilliant career.

trade with China. The premier requested the visit as one of the highlights of his trip and said, "It is a pleasure to visit the home of the Broncos. They are the champions of American football."

AN ORANGE SUNSET FOR ELWAY

After a glorious season, the biggest buzz centered on whether John Elway would return for another. Speculation was rife throughout the Denver media all through the spring, and it came to a head in late April when Gary Miller, the longest-tenured television beat reporter in team history, caught up with Elway at a golf tournament at Pebble Beach. Elway confided to Miller that he indeed had played his last game. Miller had the scoop of the offseason. The formal announcement of John Elway's retirement came in a May 2 press conference at the Inverness Hotel and Golf Club in Englewood. His career was over, as had been much anticipated, and a new era was thrust upon the Broncos.

Not surprisingly, Elway entered the team's Ring of Fame on the 1999 season's opening night, when his fabled No. 7 uniform was retired, never to be worn again by a Denver Bronco.

The decade ended with a disappointing 6-10 season, but Shannon Sharpe became the leading receiver in franchise history, surpassing the previous standards held by Lionel Taylor. Jason Elam became the Broncos' all-time leading scorer, and running back Olandis Gary set the franchise rookie rushing record by finishing the 1999 season with 1,159 yards on 276 carries. Also, wide receiver Rod Smith topped the 1,000-yard receiving mark for the third consecutive season, another franchise record. Gary worked his way into the lineup after Davis suffered a knee injury that ended his season and dramatically altered the length of his brilliant career.

But neither a losing record nor injury could diminish the glow that emanated from a franchise that had taken its place among the great teams in pro football history. The last decade of the century was marked forever as the one in which the Broncos, their fans, and their quarterback all got their due. It was Manifest Destiny in orange and blue.

JOHN ELWAY

QUARTERBACK
1983–1999

John Elway holds up his second consecutive Super Bowl trophy after defeating the Atlanta Falcons in 1998. Elway was named the MVP of Super Bowl XXXIII and is joined on the stage by announcer and fellow Hall of Fame quarterback Terry Bradshaw.

John Elway is regarded by a number of football analysts and fans to be the greatest quarterback of all time. Elway, who was inducted into the Broncos' Ring of Fame on September 13, 1999, also had his No. 7 jersey retired in a ceremony at halftime of the Broncos' season opener versus Miami. He capped his brilliant career by winning Most Valuable Player (MVP) honors in Super Bowl XXXIII—the Broncos' second consecutive world championship.

Following his playing career, Elway was inducted into the Pro Football Hall of Fame on August 8, 2004, in a ceremony held at Fawcett Stadium in Canton, Ohio.

In his final season of play, Elway posted the highest quarterback rating of his career (93.0). At the close of the 1998 season, he ranked second among active NFL players for number of appearances with one team (234) and retired having played in and started more games (231) in more seasons (16) than any player in Denver Bronco history.

Elway retired as the NFL's all-time winningest starting quarterback (148-82-1; .643) and currently trails only Brett Favre in career victories. He was voted to a franchise-record nine Pro Bowl appearances (1986, 1987, 1989, 1991, 1993, 1994, 1996, 1997, 1998)—tied with Brett Favre, Dan Marino, and Warren Moon for the most ever by a quarterback—and as a starter six times (1987, 1989, 1993, 1996, 1997, 1998). He was the NFL's Most Valuable Player in 1987 and AFC Player of the Year in 1993, and he was named AFC Offensive Player of the Week 15 times and AFC Offensive Player of the Month twice.

Elway was named the Edge NFL Man of the Year for 1992 and was inducted into the Colorado Sports Hall of Fame in 1999. He also was named to the NFL's All-Decade team for the 1990s (first team).

He ranks third behind Favre and Marino in most major NFL career passing categories, including passing yards (51,475), attempts (7,250), completions (4,123), and total offense (54,882). He also figures fourth in total touchdowns (behind Marino, Favre, and Fran Tarkenton) with 334 (300 passing/33 rushing/one receiving), fifth in passing touchdowns with 300, second among NFL quarterbacks in career rushing attempts (774), and sixth in rushing yards (3,407).

Elway is the only player in NFL history to pass for more than 3,000 yards and rush for more than 200 yards in the same season for seven consecutive years (1985–1991). He generated 4,771 of the 5,806 points (82.2 percent) scored by the Broncos during his 16-year tenure with the club.

He ranks No. 1 in NFL history in fourth-quarter game-winning or game-saving drives with 47 (46-0-1 record) and had 36 career 300-yard passing games in the regular season, third among active quarterbacks at the time of his retirement (behind Marino and Moon).

He also caught three passes in regular-season play for 61 yards, including a touchdown of 23 yards from Steve Sewell in 1986. In 1997, Elway broke his franchise record for consecutive passes without an interception, with the streak reaching 189 attempts. For his career, Elway had 19 games in which he completed 70 percent or more of his passes (with a minimum of 20 attempts) and fashioned a 17-2 record in those games. He started 2,595 drives as a pro and was replaced just 10 times due to injury (.039 percent).

As brilliant as he was the regular season, Elway extended his legend in postseason as the only NFL quarterback to start in five Super Bowl games, eventually leading the Broncos to back-to-back world titles. Elway played in a franchise-record 22 postseason games (21 starts) and produced a 14-7 record (9-2 at home, 3-2 on the road, and 2-3 at neutral sites). He has the NFL's all-time best record as a starting quarterback in conference championship games at 5-1. The other quarterbacks with four Super Bowl starts are Tom Brady, Jim Kelly, Joe Montana, Terry Bradshaw, and Roger Staubach.

Elway owns or shares 18 Bronco postseason records, including most passing yards, most touchdown passes, and total offense (combined rushing and passing yards). Elway ranks third in NFL postseason history in passing yardage (trailing only Montana, 5,772, and Brett Favre, 5,311), fourth in pass attempts (Montana, 734; Favre, 721; Marino, 687), fifth in completions (Montana, 460; Favre, 438;

Marino, 385; Brady, 372), and fifth in passing touchdowns (Montana, 45; Favre, 39; Marino, 32; Bradshaw, 30).

In Super Bowl play, Elway ranks second in pass attempts (152), fourth in completions (76), second in passing yards (1,128), and is tied for second in rushing touchdowns (4) with Franco Harris and Thurman Thomas (Emmitt Smith has 5). Six of Elway's NFL-record 47 fourth-quarter game-winning or game-saving drives came in the postseason.

Elway concluded his college career at Stanford University holding five major NCAA Division I-A records and nine major Pac-10 marks. He completed 62.1 percent of his career passes (774 of 1,243, both NCAA highs) for 9,349 yards and 77 touchdowns while setting an NCAA record for the lowest percentage of passes intercepted (3.13 percent).

A two-sport star, he played pro baseball for the New York Yankees' Oneonta (New York) single-A farm club in 1982, hitting for a .318 average and knocking in a team-high 25 RBI in 42 games. Elway, who batted left-handed and threw right-handed, was the Yankees' first selection in the 1981 summer draft on June 8.

Even in retirement, Elway is identified as the ultimate face of the Broncos and, often, the entire city. He officially announced his retirement from the Denver Broncos on May 2, 1999, but to Bronco fans and many others, John Elway and the Denver Broncos will always be one and the same.

He is now president and chief executive officer of the Colorado Crush of the Arena Football League.

A native of Port Angeles, Washington, Elway was the most highly recruited prep athlete in the nation in 1979 and was listed on *Parade*, *Scholastic Coach*, *Football News*, and National Coaches Association All-America teams. He had an unparalleled football and baseball career at Granada Hills High School. He completed 129-of-200 passes for 1,837 yards and 19 touchdowns as a senior while leading the baseball team to the Los Angeles City championship with a .491 batting average and a 4-2 pitching record. He completed 60 percent of his high school passes for 5,711 yards and 49 touchdowns. The football field at Granada Hills High School was renamed in Elway's honor in a ceremony June 5, 1998.

Elway's Denver Broncos Career Record

			PASSING									RUSHING			
Games	Starts	Att.	Comp.	Pct.	Yds.	TD	Int.	LG	Sack/Yds.	Rtg.	Att.	Yds	Avg.	LG	TD
234	231	7,250	4,123	56.9	51,475	300	226	86	516/3,785	79.8	774	3,407	4.4	31	33

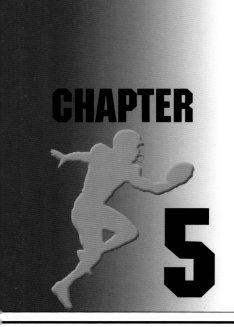

CHAPTER 5

THE 2000S
MOVING FORWARD IN BRONCOS COUNTRY

AT THE PEAK OF PRO FOOTBALL

Fifty years is a milestone for any organization, individual, or relationship, and just as much so for a professional football team. In 2009, at the end of the first decade in the new millennium, the Broncos marked their 50th year of play. The difference between the team's stature at that point and how it all began could not be more dramatic—from laughingstock loser to an elite champion member of the NFL.

Denver's pro football team entered its fifth decade as an established power and a highly respected and

The Denver Broncos opened the new century with two Super Bowl trophies under their collective belt. With his leadership and passion to win, owner Pat Bowlen—here posing with the prizes from the 1997 and 1998 championships—has played an integral role in the team's success and the extraordinary development of the franchise.

valued franchise. With two Super Bowl crowns, it no longer needed to prove anything to anyone, least of all to a vast network of fans who embraced being a part of "Broncos Country."

But the first decade of the millennium was not to be an era of championships for a team that now had so many. Still, the Broncos continued to be perennial contenders in the 2000s as they tried to meet the most demanding standards.

The Broncos began their final season of play at Mile High Stadium in 2000 with a 42-14 win over Atlanta in the home opener. The final Monday Night Football game at Mile High also produced a win—a 27-24 victory that was clinched on a 41-yard field goal by Jason Elam as time expired. Overall from 1973 to 2000, the Broncos were 16-6 in the 22 Monday Night games played at Mile High.

On December 3, 2000, rookie running back Mike Anderson rushed for 251 yards in a 38-23 win at New Orleans, setting an all-time NFL rookie rushing record for a single game. He also broke the franchise single-game rushing mark by posting the fourth-best rushing day by any player in NFL history and set a Broncos record with four touchdowns in the game. Elam also set another NFL

Quarterback Brian Griese releases a pass. In addition to earning a Pro Bowl berth as a Bronco, Griese made a great contribution to the Denver community with his opening of Judi's House, a home that provides counsel for children who have lost a parent. Judi's House is named for Brian's mother.

The offense huddles up, with Brian Griese calling the play. Griese had a hard time following in the footsteps of a legend like John Elway.

Running back Mike Anderson takes off against the Saints for some of his 251 rushing yards, then a rookie single-game record, at New Orleans on December 3, 2000. Anderson finished his great rookie season with 1,487 rushing yards.

BEHIND THE MICROPHONE

The Bronco organization has had a rich and colorful history of radio announcers since its inception in 1960, beginning with Bill Reed, a legendary radio play-by-play commentator in early Denver broadcasting.

Reed, the longtime voice of the minor-league baseball Denver Bears, was the city's first play-by-play voice in pro football on KBTR (AM 710) during the Broncos' first year. He teamed with Jerry Groom, who was a Notre Dame All-American offensive lineman in 1950. In 1961, Reed was joined by Denver television sportscaster Fred Leo. Nationally known announcer Al Helfer worked in the 1962 and 1963 seasons.

The Broncos' broadcasts moved over to KTLN (AM 1280) for the next six years (1964–1969), marking the introduction of the legendary Bob Martin to game broadcasts. Martin initially teamed with station talk show host Joe Finan and then sportscaster Dick Carlson. Martin moved over to KOA in 1969, but the Broncos had another year at KTLN, so national broadcaster Joe McConnell called the games in 1969.

The Broncos and KOA (AM 850) teamed up for the 1970 season, a partnership that continues today. Martin and Carlson called the games that year, and the next year Larry Zimmer joined Martin. The two remained in tandem through 1989, becoming arguably the most famous radio play-by-play combination in Denver sports' history.

Martin, considered by many fans and critics as the best play-by-play man in Denver sports radio, also premiered the first full-time sports talk radio show on KTLN in 1965. He passed away in 1990.

Zimmer was joined by another legend in 1990, this one from the playing field. Dave Logan—a Colorado native, former Bronco, and perhaps the finest all-around athlete to come from the University of Colorado—joined Zimmer in the KOA booth as color man in 1991. He became the play-by-play voice after seven seasons as the color analyst. Zimmer moved full time to University of Colorado broadcasts in 1997. In 2009, Logan joined Martin and Zimmer as one of three legendary broadcasters who spent 20 years doing Bronco radio broadcasts.

Versatile broadcaster and former NBA player Scott Hastings teamed with Logan on the broadcasts from 1997 to 2004. Former Bronco lineman David Diaz-Infante handled the color commentary from 2005 to 2008, and ex-quarterback Brian Griese filled that role from 2008 to 2011. Former wide receiver Ed McCaffrey joined Logan on the KOA broadcasts in 2012.

An aerial view of INVESCO Field at Mile High, before Mile High Stadium was demolished. The new stadium opened in 2001.

Below: Detron Smith wraps up Troy Brown of the Patriots on a punt return. In 1999, Smith was named to the Pro Bowl for his prowess on special teams.

another NFL record in the Crescent City, converting his 304th consecutive point-after attempt.

The Broncos played their final game at Mile High Stadium on December 23, defeating San Francisco 38-9 before the second-largest crowd in the stadium's history: 76,098. It was the largest crowd ever for a Broncos regular-season game, and those in attendance were treated to an outstanding performance from the home team. The Broncos set franchise single-season records for passing yards (4,243) and total yards (6,554), with the latter figure ranking fifth in NFL history. Wide receivers Ed McCaffrey and Rod Smith each hit the 100-catch mark for the season—just the second pair of teammates to do so in the same season in NFL history. With 101 catches, McCaffrey broke Lionel Taylor's 39-year-old franchise record of 100 catches, while Smith tied it. Smith shattered the club record with 1,602 receiving yards for the season, while Anderson set franchise rookie rushing records with 1,487 yards and 15 touchdowns for the year.

The playing field that had hosted so many moments had one more, as players celebrated after the win over San Francisco; the record crowd reveled in the final moments of one of the league's legendary venues.

The Broncos' 2000 season ended in a disappointing 21-3 defeat at the hands of the Baltimore Ravens. The AFC wild card playoff game in Baltimore took place on a blustery New Year's Eve day before 69,638 fans. Denver's

Jason Elam boots a field goal through the uprights. Elam was the most prolific scorer in Bronco history and is one of the NFL's all-time leaders.

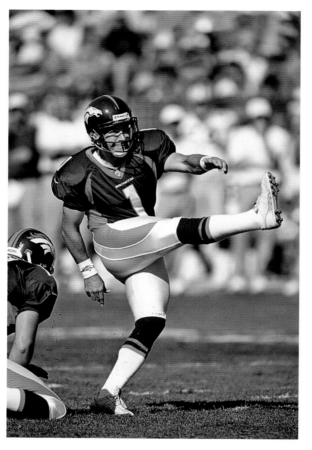

offense managed just 177 yards—the club's third-lowest output in 28 postseason games—and nine first downs. The Ravens record-setting defense put an end to the Broncos' seven-game postseason winning streak.

Baltimore put up the game's first points early in the second quarter when Jamal Lewis reached the end zone from 1 yard out to cap a 10-play, 75-yard drive. When a promising 12-play, 68-yard drive stalled after a third-and-one opportunity at the Ravens' 12 yard line, the Broncos answered with a 31-yard Elam field goal to narrow the deficit to 7-3.

What followed proved to be the play of the game, if not one of the more bizarre plays of the year. After the Ravens' Corey Harris returned the ensuing kickoff 15 yards, Baltimore had a first down on the 42 yard line. Quarterback Trent Dilfer attempted a screen pass to Lewis, who tipped the ball into and out of the hands of Denver cornerback Terrell Buckley. The loose ball then was grabbed out of the air by former Broncos tight end Shannon Sharpe, who dashed 58 yards for a touchdown, boosting the lead to 14-3 at the half. Baltimore increased its halftime lead to 21-3 late in the third quarter when Lewis ran 27 yards for his second touchdown of the day.

Denver managed just 83 yards on its eight second-half possessions and was held scoreless to preserve the lowest scoring output in franchise postseason history. The Broncos penetrated Ravens territory just once all day and ran just seven plays on the Baltimore side of the field.

Fullback Howard Griffith takes off after making a reception against the Raiders. Griffith was forced to retire at the start of the 2002 season because of a neck injury that sidelined him in the 2001 campaign.

Broncos quarterback Gus Frerotte, subbing for the injured Brian Griese, completed just 13-of-28 passes for 124 yards while Anderson led the Broncos in rushing with just 40 yards against the resolute Baltimore defense.

NEW STADIUM, NEW CHALLENGES

Denver's 32nd consecutive year of home sellouts began at a new venue, INVESCO Field at Mile High. The first preseason game at the new stadium was on August 25, 2001, versus the New Orleans Saints. Denver won the game by a score of 31-24. On September 10, the Broncos officially christened INVESCO Field at Mile High with a season-opening 31-20 win over the New York Giants on Monday Night Football. The game was marred by the fact that fan favorite Ed McCaffrey broke his leg, and was further put out of the spotlight the next morning by the 9/11 terrorist attacks on the United States.

The NFL took a week off due to the terrible tragedy and returned to action on September 23. In the matchup against Arizona, Rod Smith set a team record with 14 receptions in a 38-17 win.

America's mind was elsewhere for much of the season, but there were some highlights. Bronco cornerback Deltha O'Neal became the 18th player in league history (19th time) to intercept four passes in one game, in

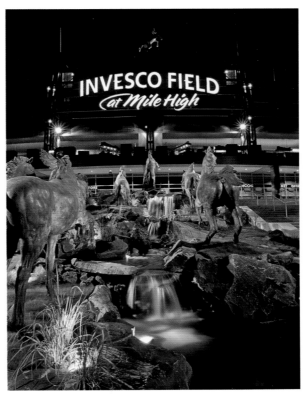

A nighttime view of INVESCO Field at Mile High's main entrance and *The Broncos* sculpture. The bronze sculpture is the largest handmade and imported piece of art on permanent display in the state. It was created in Italy by noted sculptor Sergio Benvenuti at the request of the Bowlen family.

Below: A halftime fireworks show lights up INVESCO Field at Mile High, which opened to rave reviews in 2001.

A sellout crowd celebrates a joyous moment with the regular-season opener of INVESCO Field at Mile High on September 10, 2001. The following day, Denver and the rest of the nation mourned the tragic events of the day that would live in infamy, forever remembered as 9/11.

Trevor Pryce sacks Drew Bledsoe deep in Patriot territory to snuff out a New England drive. Pryce earned Pro Bowl status four times for his pass rushing skills as a Denver defensive end.

Denver's 20-6 defeat of Kansas City at INVESCO Field at Mile High. He joined Ring of Famer Goose Gonsoulin and Hall of Famer Willie Brown on that select list—both Gonsoulin and Brown also accomplished the feat as members of the Broncos. In November, Elam became one of just 30 players in NFL history to score 1,000 career points, converting four field goals in a 38-28 loss at Oakland on Monday Night Football. His second field goal also accounted for the 20,000th point scored in the history of Monday Night Football. The statistic just proved that both the franchise and Monday Night Football games had become institutions.

The Broncos defeated the Dallas Cowboys 26-24 at Texas Stadium on Thanksgiving Day, further demonstrating that the networks could not get enough of the Broncos in this new decade. Nevertheless, Denver ended the 2001 campaign with an 8-8 record.

In 2002, the Broncos improved to 9-7. While the franchise was avoiding the pitfall of plummeting from world championship status to a complete rebuilding process, the going was slower than this team desired. There was no playoff appearance again in 2002, but another rookie running back made his mark. Clinton Portis burst onto the NFL scene in what was becoming routine for the Broncos—finding a new running back to fit the style of the most dominant rushing attack in pro football.

While Portis was captivating Bronco fans, Shannon Sharpe set an NFL record for a tight end and a franchise receiving record with 214 receiving yards on 13 receptions in Denver's 37-34 come-from-behind overtime win at Kansas City in October. Two of his receptions went for touchdowns in the game.

The second matchup against the Chiefs came in Denver on December 15, and in that one Portis tied a team record by becoming just the second player in franchise history to score four touchdowns in a game. He scored three times by rush and once receiving in Denver's 31-24 home win over Kansas City. Two weeks later, he closed out his rookie season with a 228-yard rushing effort in a win against Arizona. His 228 rushing yards tied for the best effort in the NFL in 2002 and tied for fourth most by a rookie in a single game in NFL history. Additionally, Portis' two touchdowns on the day gave him 17 for the season (15 rushing and two receiving), tied for third most by a rookie in NFL history. He finished the season with a franchise rookie record of 1,508 rushing yards, the fifth-best rushing season by a rookie in NFL history. As a result, he was named NFL Offensive Rookie of the Year by the Associated Press. Portis was only the third Bronco to be named either the offensive or defensive rookie of the year by the AP, joining running back Mike Anderson in 2000 and linebacker Mike Croel in 1991.

TRAINING CAMP MOVES BACK HOME

The times were changing in pro football's new century, and with the advent of intense offseason training programs that included NFL-allowed on-field workouts, the long and grueling training camps of pro football lore were becoming vestiges of the past. On March 17, 2003, the Broncos announced that the club would hold training

Ed McCaffrey displays some fancy footwork while making a catch near the back of the end zone against the Packers.

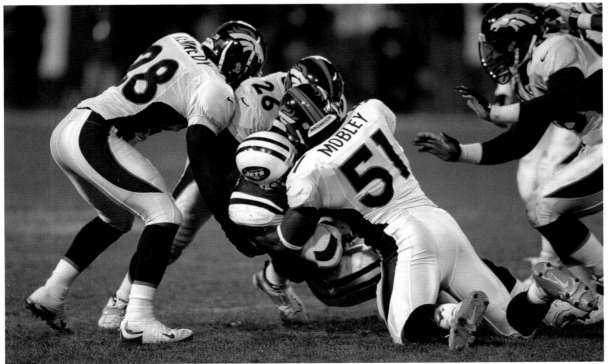

Linebacker John Mobley wraps up a Jets running back. During his career, Mobley played in 105 games, starting 102 of them, including two Super Bowls.

John Mobley waits for his unit to take part in pregame warmups.

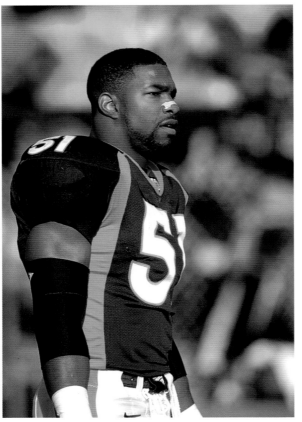

camp that year and in subsequent years at its permanent facility in Dove Valley, in suburban Denver, after 21 years at the University of Northern Colorado in Greeley.

Construction began on a third outdoor practice field, which would feature artificial turf, in the spring. By July's training camp, veteran players were able to live at home, and the local fans in Denver were able to watch practice from the closest vantage point ever offered by an NFL team.

Now playing in a new stadium and practicing closer to home than ever, the Broncos had not lost sight of returning to championship contention. They had made a major offseason acquisition in signing quarterback Jake Plummer.

With the freewheeling former Arizona State star under center, Denver went 10-6 and earned a playoff berth once again. Plummer threw 15 scoring passes during the season while Portis ran for more than 1,500 yards. Smith led all receivers with 74 catches.

Smith helped make history as a punt returner on November 16, when he returned a punt 65 yards for a touchdown against the San Diego Chargers. Coupled with Deltha O'Neal's 57-yard punt return for a score in the Broncos' previous game against the Patriots, the Broncos became the first team in NFL history to have a different player return a punt for a touchdown in back-to-back games.

Bill Romanowski's eyes say it all as he awaits the snap of the ball and the start of another collision with the opposition.

The Broncos defeated Indianapolis 31-17 at the RCA Dome in a Sunday night game to clinch the organization's first playoff berth since the 2000 season. In that game, Smith became the Bronco with the most career total yards from scrimmage, and Sharpe moved into ninth place on the all-time NFL receptions list. History ultimately showed that Sharpe was just getting started, but at the time the team's focus was on being back in the playoffs.

The excitement was short-lived, as Denver suffered a 41-10 loss to Indianapolis in the AFC wild card playoff game at the RCA Dome. On the game's opening drive, Peyton Manning led the Colts 70 yards and capped the drive when he found Brandon Stokley for a 31-yard touchdown and an early lead. Denver answered on its first drive but could only manage a 49-yard Jason Elam field goal after penalties caused the drive to stall.

Late in the first quarter, Manning hit Marvin Harrison, who fell near the Colts' 29 yard line. After not being touched by a Broncos' defender, he got up and ran the ball in for a touchdown and a 14-3 lead. With Denver unable to sustain a drive after picking up two holding penalties, Indianapolis took possession on its 20 yard line after a Broncos' punt and engineered another successful touchdown drive.

After another Denver punt, Manning hit Stokley in stride, and he scampered 87 yards for a touchdown.

Now the Colts had a 28-3 lead with less than two minutes remaining in the half. Denver began to mount a drive, but Plummer's pass intended for Smith was intercepted. The interception led to a field goal that gave the Colts a 31-3 halftime lead.

The Broncos were never able to overcome that halftime deficit but finally found the end zone on a Plummer-to-Smith 7-yard touchdown. Plummer completed 23-of-30 passes for 181 yards with a touchdown in the game but had a pair of interceptions. Smith pitched in with five catches for 66 yards and Sharpe also caught five passes, but the day belonged to Indy.

ELWAY CAPTURED IN BRONZE

Every season ends with the Super Bowl, and even though the Broncos were not in this one, they celebrated a historic day on January 31, Super Bowl Saturday. The 2004 Pro Football Hall of Fame class was announced, and former Bronco quarterback John Elway was a unanimous first ballot selection. Elway became the first Bronco in the Canton shrine to have played his entire career with the team. He joined Bob Brown, Carl Eller, and Barry Sanders in being inducted on August 8, 2004. Previous Broncos to make the hall after playing the majority of their careers elsewhere were Willie Brown and Tony Dorsett, but Elway was undoubtedly the brightest star in any Bronco fan's galaxy.

Left: Quarterback Jake Plummer led the Broncos to a 13-3 record and a berth in the AFC title game in 2005. He threw 71 touchdown passes in his four years as a Bronco.

Right: Team captain Rod Smith signals to the crowd after scoring a touchdown. He went from free-agent obscurity to a Bronco fan favorite and one of the team's all-time greatest players and leaders.

Thunder, an Arabian stallion and one of the NFL's most identifiable team symbols, rambles down the field after a Bronco touchdown.

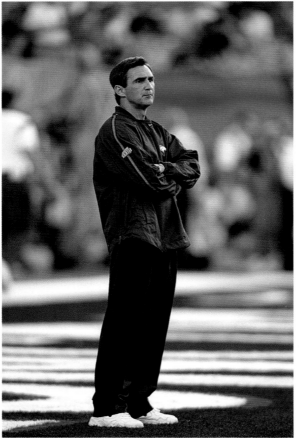

Coach Mike Shanahan watches pregame warmups from the endzone. Few elements of the game escaped the scrutiny of Shanahan, whose meticulous preparation and attention to detail were key factors in his brilliant Bronco record.

The year 2004 also featured a $4 million renovation and expansion of the team's headquarters, the Paul D. Bowlen Memorial Broncos Centre, in suburban Denver. Included in the project were adding a new strength and conditioning center to house the team's weight room, an indoor conditioning area, and a new home for the field-maintenance department. The new weight room was approximately 9,000 square feet in size, nearly three times the size of the previous weight room. Also included in the renovation were an expanded training room and a cafeteria seating approximately 120 people.

This renovation also was a reflection of the new competition in pro football, as each team needed top-notch facilities to attract an annual stream of free-agent players. Bronco owner Pat Bowlen once again wanted to make sure his team was on the cusp of this development rather than at the trailing end of the curve.

That year, the Broncos trotted out yet another 1,000-yard running back in Reuben Droughns. He put up 193 rushing yards against Carolina on a sparkling October afternoon, marking the most by a Broncos player in his first start at running back. Mike Shanahan also earned his 100th win with the team. It came in a 23-13 triumph over San Diego in September, and with it Shanahan became one of an elite group of coaches to post 100 wins in his first 10 seasons with one club.

Meanwhile, Rod Smith passed Shannon Sharpe to become the franchise leader in receptions and touchdown

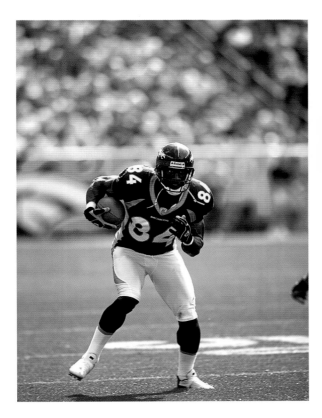

Left: Shannon Sharpe runs for yardage after a reception. He continued to be a pass-catching star for Denver as the franchise worked to move back to championship status.

Right: An intense student and observer of the game, Shannon Sharpe watches the action from the sideline. Those qualities served Sharpe well when he fashioned a television career following his playing days.

receptions, passing Sharpe's totals of 675 and 55, respectively. With Sharpe having become a virtual lock for the Pro Football Hall of Fame, Smith was quietly starting his own case for the game's highest individual honor. He kept amassing stats never before achieved by any free-agent wide receiver.

Shanahan's drive to push his team back into championship contention took a major step forward in Plummer's second season with Denver, as the Broncos finished with a 10-6 record. The team earned second place in the AFC West and a wild card playoff berth.

Plummer brought his final 2004 passing yards total to a franchise-record 4,089 yards in the regular-season finale against Indianapolis, a 33-14 Bronco win. In the same game, he tied Elway's franchise record with 27 touchdown passes in a single season. Linebacker D. J. Williams became just the second rookie in franchise history to lead the team in tackles, the first since Tom Graham paced the team with 91 stops in 1972. The Broncos' offense yielded a franchise-low 15 sacks in 2004, the third-fewest in the NFL for the year. The team earned its second consecutive trip to the postseason, while newcomers safety John Lynch and cornerback Champ Bailey both earned Pro Bowl nods.

Despite the Broncos' win at Indy in the final game of the regular season, the playoff game against the Colts again proved to be a disappointment. Peyton Manning threw for 458 yards with four touchdowns. He also ran

for a score to lead the Colts in a 49-24 victory over the Broncos in the RCA Dome.

The Colts jumped out to a 14-0 first-quarter lead on a pass by Manning and a score on the ground, and the Colts went ahead 21-0 on his second scoring pass of the day. Jason Elam put Denver on the scoreboard with a 33-yard field goal, but the Colts' offense responded quickly. Manning increased the lead to 35-3 with a 35-yard touchdown pass to Reggie Wayne and a 1-yard quarterback sneak in the closing seconds of the half.

The Broncos fought back in the third quarter when Jake Plummer capped off a 10-play, 71-yard drive with a 9-yard touchdown pass to Rod Smith. After forcing the Colts to punt for just the second time all day, Plummer led Denver downfield once again and hit tight end Jeb Putzier for a 35-yard score. The touchdown concluded an 85-yard drive, cutting the Broncos' deficit to 35-17.

Indianapolis denied a Denver comeback when Manning connected with Wayne for the second time in the game on a 43-yard touchdown pass early in the fourth quarter. The Broncos scored their final points on a run by Tatum Bell at 7:45 of the fourth quarter, but it was not enough to catch up to the potent Colts offense, which amassed 530 total yards for the game.

Smith paced the Denver receivers with seven catches for 99 yards with a touchdown to give him 39 career postseason catches, and Plummer completed 24-of-34

Safety John Lynch went to four Pro Bowls as a Bronco and was one of the team's most popular players in the first decade of the new millennium. Lynch was a fierce hitter on the field, as well as a contributor to the Denver community.

passes for 284 yards with two touchdowns, posting a passer rating of 103.1.

Still, Manning was unbeatable. His 458 passing yards were the most the Broncos ever yielded in a game and ranked as the second-most passing yards in a playoff game in NFL history.

THE BRONCOS BOUNCE BACK

The Broncos were poised for a big season in 2005, both in terms of individual honors and another appearance in the AFC Championship Game.

Rod Smith became the first undrafted player in NFL history to reach 10,000 career receiving yards, with a 19-yard catch in the third quarter of a home Monday Night Football game against the Chiefs. The team jumped out of the gate with five straight wins after an opening-day loss at Miami, and the offense was rolling up a lot of yards and points while minimizing mistakes. The Broncos tied an NFL record by not committing a turnover for the fourth consecutive game during their October 16 victory against New England.

Plummer ran up a streak of 229 consecutive passes without an interception before a second-quarter interception at Dallas. The Broncos still managed to win, 24-21, in overtime against the Cowboys on Thanksgiving Day. His 229 attempts without an interception lasted eight complete games and 34 quarters and was the fourth-longest streak in the NFL since 1996.

In December, Mike Shanahan became the Broncos' all-time leader in career victories, collecting his 118th career win with Denver's 12-10 triumph against Baltimore. Champ Bailey recorded an interception for the fifth consecutive game, setting a franchise record. On Christmas Eve, the Broncos defeated Oakland 22-3 before the home fans to post a perfect home record (8-0) for the fifth time in team history. The win also clinched the club's 10th division title and the first since the 1998 season, as well as the No. 2 seed in the AFC playoffs.

The team finished 13-3 to tie for the second-most wins in a season in franchise history. The Broncos ended the year with the second-highest rushing total—2,539 yards—in club annals. Denver's run defense ranked second in the NFL by allowing just more than 85 yards per game, and it finished the year ranked second in the NFL with a plus-20 turnover ratio, setting a franchise record with a league-low 16 giveaways.

Smith had his eighth 1,000-yard receiving season, and Denver became only the third team in NFL history to have two 900-yard rushers (Mike Anderson and Tatum Bell), a 1,000-yard receiver (Smith), and a 3,000-yard passer (Plummer) in the same season.

In their best season of the decade, the Broncos ended the New England Patriots' NFL-record 10-game postseason winning streak with a 27-13 victory in a Saturday-night AFC divisional playoff game in front of 76,238 chilled but frenzied fans at INVESCO Field at Mile High. The Broncos' win against the two-time defending Super Bowl champions was their first play-off victory since the 1998 season and the first at their new stadium. Denver forced five turnovers against the Patriots, snagging two interceptions and three fumble recoveries that led to the first 24 points the team scored.

Cornerback Champ Bailey recorded the longest non-scoring interception return and second-longest overall interception return in NFL postseason history with a key 100-yard return late in the third quarter. Bailey's play ended a potential go-ahead scoring drive by the Patriots and set up a touchdown to give the Broncos a 17-6 lead entering the final period.

The game was scoreless until Adam Vinatieri's 40-yard field goal put the Patriots ahead 3-0 at 3:48 of the second quarter. A 40-yard pass interference penalty drawn by Broncos wide receiver Ashley Lelie in the end zone with less than two minutes remaining in the first half led to a short scoring run by Mike Anderson, giving Denver a 7-3 lead. On the ensuing kickoff, Broncos kicker Todd Sauerbrun forced a fumble that Denver recovered to set up a 50-yard field goal by Jason Elam, which put the Broncos ahead 10-3 at halftime.

Vinatieri's 32-yard field goal at 7:49 of the third quarter narrowed Denver's lead to 10-6, but that would be as close as the Patriots would get. Champ Bailey intercepted Tom Brady, who finished the game with 341 passing yards, in the end zone with 1:03 left in the third quarter. After Bailey was forced out of bounds at the 1 yard line following his historic 100-yard return, Anderson scored on a run to put Denver up 17-6.

Plummer's 4-yard touchdown pass to Smith at 8:38 of the fourth quarter extended the Broncos' lead to 24-6. A Patriots touchdown moved the team to within 11 with 8:05 left to play, but Elam's 34-yard field goal on Denver's next drive sealed the Broncos' first playoff victory in their new home.

Elam became Denver's all-time postseason leader in points and field goals in the game. In addition, the win

Jake Plummer in a classic quarterback pose as he leads the Broncos to a 27-0 win over the New York Jets at INVESCO Field.

Below: Champ Bailey watches a replay on the scoreboard. Bailey exhibits a rare combination of grace and toughness in what is regarded by observers as a Hall of Fame–worthy career.

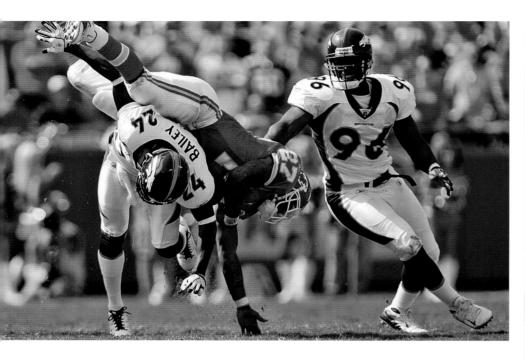

Left: A fierce and willing tackler, Champ Bailey upends the Chiefs' Larry Johnson and forces a fumble at Arrowhead Stadium.

Right: Quarterback Jake Plummer's Denver career ended with the conclusion of the 2006 season, after having been replaced by Jay Cutler.

gave head coach Mike Shanahan more postseason victories (eight) than any coach in Broncos' history.

The estatic Bronco fans had one of their greatest letdowns the following week when the club suffered its first home loss in an AFC Championship Game. The Broncos' 2005 season ended one game short of Super Bowl XL with a 34-17 loss to the Pittsburgh Steelers. The grim defeat also snapped Denver's 11-game overall home winning streak and was only the Broncos' third loss in their 15 all-time home postseason playoff games.

A week after forcing five turnovers to beat the Patriots in the divisional round, Denver recorded four giveaways against the Steelers. Pittsburgh scored 24 points off two interceptions and two fumbles by the Broncos, who surrendered only 27 points off giveaways for the entire 2005 regular season.

Pittsburgh converted 10-of-16 third-down attempts, including eight of its first nine such attempts, to take control of the game. Quarterback Ben Roethlisberger compiled a 124.9 passer rating while throwing for 275 yards with two touchdowns and no interceptions to lead Pittsburgh to its sixth Super Bowl.

Plummer completed 18-of-30 passes for 223 yards with one touchdown and two critical interceptions.

The Steelers scored the game's first points on a 47-yard field goal by Jeff Reed at 4:11 of the first quarter and extended their lead to 10-0 on a 12-yard touchdown grab by wide receiver Cedric Wilson at 14:54 of the second quarter. Elam's 23-yard field goal on Denver's next drive trimmed the Broncos' deficit, but the Steelers went ahead 17-3 on a 3-yard touchdown run by Jerome Bettis with 1:55 left in the first half.

Plummer was intercepted on the first play of Denver's ensuing series, and that turnover proved devastating as wide receiver Hines Ward caught a 17-yard touchdown pass, with seven seconds remaining in the first half, to put Denver behind 24-3.

Plummer moved the Broncos within 14 on a 30-yard touchdown pass to Lelie with 3:36 left in the third quarter. Denver closed its deficit to 10, making the score 27-17, on a 3-yard touchdown run by Anderson with 7:52 left in the game. Despite Denver's comeback, the Steelers sealed the win on Roethlisberger's 4-yard touchdown run at 2:59 of the fourth quarter.

While this was a brutal loss for Bronco fans to swallow, it marked Denver's eighth AFC Championship Game appearance, a tribute to the steady excellence of Pat Bowlen's franchise. And with Pittsburgh advancing to its sixth title game, the Steelers and the Broncos now only trailed Dallas in number of Super Bowl appearances (seven).

A NEW QUARTERBACK COMES TO TOWN

After the loss, Mike Shanahan was looking forward, not backward, and he felt a compelling need to make a bold step at the critical quarterback position. On the first day of the 2006 NFL Draft, the Broncos acquired the 11th

Coach Mike Shanahan congratulates Jay Cutler after a touchdown pass. Shanahan traded up to get the 11th pick in the first round of the 2006 draft so that he could select Cutler.

Jay Cutler demonstrates his throwing form and the Broncos' all-blue uniform combination as he finds a receiver downfield.

overall pick from St. Louis and selected highly touted Vanderbilt quarterback Jay Cutler.

Individual highlights of the 2006 season included Rod Smith becoming just the 15th player in NFL history to record 800 career receptions, while Shanahan coached his 200th career regular-season game against Baltimore on Monday Night Football. In the matchup, the Broncos defeated the Ravens, 13-3, and Shanahan's 125 wins through his first 200 games tied for the third most by a coach in the Super Bowl era (since 1966).

Defensively, Denver became the first team since the 1934 Detroit Lions to allow two or fewer touchdowns through its first six games of a season. The Broncos had not been around as long as the Lions and the other NFL originals, but the Mile High City franchise continued moving forward in the pack. On November 5, the Broncos played their 700th all-time regular-season game at Pittsburgh and defeated the Steelers, 31-20.

Shanahan and the Broncos made a big move on November 27, 2006, by naming rookie Jay Cutler as the Broncos' starting quarterback, replacing Plummer. Cutler made the first start of his career in a Sunday Night Football game against Seattle at INVESCO Field at Mile High. He completed 10-of-21 passes for 143 yards with two touchdowns and two interceptions as Denver lost to the Seahawks, 23-20. However, he threw multiple touchdown passes in each of his first four games, the first NFL rookie to do so.

The Broncos finished the year with a 9-7 record. This was the team's fifth consecutive year with a winning record, which tied the longest such streak in franchise history. Champ Bailey tied for the NFL lead with 10 interceptions and led the league with 11 takeaways as he finished second in the Associated Press' voting for NFL Defensive Player of the Year. Cutler demonstrated his spectacular potential with the second-highest touchdown percentage (6.6 percent) among NFL rookies since 1970, while Tatum Bell became the latest Bronco rusher to hit the 1,000-yard mark. Elam set a franchise single-season record for field-goal accuracy (93.1 percent) by connecting on 27-of-29 attempts.

However, the team's performance on the field became secondary for the Broncos and the entire city of Denver early New Year's Day morning in 2007 when popular and talented cornerback Darrent Williams, a 2005 second-round draft choice, died at age 24 as the result of gunshots fired into his automobile. The entire football team traveled by charter flight to Fort Worth, Texas, to attend his funeral on January 6. Then on February 24, running back Damien Nash, a second-year player who completed his first season with the Broncos in 2006, died at age 24. After never experiencing the death of an active player in franchise history, the Broncos mourned two in two months.

The team's grief was somewhat lightened when safety John Lynch was named winner of the National Football League Players Association's Byron "Whizzer" White Award for his work in the community that spring. Also, Broncos president and CEO Pat Bowlen received a well-deserved honor with induction into the Colorado Sports Hall of Fame.

Bowlen's induction, viewed by many as long over-due, brought the state's highest honor to the man most responsible for carrying the torch originally lit by men like Gerry Phipps. The only two-decade owner of a major league sports team in Colorado history, he reached the quarter-century mark of Bronco owner-ship in 2008. Whether judged by the measure of wins and championships, game attendance, national tele-vision exposure, or by his and the Broncos' reputation locally and throughout the NFL, he has been an excellent leader for this team.

Under Bowlen's regime, the Broncos arguably have brought more national and international recognition to Colorado than any other local organization or team in state history. In addition to the well-documented and almost unmatched record of on-field success during Bowlen's tenure as owner, the team has enjoyed tremen-dous off-the-field success, as well. The Broncos marked an unprecedented 40 consecutive sellout seasons in 2009.

A key figure in securing the league's labor and televi-sion contracts, Bowlen was the chair of the prestigious NFL Broadcasting Committee when it negotiated an $18 billion contract, the most lucrative single-sport con-tract in history. He currently sits as co-chair of the NFL

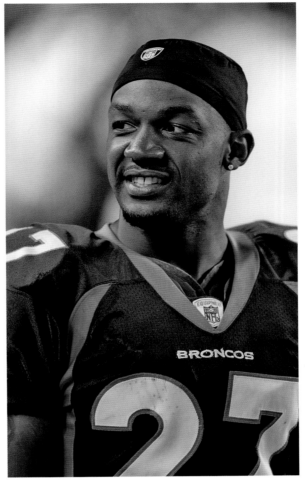

Talented and popular cornerback Darrent Williams was the victim of a tragic shooting incident on January 1, 2007. His memory lives on within the community with the founding of the Darrent Williams Memorial Teen Center.

Opposite: Linebacker Al Wilson concentrates as he watches for the snap. Wilson was a five-time Pro Bowler, heavy hitter, and team captain from his middle linebacker position.

A lucky fan gets his football autographed by Broncos Pro Bowl safety John Lynch following a practice at Dove Valley.

Diagnosed as a Type 1 diabetic at the end of the 2007 season, Jay Cutler wears a blood sugar monitor during games and practice. He has become a prominent spokesman on behalf of the diagnosis and treatment of diabetes, especially among juveniles.

Management Council Executive Committee, which represents the league in labor negotiations with the NFL Players Association.

THE FUTURE OF BRONCOS COUNTRY

The 2007 campaign was a disappointing 7-9 season for the Broncos, but it was marked by the emergence and development of the team's new starting quarterback, Jay Cutler. Both Cutler and wide receiver Brandon Marshall showed the kind of potential and star power that suggested big things for the future, and their play was a bright spot on an otherwise dismal campaign.

In the 2008 draft, the Broncos made some dramatic additions to the team, selecting tackle Ryan Clady in the first round and wide receiver/kick returner Eddie Royal in the second. Each made a major impact in his rookie year.

The Broncos had high hopes for the 2008 campaign, which began with a 41-14 win on Monday Night Football at Oakland. Royal made an impressive NFL debut, catching nine catches for 146 yards with one touchdown. His receiving yardage total marked the sixth highest by an NFL player in his debut game since 1960 and the most in five seasons. His nine receptions also were the most by a Broncos rookie playing in his first game.

In week two, the Broncos scored a two-point conversion with 24 seconds left to capture a 39-38 win against the San Diego Chargers at INVESCO Field at Mile High. The victory improved Denver's record to 2-0 for the

Brandon Marshall breaks into the open for a long gain in 2008 action. Marshall has quickly established himself as one of the NFL's most spectacular receivers. The Broncos wore their alternate orange jerseys for this contest against New Orleans.

Left tackle and 2008 first-round draft pick Ryan Clady zeros in on a block during a game against the Tampa Bay Buccaneers in his rookie season. Clady quickly established himself as one of the game's best young offensive linemen.

Daniel Graham hauls in a pass and rambles downfield against the San Diego Chargers at INVESCO Field on September 14, 2008. A Denver native, Graham was a college star at the University of Colorado.

Wide receiver Brandon Marshall displays the fiery emotion that is part of his game. Marshall is one of several young stars on offense that provide the core talent for the Broncos.

second consecutive year and marked the Broncos' ninth consecutive victory in their home opener.

Marshall's franchise-record 18 receptions (for 166 yards and a touchdown) in the game tied for the second most by a player in NFL history. He had 10 grabs in the first half alone, helping the Broncos take an early 21-3 lead and enter halftime ahead 31-17.

Cutler finished the game with a career-high 350 yards, completing 36-of-50 passes with four touchdowns. His 36 completions tied a Broncos franchise record, and his 350 passing yards marked his second consecutive 300-yard game.

Then, for the first time since 2003 and the 10th time in club history, the Broncos improved to 3-0 with their 34-32 victory over the New Orleans Saints. Denver earned the win despite allowing 502 yards of offense by New Orleans, which was led by Drew Brees' 421 passing yards.

Unable to overcome four turnovers, the Broncos suffered their first loss of the season in a 33-19 defeat to the Kansas City Chiefs at Arrowhead Stadium the following week. Kicker Matt Prater became only the third Bronco

in club history to post two field goals of at least 50 yards in the same game; the second-year player finished the game accounting for 13 of Denver's 19 points (four-of-five field goals, one-of-one extra-point attempts).

The Broncos bounced back into the victory column with a 16-13 win over Tampa Bay that marked the team's sixth consecutive home win. Three different Broncos registered sacks, including defensive end Elvis Dumervil, who notched his first takedown of the season.

The season took on a different tone when the Broncos faced New England in 41-7 pummeling loss. Turnovers plagued the Broncos for the second consecutive week, this time New England scoring 20 points off of five takeaways. The Miami Dolphins added to Denver's misery with a 26-17 win at INVESCO Field at Mile High. More than 75,000 disgruntled Bronco fans watched Denver's 3-0 record slide to a very disappointing 4-4. Three Cutler interceptions led to 13 points by Miami, whose defense held Denver to a paltry and embarrassing 14 rushing yards.

The Broncos then went on the road for two straight, winning both and earning their 400th overall franchise vic-

tory. Denver rallied from a 13-point deficit at Cleveland in the third quarter to defeat the Browns 34-30. Cutler engineered his fifth-career game-winning or game-saving drive in the win while tying for the third-highest single-game passing yardage total (447) in club history. He also tossed three touchdown passes in the win.

During the 24-20 win against Atlanta the following week, Broncos rookie Peyton Hillis started at running back and posted two rushing touchdowns. Another Denver rookie, Spencer Larsen, became the first Bronco in club history and the fourth NFL player since 1990 to start on offense and defense as he opened the game at fullback and middle linebacker.

Unfortunately, the Broncos' two-game winning streak came to an end with a 31-10 loss to the Oakland Raiders at home before an increasingly disgruntled fan base. Oakland, which came into the game with one of the lowest scoring offenses in the NFL, scored 21 unanswered points to break a 10-10 tie in the third quarter. The Raiders handed Denver its third consecutive home defeat before a shocked crowd.

The inconsistent Broncos won their third consecutive road game and snapped the AFC East–leading New York Jets' five-game winning streak with a 34-17 victory the following week. Cutler set a Denver single-season record with his sixth 300-yard passing game, completing 27-of-43 passes for 357 yards with two touchdowns. He also became the fastest player in Bronco history to complete 50 touchdown passes, reaching that total in just 33 games.

Denver next overcame a 17-7 second-quarter deficit to defeat the Kansas City Chiefs 24-17 at home, posting its highest time-of-possession total (36:38) in more than a year and snapping a three-game home losing streak. The win over Kansas City put the Broncos in position to win the AFC West with either one win or a loss by the Chargers in the season's final three weeks.

Again, the Broncos stumbled and became the only team in NFL history to have led its division by three games so late in the season and then fail to make the playoffs. The team lost 30-10 to the Carolina Panthers on the road, 30-23 to the Buffalo Bills in a cold game at home, and 52-21 to the Chargers in San Diego.

Pass-rushing defensive end Elvis Dumervil celebrates a sack. Although only 6 feet tall and shorter than many defensive ends, Dumervil had the second-highest sack total in NCAA history at the University of Louisville and has been among the NFL sack leaders since joining the Broncos in 2006.

Right: Josh McDaniels greets the media after being named as the new head coach of the Denver Broncos in January 2009. McDaniels served as the offensive coordinator in New England before being hired by Pat Bowlen.

Below: Brian Dawkins was a key free-agent acquisition who brought a renewed passion to the Denver defense. He made the Pro Bowl twice as a Bronco and was a team captain for all three of his Bronco seasons.

The Broncos were unable to stop a San Diego offense that gained 491 yards, including a club-record 289 rushing yards, while controlling the ball for more than 36 minutes. The disappointing loss was a wretched conclusion to a once-promising season.

Individually, Royal finished the year with the second-most receptions (91) by a rookie in NFL history. Cutler had a club-record 4,526 passing yards, becoming just the third player in NFL history with three years' experience or less to reach the 4,500-yard passing mark for a season. The Broncos' outstanding offensive line allowed a franchise-low 12 sacks. Cutler, Marshall, and center Casey Wiegmann all earned Pro Bowl trips.

But Bronco fans everywhere were completely miserable with the club's 8-8 record, especially in light of the team's late-season collapse. None was more disenchanted than the team owner, Pat Bowlen. Just two days after the season ended, he fired Mike Shanahan, the Broncos' longtime head coach.

After an extensive search, Bowlen named former New England Patriots offensive coordinator Josh McDaniels as the Broncos' new head coach on January 12, 2009. The 32-year-old McDaniels came to Denver as the youngest head coach in team history, and he brought three Super Bowl rings from his successful stint with the Patriots.

But sometimes things do not work out as expected and instead lay the groundwork for success in an entirely different way.

Initially, McDaniels infused new energy into the organization, and those in Broncos Country quickly picked up on the new coach's dynamic personality as they prepared for the 50th season of Broncos football.

During the 2009 offseason, the Broncos were aggressive in pursuing free agents, signing 16 new players to the roster. One of the newcomers was veteran safety Brian Dawkins, who had been a seven-time Pro Bowl selection as a member of the Philadelphia Eagles.

But Denver became immersed in controversy almost immediately under McDaniels. Cutler became disgruntled when his name surfaced in trade discussions, and he indicated through his agent that he no longer wished to play in Denver. After several failed attempts to iron out the differences and bring Cutler back into the fold, the Broncos made a blockbuster trade with Chicago, sending Cutler to the Bears in return for two first-round draft choices, a third-round selection, and starting quarterback Kyle Orton, who would be the Broncos' new starting signal-caller.

Fans were excited by new hope, as reflected by the 40th straight season of home sellouts. That offseason, tight end Shannon Sharpe was named as the 22nd member of the team's Ring of Fame.

Denver kicked off its 50th season of professional football, and the McDaniels era began with signs of great promise.

In the season opener, Denver was trailing Cincinnati 7-6 with 28 seconds to play when Orton's pass intended for Brandon Marshall was tipped by a Bengals defender into the hands of Broncos wide receiver Brandon Stokley, who raced 62 yards down the left sideline for the game-winning score. In all, the 87-yard touchdown marked the longest game-winning touchdown from scrimmage in the final minute of the fourth quarter of a game in NFL history. Josh McDaniels had earned his first victory as an NFL head coach, and it would be the first of six straight.

Sharpe was inducted into the Ring of Fame in a half-time ceremony during Denver's regular-season home opener against Cleveland, and during the game, defensive end Elvis Dumervil tied a club record with four sacks.

In celebration of the 50th season of play for AFL teams, on October 11 the Broncos donned their "throwback" uniforms from the 1960–1961 seasons for what would be a 20-17 overtime win over New England. The team wore mustard-gold jerseys with brown pants, vertically striped brown and gold socks, and brown helmets with numbers on the sides.

Wide receiver Eddie Royal returned a kickoff 93 yards and a punt 71 yards for touchdowns in Denver's 34-23 win at San Diego to help the Broncos improve

Kyle Orton came to the Broncos prior to the 2009 seasons in a blockbuster trade with the Bears. He had the best season of his career statistically that year, throwing for 3,802 yards and 21 touchdowns, but he only lasted two and a half years with the organization.

SHANNON SHARPE

TIGHT END

1990–1999, 2002–2003

On May 12, 2009, Shannon Sharpe became the 22nd member elected to the Denver Broncos Ring of Fame after 12 record-setting seasons with the club. A Pro Football Hall of Fame inductee in 2011, Sharpe tied a Broncos record with seven consecutive Pro Bowl selections (1992–1998) while becoming the NFL's all-time leader in receptions, receiving yards, and receiving touchdowns by a tight end (currently second to Tony Gonzalez). A key member of the Broncos' back-to-back Super Bowl championship teams in 1997 and 1998, Sharpe also was a four-time first-team All-Pro selection by the Associated Press as a Bronco. In 172 career regular-season games with Denver, he registered the second-most receptions (675), receiving yards (8,439), and receiving touchdowns (55) by a player in club annals, trailing only wide receiver Rod Smith.

Sharpe also played two seasons with Baltimore, from 2000 to 2001, earning the third Super Bowl ring of his career during the 2000 campaign and his eighth trip to the Pro Bowl in 2001 with the Ravens.

Over his 14-year NFL career, Sharpe played 204 regular-season games and had 815 receptions for 10,060 yards (12.3 average) with 62 touchdowns. Sharpe owns more receptions, receiving yards, receiving touchdowns, Super Bowl wins, and Pro Bowl selections than any of the other seven tight ends enshrined in the Pro Football Hall of Fame.

Selected by the Broncos in the seventh round (192nd overall) of the 1990 NFL Draft from Savannah State University, Sharpe was named the first-team tight end on the NFL 1990s All-Decade Team, as chosen by the Hall of Fame Selection Committee.

Sharpe's Denver Broncos Career Record

Games	Starts	Rec.	Yds.	Avg.	LG	TD
172	139	675	8,439	12.5	82t	55

Sharpe's NFL Career Record

Games	Starts	Rec.	Yds.	Avg.	LG	TD
204	169	815	10,060	12.3	82t	62

This banner from the Broncos-Patriots 50-year AFL anniversary "throwback" game in 2009 commemorates the cover art from the very first AFL program, between Denver at Boston on September 9, 1960, the first regular-season game in AFL history.

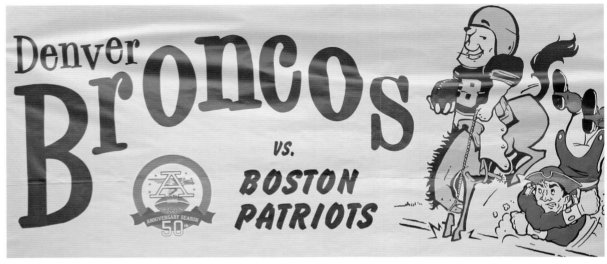

The Broncos and Patriots wore throwback uniforms for that game, and it was particularly significant for the Broncos, giving new generations of Denver fans a live look at the team's original uniform worn in 1960 and 1961.

to 6-0 on the season. It marked just the 11th time in NFL history and just the 6th since the AFL-NFL merger that a player had accomplished that feat in a game. The 6-0 start tied McDaniels for the third-best start by a rookie head coach since 1930, while joining Red Miller (1977) as only the second head coach in Denver history to win his first six games with the club.

But it quickly went downhill from there for McDaniels.

The Broncos won just two games the entire rest of the season. Individual honors, such as Dumervil setting a new single-season club sack record with 17, were the biggest highlights by season's end.

Denver finished with an 8-8 record following a 44-24 loss to the Kansas City Chiefs in the finale. Cornerback Champ Bailey, tackle Ryan Clady, safety Brian Dawkins, defensive end Elvis Dumervil, and wide receiver Brandon Marshall were chosen for the Pro Bowl, but the natives were restless. There were strong sentiments from fans and the media that the young head coach was in over his head. The tickets were sold, but the grumbling was loud.

In one of the most remarkable end-of-game plays in Broncos history, fan favorite Brandon Stokley caught a deflected pass and dashed 87 yards for the game-winning touchdown on opening day of the 2009 season at Cincinnati.

Below: Left tackle Ryan Clady is one of just four offensive linemen in NFL history to start every game and make three Pro Bowls in his first five seasons. He was one of five Bronco Pro Bowlers in 2009.

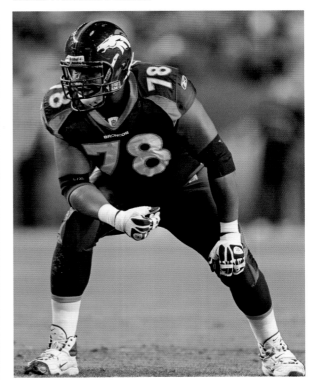

2000s

DENVER BRONCOS
YEAR BY YEAR

2000	11-5
2001	8-8
2002	9-7
2003	10-6
2004	10-6
2005	13-3
2006	9-7
2007	7-9
2008	8-8
2009	8-8

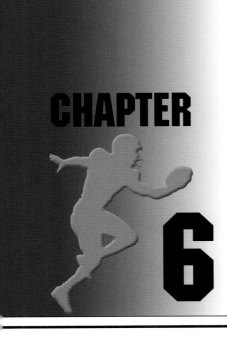

CHAPTER 6

THE 2010S
FROM LOW EBB TO AN AMAZING NEW ERA

The Broncos played their first regular-season game on foreign soil when they faced the San Francisco 49ers before 83,941 fans at London's Wembley Stadium on October 31, 2010.

TEBOWING INTO THE PLAYOFFS

The new decade began with one of the greatest moments ever for longtime fans, as running back Floyd Little was elected to the Pro Football Hall of Fame, joining John Elway and Gary Zimmerman as one of three Hall of Famers who spent major portions of their careers with the

Broncos. It was the culmination of a long but rewarding process for Little, the Broncos, and their legions of fans.

But the 2010 season was a grim one, with discontent growing at a rapid pace. The Broncos played their first regular-season game on foreign soil when they dropped a 24-16 decision to the San Francisco 49ers in London

as part of the NFL's International Series. That loss to San Francisco was the fourth straight for McDaniels, who saw his team go 5-17 over his final 22 games.

On December 6, with that record and a trail of embarrassing moments for the franchise, McDaniels was relieved of his duties as head coach of the Broncos. Eric Studesville, who tutored the running backs in his first season with the Broncos, took over as interim head coach for the season's final four games, and he did a commendable job restoring order, respect, and popularity.

No one could have predicted what would lie ahead.

Rookie quarterback Tim Tebow made his first career start in a 39-23 loss against Oakland, but he finished with the highest passer rating (100.5) by a Broncos rookie making his first NFL start. He added 78 yards rushing to mark the third-highest rushing total by a quarterback in team history. Wide receiver Brandon Lloyd was named to the Pro Bowl after finishing the season as the first Bronco ever to lead the NFL in receiving yards (1,448).

On January 2, 2011, Denver concluded the regular season with a 4-12 record. Three days later, owner Pat Bowlen took the dramatic step of naming Hall of Fame quarterback John Elway as executive vice president of football operations. Choosing to step back from the grueling role of running the Broncos on a daily basis, Bowlen also appointed Joe Ellis as president of the

The triumvirate of John Elway, Pat Bowlen, and John Fox pose at the press conference announcing Fox as Denver's new head coach. Bowlen's dramatic move to hire Elway as head of football operations put an immediate charge into the entire organization and fan base.

Eric Studesville did a fine job as interim head coach for the last four games of 2010, helping the Broncos take the first steps back toward stability and earning respect from Broncos Country.

Tim Tebow runs for the winning touchdown as the Broncos defeat Houston, 24-23, in his 2010 rookie season. Tebow scored 12 rushing touchdowns and added 17 scoring passes in his two years with the Broncos, leading them to the AFC West title in 2011.

Tebow often would drop to a knee to pray on the sidelines. "Tebowing" rapidly became an international phenomenon in 2011, spurred on by network television and the social media.

Broncos, giving him complete control over all aspects of the organization.

Elway quickly infused the team with a winning culture and a positive approach toward building a championship team. His first major decision was to hire widely respected NFL veteran John Fox as the 14th head coach in team history, on January 13, 2011.

Like Elway, Fox proved to be a perfect fit for the Broncos.

In all, it was an eventful offseason for Denver fans. Shannon Sharpe was elected to the Pro Football Hall of Fame, the stadium was renamed Sports Authority Field at Mile High, and Elway began to put his winning stamp on the organization from the front office.

Elway showed his aptitude for player evaluation with his very first draft, as his 2011 rookie class accounted for the second-highest number of starts (56) in the league. Linebacker Von Miller was named the Associated Press NFL Defensive Rookie of the Year—the first Broncos player to win the award since linebacker Mike Croel in 1991—after being the highest draft choice in team history as the second overall selection.

Elway's impact was proving to be enormous, but on the playing field, 2011 was most memorable for being all about Tim Tebow.

A number-one draft choice by McDaniels, Tebow had an entirely different style of play from the typical NFL quarterback and had mostly languished on the bench in Denver in 2010. But the fans were calling for him.

Orton was replaced by Tebow at halftime during the Broncos' 29-24 loss to the San Diego Chargers on October 9, 2011.

The Broncos were 1-4 at that point, and the team and its fan base both needed a boost. Tebow's style was completely unconventional, but he went on to lead the Broncos to a 7-4 record down the stretch—including six consecutive wins at one point—as a starter.

Despite a pass completion figure of just 46.5 percent, Tebow featured the running dimension as an integral part of his game and pounded away for 660 yards on the ground. He accounted for 18 touchdowns, 6 rushing and 12 passing. Tebow also gave new meaning to the last-minute comeback with his six straight wins, each one delivered in a seemingly more dramatic manner.

Tebow was a polarizing figure known for his fervent religious beliefs and community involvement, while also being widely criticized by many football people for his unconventional play, particularly as a passer.

But there was no question that he rejuvenated Bronco fans and gave them new hope at a low point in team history. He became a national and even international phenomenon, introducing "Tebowing" into popular culture—a reference to his habit of dropping to one knee and placing his head against his fist to pray.

One of the most dramatic endings in NFL playoff history was the 80-yard touchdown reception by Demaryius Thomas against the Steelers in the 2011 Wild Card game. It was the first playoff game in NFL history to be decided on the first play from scrimmage in overtime.

Denver captured its first AFC West title and post-season berth in six seasons, and the Broncos set a team record with 2,632 rushing yards in 2011.

In one of the most dramatic home playoff games in team history, Tebow found wide receiver Demaryius Thomas for an 80-yard touchdown on the first play of overtime to give Denver a 29-23 win over the Pittsburgh Steelers in their AFC Wild Card matchup. John Fox became just the third head coach since the 1970 merger to take over a team with four or fewer victories the season before and lead it to a division title and a playoff win

in his first season. The Broncos fell to the New England Patriots 45-10 to end their 2011 season, but fans were left with high hopes for the year ahead.

Bailey, Dumervil, and Miller were named to the Pro Bowl, Miller just the second Broncos rookie to be selected to the league's annual All-Star Game. Ryan Clady and running back Willis McGahee also played in the game, McGahee after rushing for 1,199 yards.

Things were looking up, and Elway was about to give new meaning to "up."

MANNING BRINGS SUPERSTARDOM BACK TO DENVER

In free agency, Elway executed arguably the highest-profile signing in NFL history when quarterback Peyton Manning, the league's only four-time MVP, signed with the Broncos on March 21, 2012. If there was any way for Broncomania to reach an even greater fever pitch, the Manning signing accomplished it.

Manning came to Denver with an unprecedented record in NFL annals—how do you say number one among greats? That was the status he brought to Denver.

A 43rd consecutive year of home sellouts was assured—in fact, Denver would go on to set a new home attendance record in 2012. Tebow, meanwhile, was traded to the New York Jets.

Adding to the euphoria in the Mile High City, the Broncos in 2012 returned to orange as their primary jersey color and announced that former wide receiver Rod Smith, one of the most respected Broncos ever, had been selected as the 23rd member of the Denver Broncos Ring of Fame.

The bond between Elway and Manning as Hall of Fame quarterbacks cannot be overstated as a factor in Manning's final decision to choose Denver. In fact, Peyton Manning's contract with the Broncos is the only one in NFL history to have the signatures of two present or future Hall of Fame quarterbacks, Elway as team executive and Manning as player.

Elway also brought in key veteran free agents to a

The greatest free-agent signing in NFL history is made official as Peyton Manning inks his Bronco pact. This contract is the only one ever to bear the signatures of two Hall of Fame quarterbacks, present member Elway and future member Manning.

mix that included another good draft class. By the end of the 2012 season, 33 different players started at least one game for Denver, and 23 of those starters were brought in by Elway.

The year blended individual and team greatness, extraordinary frustration, and the promise of things to come.

Manning capped his Broncos regular-season debut by delivering a comeback win for the club in a 31-19 victory over the Pittsburgh Steelers in the 2012 season opener. Appearing in his first game after sitting out the entire 2011 season due to injury, Manning became just the third player in NFL history to reach 400 career passing touchdowns, with the historic throw coming on a 71-yard pass to Demaryius Thomas. Denver put up 17 unanswered points to seal the win, capped by a 43-yard pick-six by cornerback Tracy Porter.

The next week at Atlanta, in front of a crowd of 70,427 at the Georgia Dome and a national Monday Night Football television audience, Denver mounted a fourth-quarter rally, but four early turnovers proved too much to overcome and the Broncos lost to the Falcons, 27-21. Atlanta handed Denver its first loss of 2012, and the team would falter to 2-3 against tough competition before righting the ship in a big way.

Manning crossed the 300-yard passing threshold for the first time as a Bronco and for an NFL-record 64th time in his career the following week against Houston. Again the Broncos mounted a fourth-quarter comeback that ended short of the win, falling to the Texans by a final score of 31-25.

But the Broncos earned their biggest win against their AFC West Division rival in 50 years and snapped a two-game losing streak in their 37-6 win against the Oakland Raiders the following week.

Manning and the Denver offense clicked the entire afternoon, as the Broncos became just the eighth team in NFL history to post a 30-plus-point win without the benefit of a takeaway. The home fans were ecstatic as the Broncos dominated the second half, outscoring the Raiders 27-0 to end the game. Denver produced touchdowns on all three offensive possessions in the third quarter and scored on five straight drives overall during the second half in a dominating 37-6 victory.

The Denver Broncos executed another late rally but ultimately couldn't overcome a 24-point second-half deficit in an eventual 31-21 loss to the New England Patriots in front at Gillette Stadium.

The Patriots forced three fumbles on defense and totaled a franchise-best 35 first downs on offense to keep Denver's offense off the field for much of the game. Everyone felt that the Broncos had to survive a tough early season schedule to challenge for the playoffs, and now they faced another tough road game at traditional rival San Diego.

Above: Manning led the Broncos to a Sunday Night Football win over the Steelers to start what would be a Comeback Player of the Year season for the 12-time Pro Bowler. He shattered virtually every significant Bronco passing record in his first season wearing orange and blue.

Right: The popular Eric Decker celebrates a touchdown with Denver fans during the 37-6 win over the Raiders. Decker's 21 reception touchdowns over the 2011 and 2012 seasons are the highest two-year total by any receiver in Bronco history.

It was a must-win game, it was Monday Night Football on the road, and the Broncos used that venue to make NFL history. The Broncos matched the largest comeback in franchise history and knotted the AFC West race with a historic 35-24 victory over the division-rival Chargers before that national audience.

Trailing 24-0 at halftime, the Broncos stormed back with five unanswered touchdowns, including two defensive scores and strikes from quarterback Peyton Manning to three different receivers. Manning engineered his 47th career game-winning drive in the fourth quarter or overtime, passing for 309 yards, his fourth consecutive 300-yard game and the 67th in his career, extending his league record.

On defense, Denver harassed San Diego quarterback Philip Rivers throughout the evening, picking him off a career-high four times and forcing six total turnovers. Second-year cornerback Chris Harris recorded two of the interceptions and returned one for a touchdown, and fellow cornerback Tony Carter added another defensive score with a 65-yard fumble return.

San Diego led 24-14 entering the final frame, but Denver's momentum continued as Manning capped a

One more hurrah for Rod Smith, acknowledging the fans at his Ring of Fame induction ceremony. His attire says it all—Rod Smith was orange and blue, a great team player whose proudest accomplishment was winning.

ROD SMITH
WIDE RECEIVER
1995–2007

Rod Smith, the franchise's all-time leading receiver, was elected to the Denver Broncos Ring of Fame in 2012. A three-time Pro Bowl selection (2000–2001, 2005), Smith played 183 regular-season games (158 starts) over 12 seasons while setting club records for receptions (849), receiving yards (11,389), and receiving touchdowns (68). He also set the team's career postseason receiving marks with 49 catches for 860 yards and six touchdowns in 13 playoff games, including Denver's back-to-back Super Bowl championships following the 1997 and 1998 seasons.

Originally signed by the Broncos as a college free agent from Division II Missouri Southern University in 1994, Smith spent his rookie season on Denver's practice squad. His first NFL reception came against the Washington Redskins on September 17, 1995, on a 43-yard catch from quarterback John Elway as time expired, giving the Broncos a dramatic 38-31 victory.

Smith eclipsed the 1,000-yard receiving mark in six consecutive seasons (1997–2002) and in a club-record eight seasons overall (also in 2004 and 2005). His career totals feature a franchise-best 30 100-yard receiving games in the regular season, including in a career-high eight contests during the 2000 season.

Following his final game as a Bronco at the conclusion of the 2006 regular season, Smith was ranked 11th in NFL history in career receptions (849), 17th in career receiving yards (11,389), and tied for 30th in career receiving touchdowns (68). His string of posting 70 or more catches for nine consecutive seasons (1997–2005) is tied for the second-longest streak in NFL history, and his career reception, receiving yardage, and reception touchdown totals still lead all undrafted wide receivers in league annals.

Smith's Denver Broncos Career Record

Games	Starts	Rec.	Yds.	Avg.	LG	TD
183	158	849	11,389	13.4	85t	68

Sideline reaction tells the story as cornerback Chris Harris returns this interception for a score at San Diego in one of the greatest Monday Night Football games ever. Denver overcame a 24-0 halftime deficit to beat the Chargers 35-24 and start an 11-game winning streak.

quick scoring drive with a seven-yard pass to Eric Decker. After Carter made another big play by picking off Rivers at midfield, Manning hit Brandon Stokley from 21 yards out to cap a four-play series that gave Denver a lead it would not relinquish. Harris recorded his first interception on the Chargers' next possession, but the Broncos' offense was unable to score off the turnover. After a Denver punt, Harris picked off Rivers again and took care of business himself, racing to the end zone from 46 yards out to seal the win for the Broncos. This game marked the only one in NFL history in which a team that trailed by 24 points went on to win by double digits.

Rejuvenated by the big win in San Diego and by the annual bye week, the Broncos returned home to string together consecutive wins for the first time in 2012 as they defeated the New Orleans Saints 34-14 before another national audience, this one on Sunday Night Football. Manning passed for more than 300 yards for a team-record fifth consecutive game while a strong running game complemented the Broncos' aerial display, led by tailback Willis McGahee, who had 122 yards.

Denver seized sole possession of first place in the AFC West with a 34-14 win and had won two straight.

For the Broncos, the winning was just beginning.

The team earned its second straight road victory and third consecutive win overall at Cincinnati, 31-23, as all three phases of the game were clicking for a Denver team that looked to maintain its lead in the AFC West. Manning orchestrated his NFL-record 48th game-winning drive in the fourth quarter and improved to 8-0 in his career against the Bengals.

Denver's special teams provided a spark to begin the second half as Trindon Holliday—the shortest player in Broncos history at just 5-foot-5—took the opening kick-off and returned it 105 yards for a score to mark the longest play in team history and give Denver a 17-3 lead. The game went back and forth until Manning's one-yard game-clinching scoring strike in Denver's eventual 31-23 win.

Three straight wins and on the road again, this time to Charlotte, a city with which Head Coach John Fox had plenty of familiarity in his nine years coaching the Panthers.

The Broncos gave Coach Fox a happy homecoming and began the second half of their season with a 36-14 win over the Carolina Panthers, and everyone in America was taking note of how well the Broncos were playing. All three phases of the team reached the end zone in the Broncos' most complete all-around performance of the year. Manning's scoring strike to wide receiver Stokley was the 420th of Manning's career, tying him with Dan Marino for second all-time. The Broncos' signal-caller also earned his 147th career win, pulling even with Marino for third in league annals. The Broncos sacked Cam Newton seven times on the afternoon, and Holliday continued to prove his value, scoring on a 76-yard punt return to mark his second special-teams touchdown in as many weeks.

The Broncos were sizzling when they returned home for the rematch with San Diego, and the Denver defense quickly set the pace by limiting the Chargers to 277 yards of total offense and forcing three takeaways en route to a 30-23 win. Denver had four quarterback sacks on the afternoon, including three takedowns from brilliant second-year linebacker Von Miller, to sweep the season series from their AFC West rivals for the first time since 2005. Miller was making a strong case for Defensive Player of the Year consideration. The defense was at its best in the clutch, stopping the Chargers on their first 11 third-down attempts of the game.

Meanwhile, Manning reached two more personal milestones. The Broncos' signal-caller earned his 148th career win as a starter to tie John Elway for second on the all-time list.

Manning also threw three touchdown passes during the game to raise his lifetime mark to 423, taking sole possession of second place from Dan Marino. The trio of scores represented the sixth time he totaled three touchdown passes to set a franchise single-season mark, and the Broncos had won five in a row.

The following week Denver's defense held Kansas City out of the end zone as the Broncos opened up a four-game lead in the AFC West to earn their sixth consecutive victory in a 17-9 decision at Arrowhead Stadium. With the win over the Chiefs, the Broncos improved to 4-0 in AFC West play to secure their first winning record inside the division since 2005, when the team reached the AFC Championship Game. Every week, Manning did something new to the record books, and at KC he earned his 149th win and passed his boss John Elway for second place on the NFL's all-time list.

Manning threw touchdown passes to wide receiver Demaryius Thomas and tight end Jacob Tamme to bring his season total to 26 and extend his NFL record for seasons with at least 25 passing touchdowns to 14.

Every week there were new stats—Monday Morning Manning was a vital part of every game summary.

It was obvious that the Broncos were not going to be denied in their bid for postseason play. The previous year with Tebow had been a magical one, six straight wins in crazy manners as the final gun sounded, but the 2012 Broncos under Manning bore no comparison to

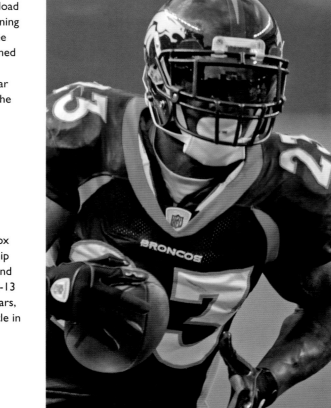

Left: The Broncos counted on and got a heavy workload of professionalism as running back from Willis McGahee in 2011 and 2012. He gained over 2,200 yards from scrimmage in the two-year span and was named to the 2011 Pro Bowl team.

Right: Head coach John Fox brought veteran leadership to the Broncos sideline and produced a combined 22-13 record in his first two years, winning the AFC West title in both 2011 and 2012.

the team's previous edition. And it was not just Manning; Denver's defense had grown to the point that it would end the season ranked second in the NFL in yards allowed and first in the league in sacks.

The team clinched its second consecutive AFC West title, defeating the Tampa Bay Buccaneers 31-23, behind a strong defensive performance and the usual record-setting day from Manning.

Denver's 12th AFC West crown tied Oakland for the most all-time and ushered Fox into an exclusive club of 10 NFL head coaches to win division championships in each of their first two years with a team.

Linebacker Von Miller's play continued to glow with six tackles, one sack, and his first career interception, which he returned 26 yards for a touchdown. Manning tossed two scoring passes to Thomas, the first of which brought Manning's season total to 28 to set a franchise record.

But just to add some spice to the offensive stew, the Broncos jumped out to a quick lead as Manning culminated their first touchdown drive with a short toss to Eaton, Colorado, native and defensive lineman Mitch Unrein, who was eligible on the play.

Seven straight wins, and on to Oakland.

The Broncos' ground game supported a strong aerial attack as the newly crowned AFC West champions completed a season sweep of a division opponent for the second time in 2012 with a 26-13 win over the Raiders in Oakland. Tailback Knowshon Moreno rushed for 119 yards and one touchdown on a career-high 32 carries, crossing the century mark for the third time in his career. Manning did the routine—for him—completing the 5,000th pass of his career and becoming just the second player in NFL history to connect on 5,000 attempts. Kicker Matt Prater was perfect on four field-goal attempts for Denver to match a career best, and Denver ran out the clock to earn its eighth consecutive victory. It is really hard to win in the NFL, and especially so on the road. But Manning and the Broncos were making it look easy.

The next week they earned their first-ever road win against the Baltimore Ravens, holding the home team without a touchdown through the first three quarters in a 34-17 win, with the defense getting a pair of takeaways that led to 10 points. Denver's defense sacked Baltimore quarterback Joe Flacco three times and limited the Ravens to just 56 rushing yards, while Manning topped 4,000 yards passing on the year for the 12th time in his legendary career. Decker was Manning's primary target on the afternoon, hauling in eight passes for 133 yards and his ninth touchdown of the season to set a career high.

Baltimore threatened to score just before halftime, but cornerback Chris Harris swung the momentum in Denver's favor by stepping in front of Ravens receiver

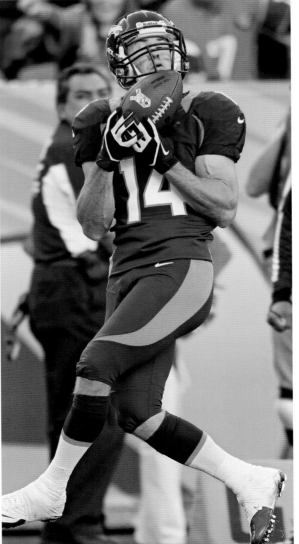

Above: Manning prepares to take a snap from center Dan Koppen. Manning directed his ninth 12-win season and was named AFC Offensive Player of the Year by the Kansas City 101 Club for a record seventh time in 2012.

Left: Stokley was an ideal fit as the slot receiver for the Broncos in 2012, and his experience working with Manning showed in a fine season that resulted in 45 receptions and five touchdowns. Stokley was also an excellent mentor for the team's younger receivers.

Linebacker Von Miller was the NFL Defensive Rookie of the Year in 2011 and was runner-up for Defensive Player of the Year in 2012. He made the Pro Bowl both seasons, becoming the first Bronco ever to earn that honor in each of his first two years.

all of its division contests. Winning streaks are nothing new to Peyton Manning. In his career, combining Denver and Indianapolis, he has now had a winning streak of 10 games or longer in a single season four times.

Denver outgained Kansas City 488-119 to represent the third-largest total yardage margin in a single game in Bronco history. On offense, Manning completed 23 of 29 passes for 304 yards and three touchdowns (a 144.8 passer rating), setting team standards for yards (4,659) and completions (400) while extending his team record with his 37th touchdown pass. Two of Manning's scoring tosses went to Decker, who topped 1,000 yards on the season and ended the year with 13 touchdown grabs. Thomas and Decker each topped the 1,000-yard reception threshold for the Broncos.

But regular seasons and streaks end, and there is truth in the cliché that the playoffs are a whole new season.

The number-one-seeded Broncos played the fourth-longest game in NFL history, falling in the end to the eventual world-champion Baltimore Ravens 38-35 in the second overtime in front of 76,732 fans at Sports Authority Field at Mile High. Despite a temperature of 13 degrees at kickoff, marking the coldest postseason game in Broncos history, the teams combined for 877 yards and 73 points in the thriller. Special teams played a key role for the Broncos early on as midseason acquisition Trindon Holliday returned his first punt 90 yards for a touchdown to give Denver an early 7-0 advantage.

Manning completed 28 of 43 passes for 290 yards and three touchdowns with two interceptions on the day, but both picks led to Baltimore scores.

Tied at 14 after one quarter, the teams traded touchdown passes in the second frame. Holliday swung the momentum in Denver's favor again by taking the opening second-half kickoff 104 yards for a touchdown to become the first player in NFL history to score a touchdown on a punt return and a kickoff return in the same game.

Thomas caught a 17-yard touchdown pass from Manning with 7:18 remaining, capping a magnificent 88-yard drive, and Denver stopped Baltimore on fourth down on its ensuing possession, but Flacco was able to hit wide receiver Jacoby Jones for a 70-yard touchdown with 31 seconds remaining to send the game into overtime. The teams battled through a scoreless first overtime, but after Manning threw an interception near midfield at the end of the fifth frame, the Ravens ended Denver's season with a 47-yard field goal.

This was a level of frustration and disappointment for the Broncos and their multitudes not experienced since that infamous loss to Jacksonville in 1996. It was a crushing end to the dreams of 2012.

But it still was a season of exhilaration for fans and of highs for so many players. Thomas had 94 catches for 1,434 yards and 10 scores, Decker had 85 receptions

Anquan Boldin at the Broncos' two-yard line and racing 98 yards the other way for a touchdown. The pick-six was Harris' second of the season, following his 46-yard score that sealed Denver's Week 6 win in San Diego.

The Broncos extended their winning streak to 10 games and earned a season sweep of their four AFC North opponents with a 34-12 victory over the Cleveland Browns at home. They followed that up by securing the number-one seed in the AFC playoffs and completing a season sweep of their three division foes with a 38-3 win over the Kansas City Chiefs before 76,502 playoff-crazed fans at Sports Authority Field at Mile High.

The Broncos' 11th consecutive win gave them a perfect 6-0 record in AFC West games, marking just the second time in franchise history that Denver won

for 1,064 yards and 13 scores, and the tight ends pitched in as well—Jacob Tamme had 52 receptions, while Fort Morgan, Colorado, native Joel Dreessen had 41 catches and scored 5 times. Stokley caught 45 passes and also scored 5 times. Miller set a new team sack record with 18.5 and had 30 total in his first two years, the most in Denver history.

Seven Broncos received Pro Bowl honors at season's end, including Bailey, Clady, Dumervil, Manning, Miller, Thomas, and guard Zane Beadles. Bailey became the first NFL defensive back to be named 12 times, and Manning also was named for the 12th time, the most by a quarterback in history in addition to becoming the first quarterback to be selected after missing the previous year due to injury. Manning also is the 14th player ever (and the only quarterback) to make 10 consecutive Pro

Bowls in years he played.

The league's active leader in nearly every passing category, Manning was named the Associated Press Comeback Player of the Year and finished second in the MVP voting. He was also named the winner of the prestigious Kansas City 101 Club AFC Offensive Player of the Year award, his seventh time winning that honor. He set Bronco single-season records in nearly every major passing category in 2012, including completions (400), completion percentage (68.2), passing yards (4,659), touchdown passes (37), and passer rating (105.8).

The Broncos in 2013 will again be led by the quarterback who is second all-time in passing touchdowns (436) and third in passing yards (59,487), and who has the most wins (154) by a quarterback in NFL history, including a league-record 12 double-digit win seasons.

This spectacular one-handed touchdown catch against the Chiefs was just one of Demaryius Thomas' 10 scoring receptions in 2012. Thomas played in the Pro Bowl following a breakthrough season in which he finished with 94 pass receptions.

Left: One of the NFL's best pass rushers, Elvis Dumervil records a quarterback sack against the Browns in late December 2012. Dumervil was named to the Pro Bowl for the third time in 2012 and had 11 sacks to raise his career total to 63.5.

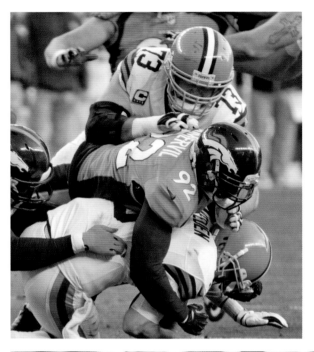

Right: The only multiple-decade franchise owner in Denver sports history, Pat Bowlen celebrates his 30th year as owner of the Denver Broncos in 2013. His 276 regular-season wins and five Super Bowl appearances both rank second in the NFL during his brilliant tenure.

Hats off to the fans! The 2012 season marked the 43rd straight sellout campaign for the Broncos, one of the longest streaks in NFL history and by far the longest of any original AFL franchise. From the original Bears Stadium to the latest incarnation of Sports Authority Field at Mile High, Denver fans have always loved coming out to cheer for their Broncos.

Manning owns the most 4,000-yard passing seasons (12) and is the only player ever to throw for more than 3,000 yards in each of his first 13 NFL seasons.

This talented team gives Bronco fans plenty to look forward to in the future.

The Broncos made a number of roster changes as they prepared for the 2013 season, most notably the addition of wide receiver Wesley Welker. Welker joined the Broncos as a free agent after six seasons in New England. He had more receptions in that six-year period than any receiver in NFL history and had an astonishing five 100-catch campaigns to go along with five Pro Bowl appearances.

And while free agency brings in new players, it also results in departures. After a fine six-year career with the Broncos, Elvis Dumervil signed with the Baltimore Ravens.

The 2013 season marks Pat Bowlen's 30th as owner of the Broncos, and he enters the new season presiding over a franchise that is one of the crown jewels among NFL clubs. By any definition, the Broncos are at the pinnacle of professional sports teams. His 30-year tenure of ownership is indelibly stamped as one of the most successful periods for any team in NFL history.

The team's fan following is as strong as ever, with season ticket holders from all 50 states as well as Canada, Spain, and the United Kingdom. Every game continues to be an event for the orange and blue faithful, as the Broncos set their all-time home attendance record in 2013 with an amazing 613,062, and some of those fans come to every game from as far away as Arkansas, Pennsylvania, and Maryland.

The orange-clad frenzy does not end within the confines of Sports Authority Field at Mile High either, as America's television networks long ago became captivated by the sunshine, mountain vistas, and sea of orange and blue on display at Denver's home venue. The Broncos will have their 44th straight sellout season in 2013 and they come into it with a 21-year streak of being on Monday Night Football, longest active streak in the NFL. Denver has been featured on 285 nationally televised games during the Bowlen era of ownership.

Broncos Country is more than a place. It's a state of mind represented not only by a frenzied audience at a home game, but also by a bumper sticker on an old pickup truck in Montana or a flag planted by a rabid Denver fan at the South Pole. The Broncos are in their sixth decade of existence as a driving emotional force within the city of Denver and the state of Colorado. They live in Broncos Country, a region that is not defined merely by geography but by the raw and passionate commitment of football's greatest fans.

Armed and dangerous. The greatest quarterback of his generation looks downfield for an open receiver. Manning's 48 game-winning drives in the fourth quarter or overtime are the most in football history since the NFL merger.

2010s
DENVER BRONCOS
YEAR BY YEAR

2010	4-12
2011	8-8
2012	13-3

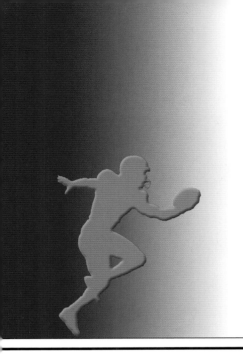

APPENDIX
DENVER BRONCOS RECORD BOOK
THROUGH THE 2012 SEASON

PLAYER RECORDS

Service
Seasons

16	John Elway, 1983–1998
15	Jason Elam, 1993–2007
14	Tom Jackson, 1973–1986
14	Tom Nalen, 1994–2007
14	Dennis Smith, 1981–1994

Games

236	Jason Elam, 1993–2007
234	John Elway, 1983–1998
194	Tom Nalen, 1994–2007
191	Tom Jackson, 1973–1986
187	Paul Howard, 1973–1975, 1977–1986

Starts

231	John Elway, 1983–1998
188	Tom Nalen, 1994–2007
178	Bill Thompson, 1969–1981
177	Barney Chavous, 1973–1985
170	Dennis Smith, 1981–1994

Consecutive Games

172	Simon Fletcher, 1985–1995
166	Ken Lanier, 1981–1992
156	Bill Thompson, 1971–1981

OFFENSE

Scoring
Most Points Scored
Career

1,786	Jason Elam, 1993–2007
742	Jim Turner, 1971–1979
655	Rich Karlis, 1982–1988
532	Matt Prater, 2007–2012
429	David Treadwell, 1989–1992

Season

138	Terrell Davis, 1998
137	Gene Mingo, 1962
133	Matt Prater, 2012
132	Jason Elam, 1995
129	Jason Elam, 2004

Game

30	Clinton Portis, vs. Kansas City, 12/7/2003
24	Clinton Portis, vs. Kansas City, 12/15/2002
24	Mike Anderson, at New Orleans, 12/3/2000
21	Gene Mingo, at L.A. Chargers, 12/10/1960
20	Bob Scarpitto, at Buffalo, 12/18/1966
20	Gene Mingo, vs. San Diego, 10/6/1963

Touchdowns Scored
Career

71	Rod Smith, 1995–2007 (1 rush, 68 rec., 2 ret.)
65	Terrell Davis, 1995–2002 (60 rush, 5 rec.)
55	Shannon Sharpe, 1990–1998, 2002–2003 (55 rec.)
54	Floyd Little, 1967–1975 (43 rush, 9 rec., 2 ret.)
48	Sammy Winder, 1982–1990 (39 rush, 9 rec.)

Season

23	Terrell Davis, 1998 (21 rush, 2 rec.)
17	Clinton Portis, 2002 (15 rush, 2 rec.)
15	Mike Anderson, 2000 (15 rush)
15	Terrell Davis, 1997 (15 rush)
15	Terrell Davis, 1996 (13 rush, 2 rec.)

Game

5	Clinton Portis, vs. Kansas City, 12/7/2003
4	Clinton Portis, vs. Kansas City, 12/15/2002
4	Mike Anderson, at New Orleans, 12/3/2000
3	28 times (last: Javon Walker, at Pittsburgh, 11/5/2006)

Total Yards
Combined Passing, Rushing, and Receiving Attempts
Career

8,543	John Elway, 1983–1998
1,961	Brian Griese, 1998–2002
1,887	Craig Morton, 1977–1982
1,866	Floyd Little, 1967–1975
1,846	Jake Plummer, 2003–2006

Season

693	John Elway, 1985
634	John Elway, 1993
605	John Elway, 1995
598	Jake Plummer, 2004
598	John Elway, 1994

Game

68	John Elway, at Green Bay, 10/10/1993
64	Gus Frerotte, vs. San Diego, 11/19/2000
60	Mickey Slaughter, at Houston, 12/20/1994
59	Frank Tripucka, at Buffalo, 9/15/1962
58	Brian Griese, at Baltimore, 9/30/2002

Combined Rushing and Passing Yardage
Career

54,882	John Elway, 1983–1998 (3,407 rush, 51,475 pass)
12,301	Jake Plummer, 2003–2006 (670 rush, 11,631 pass)
12,279	Brian Griese, 1998–2002 (516 rush, 11,763 pass)
12,155	Craig Morton, 1977–1982 (260 rush, 11,895 pass)
9,447	Jay Cutler, 2006–2008 (423 rush, 9,024 pass)

Season

4,726	Jay Cutler, 2008 (200 rush, 4,526 pass)
4,665	Peyton Manning, 2012 (6 rush, 4,659 pass)
4,291	Jake Plummer, 2004 (202 rush, 4,089 pass)
4,183	John Elway, 1993 (153 rush, 4,030 pass)
4,146	John Elway, 1995 (176 rush, 3,970 pass)

Game

504	Jake Plummer, vs. Atlanta, 10/31/2004 (5 rush, 499 pass)
487	Kyle Orton, vs. Indianapolis, 9/26/2010 (11 rush, 476 pass)
476	Jay Cutler, at Cleveland, 11/6/2008 (29 rush, 447 pass)
458	Gus Frerotte, vs. San Diego, 11/19/2000 (-4 rush, 462 pass)
447	Frank Tripucka, at Buffalo, 9/15/1962 (0 rush, 447 pass)

Combined Rushing, Receiving, and Return Yardage
Career

12,488	Rod Smith, 1995–2007 (348 rush, 11,389 rec., 751 ret.)
12,173	Floyd Little, 1967–1975 (6,323 rush, 2,418 rec., 3,432 ret.)
10,081	Rick Upchurch, 1975–1983 (349 rush, 4,369 rec., 5,363 ret.)
8,880	Terrell Davis, 1995–2002 (7,607 rush, 1,280 rec., -7 ret.)
8,448	Shannon Sharpe, 1990–1999, 2002–2003 (9 rush, 8,439 rec., 0 ret.)

Season

2,225	Terrell Davis, 1998 (2,008 rush, 217 rec., 0 ret.)
2,198	Otis Armstrong, 1974 (1,407 rush, 405 rec., 386 ret.)
2,080	Glyn Milburn, 1995 (266 rush, 191 rec., 1,623 ret.)
2,037	Terrell Davis, 1997 (1,750 rush, 287 rec., 0 ret.)
1,929	Rick Upchurch, 1975 (97 rush, 436 rec., 1,396 ret.)

Game

404*	Glyn Milburn, vs. Seattle, 12/10/1995 (131 rush, 45 rec., 228 ret.)
295	Floyd Little, vs. Buffalo, 11/24/1968 (71 rush, 165 rec., 59 ret.)
290	Shane Swanson, at Kansas City, 10/18/1987 (0 rush, 87 rec., 203 ret.)
289	Otis Armstrong, vs. Pittsburgh, 9/22/1974 (131 rush, 86 rec., 72 ret.)
284	Rick Upchurch, vs. Kansas City, 9/21/1975 (13 rush, 153 rec., 118 ret.)

* NFL record

Yards from Scrimmage (Rushing and Receiving)
Career

11,737	Rod Smith, 1995–2007 (348 rush, 11,389 rec.)
8,887	Terrell Davis, 1995–2002 (7,607 rush, 1,280 rec.)
8,741	Floyd Little, 1967–1975 (6,323 rush, 2,418 rec.)

8,448	Shannon Sharpe, 1990–1999, 2002–2003 (9 rush, 8,439 rec.)
6,892	Lionel Taylor, 1960–1966 (20 rush, 6,872 rec.)

Season

2,225	Terrell Davis, 1998 (2,008 rush, 217 rec.)
2,037	Terrell Davis, 1997 (1,750 rush, 287 rec.)
1,905	Clinton Portis, 2003 (1,591 rush, 314 rec.)
1,872	Clinton Portis, 2002 (1,508 rush, 364 rec.)
1,848	Terrell Davis, 1996 (1,538 rush, 310 rec.)

Game

256	Mike Anderson, at New Orleans, 12/3/2000 (251 rush, 5 rec.)
254	Clinton Portis, vs. Kansas City, 12/7/2003 (218 rush, 36 rec.)
246	Clinton Portis, vs. Arizona, 12/29/2002 (228 rush, 18 rec.)
236	Terrell Davis, at Buffalo, 10/26/1997 (OT) (207 rush, 29 rec.)
236	Floyd Little, vs. Buffalo, 11/24/1968 (71 rush, 165 rec.)

Rushing
Attempts
Career

1,655	Terrell Davis, 1995–2002
1,641	Floyd Little, 1967–1975
1,495	Sammy Winder, 1982–1990
1,023	Otis Armstrong, 1973–1980
865	Mike Anderson, 2000–2005

Season

392	Terrell Davis, 1998
369	Terrell Davis, 1997
345	Terrell Davis, 1996
297	Mike Anderson, 2000
296	Sammy Winder, 1984

Game

42	Terrell Davis, at Buffalo, 10/26/1997 (OT)
38	Reuben Droughns, at Oakland, 10/17/2004
38	Clinton Portis, vs. Cleveland, 12/14/2003 (OT)
37	Mike Anderson, at New Orleans, 12/3/2000
37	Olandis Gary, vs. Green Bay, 10/17/1999

Yards
Career

7,607	Terrell Davis, 1995–2002
6,323	Floyd Little, 1967–1975
5,427	Sammy Winder, 1982–1990
4,453	Otis Armstrong, 1973–1980
3,822	Mike Anderson, 2000–2005

Season

2,008	Terrell Davis, 1998
1,750	Terrell Davis, 1997
1,591	Clinton Portis, 2003
1,538	Terrell Davis, 1996
1,508	Clinton Portis, 2002

Floyd Little poses on horseback to help promote the team. He didn't need much help galloping into the Bronco and pro football record books. Little retired as one of the leading running backs and is a member of the Pro Football Hall of Fame.

Game

251	Mike Anderson, at New Orleans, 12/3/2000
228	Clinton Portis, vs. Arizona, 12/29/2002
218	Clinton Portis, vs. Kansas City, 12/7/2003
215	Terrell Davis, vs. Cincinnati, 9/21/1997
208	Terrell Davis, at Seattle, 10/11/1998

Rushing Yards per Carry
Career (min. 100 carries)

5.50	Clinton Portis, 2002–2003 (563–3,099)
5.38	Tim Tebow, 2010–2011 (165–887)
5.21	Selvin Young, 2007 (140–729)
4.87	Tatum Bell, 2004–2006 (481–2,342)
4.81	Vaughn Hebron, 1996–1998 (107–515)

Season (min. 100 carries)

5.52	Clinton Portis, 2002 (273–1,508)
5.49	Clinton Portis, 2003 (290–1,591)
5.41	Tim Tebow, 2011 (122–660)
5.35	Correll Buckthaler, 2009 (120–642)
5.35	Otis Armstrong, 1974 (263–1,407)

Game (min. 8 rushes)

12.25	Gaston Green, vs. Houston, 10/18/1992 (8–98)

11.79   Clinton Portis, vs. Chicago, 11/23/2003 (14–165)
11.00   Dave Rolle, vs. Oakland, 10/2/1960 (9–99)
10.75   Clinton Portis, at San Diego, 9/14/2003 (12–129)
10.75   Tatum Bell, at San Diego, 12/28/2008 (8–86)

Rushing Touchdowns

Career
60   Terrell Davis, 1995–2002
43   Floyd Little, 1967–1975
39   Sammy Winder, 1982–1990
36   Mike Anderson, 2000–2005
33   John Elway, 1983–1998

Season
21   Terrell Davis, 1998
15   Clinton Portis, 2002
15   Mike Anderson, 2000
15   Terrell Davis, 1997
14   Clinton Portis, 2003

Game
5   Clinton Portis, vs. Kansas City, 12/7/2003
4   Mike Anderson, at New Orleans, 12/3/2000
3   11 times (last: Tatum Bell, at San Diego, 12/31/2005)

Consecutive Games with a Rushing Touchdown
8   Terrell Davis, 1998
6   Terrell Davis, 1997–1998
5   Mike Anderson, 2005
5   Terrell Davis, 1997
5   Sammy Winder, 1985

Longest Scoring Run from Scrimmage
82   Gene Mingo, vs. Oakland, 10/5/1962
80   Mike Anderson, at Seattle, 11/26/2000
80   Floyd Little, at San Francisco, 10/25/1970
72   Javon Walker, at Pittsburgh, 11/5/2006
72   Joe Dawkins, at Kansas City, 10/7/1973

Passing

Winning Percentage as Starting Quarterback (min. 25 starts)
.722   Jake Plummer, 2003–2006 (39–15)
.643   John Elway, 1983–1998 (148–82–1)
.641   Craig Morton, 1977–1982 (41–23)
.529   Brian Griese, 1998–2002 (27–24)
.524   Charley Johnson, 1972–1975 (20–18–3)

Yards
Career
51,475   John Elway, 1983–1998
11,895   Craig Morton, 1977–1982
11,763   Brian Griese, 1998–2002

11,631   Jake Plummer, 2003–2006
9,024   Jay Cutler, 2006–2008
Season
4,659   Peyton Manning, 2012
4,526   Jay Cutler, 2008
4,089   Jake Plummer, 2004
4,030   John Elway, 1993
3,970   John Elway, 1995
Game
499   Jake Plummer, vs. Atlanta, 10/31/2004 (31–55)
476   Kyle Orton, vs. Indianapolis, 9/26/2010 (37–57)
462   Gus Frerotte, vs. San Diego, 11/19/2000 (36–58)
447   Jay Cutler, at Cleveland, 11/6/2008 (24–42)
447   Frank Tripucka, at Buffalo, 9/15/1962 (29–56)

Attempts
Career
7,250   John Elway, 1983–1998
1,678   Brian Griese, 1998–2002
1,596   Jake Plummer, 2003–2006
1,594   Craig Morton, 1977–1982
1,277   Frank Tripucka, 1960–1963
Season
616   Jay Cutler, 2008
605   John Elway, 1985
583   Peyton Manning, 2012
551   John Elway, 1993
542   John Elway, 1995
Game
59   John Elway, at Green Bay, 10/10/1993
58   Gus Frerotte, vs. San Diego, 11/19/2000
57   Kyle Orton, vs. Indianapolis, 9/26/2010
56   Frank Tripucka, at Buffalo, 9/15/1962
56   Kyle Orton, vs. Kansas City, 1/3/2010

Completions
Career
4,123   John Elway, 1983–1998
1,044   Brian Griese, 1998–2002
944   Jake Plummer, 2003–2006
907   Craig Morton, 1977–1982
762   Jay Cutler, 2006–2008
Season
400   Peyton Manning, 2012
384   Jay Cutler, 2008
348   John Elway, 1993
336   Kyle Orton, 2009
327   John Elway, 1985
Game
37   Kyle Orton, vs. Indianapolis, 9/26/2010
36   Jay Cutler, at Cleveland, 11/6/2008
36   Gus Frerotte, vs. San Diego, 11/19/2000
36   John Elway, vs. San Diego, 9/4/1994

Consecutive Completions
20   Hugh Millen, 12/11/1994–12/17/1994
18   Steve DeBerg, 12/12/1982–12/19/1982

17   Brian Griese, 9/23/2001
16   Craig Morton 12/10/1978
16   Jake Plummer, 9/28/2003

Completion Percentage
Career (min. 100 attempts)
.686   Peyton Manning, 2012 (400–583)
.626   Hugh Millen, 1994–1995 (107–171)
.625   Jay Cutler, 2006–2008 (762–1,220)
.622   Brian Griese, 1998–2002 (1,044–1,678)
.603   Kyle Orton, 2009–2011 (720–1,194)
Season (min. 50 attempts)
.686   Peyton Manning, 2012 (400–583)
.667   Brian Griese, 2002 (291–436)
.643   Brian Griese, 2000 (216–336)
.636   Jay Cutler, 2007 (297–467)
.632   Norris Weese, 1978 (55–87)
Game (min. 10 attempts)
.944   Craig Morton, vs. San Diego, 9/27/1981 (17–18)
.917   John Elway, at L.A. Raiders, 11/2/1986 (11–12)
.864   Craig Morton, vs. Kansas City, 12/20/1978 (19–22)
.842   John Elway, vs. Minnesota, 11/18/1984 (16–19)
.833   Steve Ramsey, vs. Cleveland, 10/19/1975 (10–12)

Touchdown Passes
Career
300   John Elway, 1983–1998
74   Craig Morton, 1977–1982
71   Jake Plummer, 2003–2006
71   Brian Griese, 1998–2002
54   Jay Cutler, 2006–2008
Season
37   Peyton Manning, 2012
27   Jake Plummer, 2004
27   John Elway, 1997
26   John Elway, 1996
26   John Elway, 1995
Game
5   Gus Frerotte, vs. San Diego, 11/19/2000
5   John Elway, vs. Minnesota, 11/18/1984
5   Frank Tripucka, vs. Buffalo, 10/28/1962
4   23 times (last: Kyle Orton, vs. Kansas City, 11/14/10)

Consecutive Games with a Touchdown Pass
23   Brian Griese, 2001–2002
17   Kyle Orton, 2009–2010
15   John Elway, 1995–1996
13   John Elway, 1985–1986
12   John Elway, 1992–1993

Longest Touchdown Pass from Scrimmage
97   George Shaw to Jerry Tarr, at Boston, 9/21/1962
96   Frank Tripucka to Al Frazier, at Buffalo, 9/15/1962

95	Craig Morton to Steve Watson, vs. Detroit, 10/11/1981
93	Jay Cutler to Eddie Royal, at Cleveland, 11/6/2008
93	Craig Morton to Steve Watson, vs. San Diego, 9/27/1981

Most Interceptions Thrown
Career
226	John Elway, 1983–1998
85	Frank Tripucka, 1960–1963
65	Craig Morton, 1977–1982
58	Steve Ramsey, 1971–1976
53	Brian Griese, 1998–2002
Season
34	Frank Tripucka, 1960
25	Frank Tripucka, 1962
23	John Elway, 1985
22	George Herring, 1961
21	Frank Tripucka, 1961
Game
6	Don Horn, at Green Bay, 9/26/1971
6	George Herring, at Houston, 11/26/1961
5	9 times (last: John Elway, vs. Kansas City, 12/14/1985)

Interception Avoidance
Career Percentage (min. 100 attempts)
.018	Hugh Millen, 1994–1995 (3–171)
.019	Peyton Manning, 2012 (11–583)
.023	Kyle Orton, 2009–2011 (28–1,194)
.025	Tim Tebow, 2010–2011 (9–353)
.029	Gus Frerotte, 2000–2001 (8–280)
Season Percentage (min. 50 attempts)
.012	Brian Griese, 2000 (4–336)
.012	Chris Miller, 1999 (1–81)
.013	Gary Kubiak, 1984 (1–75)
.015	Jake Plummer, 2005 (7–456)
.018	Kyle Orton, 2010 (9–498)
Consecutive Passes Without an Interception
229	Jake Plummer, 2005
190	John Elway, 1997
179	Peyton Manning, 2012

Passer Rating
Career (min. 100 attempts)
105.8	Peyton Manning, 2012 (583 att.)
87.1	Jay Cutler, 2006–2008 (1,220 att.)
86.5	Bubby Brister, 1997–1999 (160 att.)
85.7	Kyle Orton, 2009–2011 (1,194 att.)
85.5	Gus Frerotte, 2000–2001 (280 att.)
Season (min. 50 passes)
105.8	Peyton Manning, 2012 (583 att.)
102.9	Brian Griese, 2000 (336 att.)
99.0	Bubby Brister, 1998 (131 att.)
93.0	John Elway, 1998 (356 att.)
92.8	John Elway, 1993 (551 att.)

Receiving
Receptions
Career
849	Rod Smith, 1995–2007
675	Shannon Sharpe, 1990–1999, 2002–2003
543	Lionel Taylor, 1960–1966
462	Ed McCaffrey, 1995–2003
415	Vance Johnson, 1985–1993, 1995
Season
113	Rod Smith, 2001
104	Brandon Marshall, 2008
102	Brandon Marshall, 2007
101	Brandon Marshall, 2009
101	Ed McCaffrey, 2000
Game
21*	Brandon Marshall, at Indianapolis, 12/13/2009
18	Brandon Marshall, vs. San Diego, 9/14/2008
14	Jabar Gaffney, vs. Kansas City, 1/3/2010
14	Rod Smith, at Arizona, 9/23/2001
13	Rod Smith, vs. New England, 10/1/2000
13	Shannon Sharpe, vs. San Diego, 10/6/1996
13	Bobby Anderson, vs. Chicago, 9/30/1973
13	Lionel Taylor, vs. Oakland, 11/29/1964
* NFL record	
Consecutive Games with a Reception
124	Rod Smith, 1999–2006
68	Ed McCaffrey, 1997–2003
62	Lionel Taylor, 1960–1964
60	Shannon Sharpe, 1995–1999
53	Brandon Marshall, 2006–2009

Receiving Yards
Career
11,389	Rod Smith, 1995–2007
8,439	Shannon Sharpe, 1990–1999, 2002–2003
6,872	Lionel Taylor, 1960–1966
6,200	Ed McCaffrey, 1995–2003
6,112	Steve Watson, 1979–1987
Season
1,602	Rod Smith, 2000
1,448	Brandon Lloyd, 2010
1,434	Demaryius Thomas, 2012
1,343	Rod Smith, 2001
1,325	Brandon Marshall, 2007
Game
214	Shannon Sharpe, at Kansas City, 10/20/2002 (OT)
213	Jabar Gaffney, vs. Kansas City, 1/3/2010
208	Rod Smith, vs. Atlanta, 10/31/2004
200	Brandon Marshall, at Indianapolis, 12/13/2009
199	Lionel Taylor, vs. Buffalo, 11/27/1960

Yards per Reception
Career (min. 50 receptions)
20.5	Bill Van Heusen, 1968–1976 (82–1,684)
18.0	Haven Moses, 1972–1981 (302–5,450)
17.9	Ashley Lelie, 2002–2005 (168–3,007)

Season (min. 20 receptions)
22.0	Bob Scarpitto, 1963 (21–463)
20.7	Steve Watson, 1981 (60–1,244)
20.3	Ricky Nattiel, 1987 (31–630)
Game (min. 4 receptions)
41.3	Floyd Little, vs. Buffalo, 11/24/1968 (4–165)
38.0	Jerry Tarr, at Boston, 9/21/1962 (4–152)
36.4	Steve Watson, vs. Detroit, 10/11/1981 (5–182)

Touchdown Receptions
Career
68	Rod Smith, 1995–2007
55	Shannon Sharpe, 1990–1999, 2002–2003
46	Ed McCaffrey, 1995–2003
44	Haven Moses, 1972–1981
44	Lionel Taylor, 1960–1966
Season
14	Anthony Miller, 1995
13	Eric Decker, 2012
13	Steve Watson, 1981
12	Rod Smith, 1997
12	Lionel Taylor, 1960

Consecutive Games with a Touchdown Reception
6	Anthony Miller, 1995
6	Vance Johnson, 1987
6	Al Denson, 1969
6	Lionel Taylor, 1960–1961

Kicking
PAT Attempts
Career
604	Jason Elam, 1993–2007
301	Jim Turner, 1971–1979
254	Rich Karlis, 1982–1988
186	Matt Prater, 2007–2012
136	David Treadwell, 1989–1992
Season
58	Jason Elam, 1998
55	Matt Prater, 2012
49	Jason Elam, 2000
46	Jason Elam, 1997
46	Jason Elam, 1996

PATs Made
Career
601	Jason Elam, 1993–2007
283	Jim Turner, 1971–1979
244	Rich Karlis, 1982–1988
184	Matt Prater, 2007–2012
132	David Treadwell, 1989–1992
Season
58	Jason Elam, 1998
55	Matt Prater, 2012
49	Jason Elam, 2000

46	Jason Elam, 1997
46	Jason Elam, 1996
44	Rich Karlis, 1986

Game

7	Matt Prater, vs. Kansas City, 11/14/2010
7	Jason Elam, vs. Philadelphia, 10/30/2005
6	Jason Elam, vs. Kansas City, 12/7/2003
6	Jason Elam, vs. Dallas, 9/13/1998

Consecutive PATs Made

371*	Jason Elam, 1993–2002
131	Jason Elam, 1992–2005
96	Matt Prater, 2010–2012
82	Rich Karlis, 1986–1988
82	Jim Turner, 1971–1973

* NFL Record

PAT Percentage

Career (min. 30 attempts)

.995	Jason Elam, 1993–2007 (601–604)
.989	Matt Prater, 2007–2012 (184–186)
.983	Gary Kroner, 1965–1967 (57–58)
.979	Bobby Howfield, 1968–1970 (93–95)
.971	Fred Steinfort, 1979–1981 (68–70)

Field Goal Attempts

Career

490	Jason Elam, 1993–2007
232	Jim Turner, 1971–1979
193	Rich Karlis, 1982–1988
144	Matt Prater, 2007–2012
127	David Treadwell, 1989–1992

Season

39	Gene Mingo, 1962
38	Jason Elam, 1995
38	Rich Karlis, 1985
38	Jim Turner, 1971
37	Jason Elam, 1994

Field Goals Made

Career

395	Jason Elam, 1993–2007
151	Jim Turner, 1971–1979
137	Rich Karlis, 1982–1988
116	Matt Prater, 2007–2012
99	David Treadwell, 1989–1992

Season

31	Jason Elam, 2001
31	Jason Elam, 1995
30	Matt Prater, 2009
30	Jason Elam, 1994
29	Jason Elam, 2004
29	Jason Elam, 1999

Game

5	Jason Elam, vs. Miami, 10/13/2002
5	Jason Elam, at Kansas City, 11/16/1997
5	Jason Elam, vs. Buffalo, 9/3/1995
5	Rich Karlis, vs. Seattle, 11/20/1983
5	Gene Mingo, vs. San Diego, 10/6/1963

Most Consecutive Games with a Field Goal

18	Jason Elam
16	Jason Elam
15	Matt Prater
15	Rich Karlis

Most Consecutive Field Goals Made

19	Jason Elam
19	Jason Elam
18	Matt Prater

Longest Field Goal

63*	Jason Elam, vs. Jacksonville, 10/25/1998
59	Matt Prater, vs. Chicago, 12/11/2012
59	Matt Prater, vs. NY Jets, 10/17/2010
57	Fred Steinfort, vs. Washington, 10/13/1980
56	Matt Prater, vs. Kansas City, 9/28/2008
56	Jason Elam, at Houston, 11/26/1995

* NFL record (tie)

Field Goal Percentage

Career (min. 20 attempts)

.806	Jason Elam, 1993–2007 (395–490)
.806	Matt Prater 2007–2012 (116–144)
.780	David Treadwell, 1989–1992 (99–127)
.710	Rich Karlis, 1982–1988 (137–193)
.672	Fred Steinfort, 1979–1981 (43–64)

Season (min. 10 attempts)

.931	Jason Elam, 2006 (27–29)
.889	Matt Prater, 2010 (16–18)
.871	Jason Elam, 2007 (27–31)
.871	Jason Elam, 2003 (27–31)
.861	Jason Elam, 2001 (31–36)

Punting

Most Punts

Career

641	Tom Rouen, 1993–2002
574	Bill Van Heusen, 1968–1976
377	Luke Prestridge, 1979–1983

Season

105	Bob Scarpitto, 1967
101	Britton Colquitt, 2011
96	Chris Norman, 1984
96	Bucky Dilts, 1978

Game

12	Luke Prestridge, at Buffalo, 10/25/1981
12	Bill Van Heusen, vs. Cincinnati, 10/6/1968
12	Bob Scarpitto, at Oakland, 9/19/1967

Net Yards per Punt (since 1976)

Career (min. 100 punts)

39.5	Britton Colquitt, 2010–2012 (254–10,025)
37.2	Todd Sauerbrun, 2005, 2007 (122–4,538)
36.5	Mike Horan, 1986–1992 (379–13,851)

Season (min. 50 punts)

42.1	Britton Colquitt, 2012 (67–2,822)
40.2	Britton Colquitt, 2011 (101–4,045)
38.9	Mike Horan, 1990 (59–2,296)

Game (min. 4 punts)

52.8	Mike Horan, vs. L.A. Raiders, 9/26/1988 (OT) (5–264)
52.3	Tom Rouen, vs. San Diego, 11/11/2001 (6–314)
52.3	Bucky Dilts, at Houston, 12/4/1977 (4–209)

Longest Punt

83	Chris Norman, vs. Kansas City, 9/23/1984
78	Bill Van Heusen, vs. Dallas, 12/2/1973
76	Tom Rouen, at Oakland, 9/20/1998

Punt Returns

Most Punt Returns

Career

248	Rick Upchurch, 1975–1983
157	Bill Thompson, 1969–1981
128	Deltha O'Neal, 2000–2003
112	Glyn Milburn, 1993–1995
101	Gerald Willhite, 1982–1988

Season

51	Rick Upchurch, 1977
44	Chris Watson, 1999
42	Gerald Willhite, 1986
41	Glyn Milburn, 1994
41	Wade Manning, 1981

Game

8	Trindon Holliday, at Carolina 11/11/2012
8	Quan Cosby, vs. Chicago, 12/11/2011
8	Rick Upchurch, vs. Baltimore, 10/22/1978

Punt Return Yardage

Career

3,008	Rick Upchurch, 1975–1983
1,814	Bill Thompson, 1969–1981
1,325	Deltha O'Neal, 2000–2003
1,158	Glyn Milburn, 1993–1995
1,012	Gerald Willhite, 1982–1988

Season

653	Rick Upchurch, 1977
543	Darrien Gordon, 1997
536	Rick Upchurch, 1976
493	Rick Upchurch, 1978
481	Trindon Holliday, 2012

Game

168	Darrien Gordon, vs. Carolina, 11/9/1997
167	Rick Upchurch, vs. Pittsburgh, 11/6/1977
144	Kevin Clark, vs. San Diego, 12/27/1987

Yards per Punt Return

Career (min. 20 punt returns)

12.46	Darrien Gordon, 1997–1998 (74–922)
12.21	Rod Smith, 1995–2007 (53–647)
12.13	Rick Upchurch, 1975–1983 (248–3,008)
11.95	Charlie Mitchell, 1963–1967 (21–251)
11.94	Eddie Royal, 2008–2011 (81–967)

Season (min. 10 punt returns)

| 16.88 | Floyd Little, 1967 (16–270) |
| 16.17 | Eddie Royal, 2011 (12–194) |

16.13	Rick Upchurch, 1982 (15–242)
13.74	Rick Upchurch, 1976 (39–536)
13.69	Rick Upchurch, 1978 (36–493)

Punts Returned for Touchdown
Career
8	Rick Upchurch, 1975–1983
3	Darrien Gordon, 1997–1998
2	Eddie Royal, 2008–2011
2	Deltha O'Neal, 2000–2003
2	Floyd Little, 1967–1975

Season
4	Rick Upchurch, 1976
3	Darrien Gordon, 1997
2	Rick Upchurch, 1982

Game
2	Darrien Gordon, vs. Carolina, 11/9/1997 (75 and 82 yards)
2	Rick Upchurch, vs. Cleveland, 9/26/1976 (36 and 73 yards)

Longest Punt Return for Touchdown
94	Darrien Gordon, vs. St. Louis, 9/14/1997
92	Rick Upchurch, vs. San Diego, 10/3/1976
90	Eric Decker, vs. Oakland, 9/12/2011

Kickoff Returns
Most Kickoff Returns
Career
134	Vaughn Hebron, 1996–1998
104	Ken Bell, 1986–1989
104	Floyd Little, 1967–1975
96	Glyn Milburn, 1993–1995
95	Rick Upchurch, 1975–1983

Season
48	Chris Cole, 2001
48	Chris Watson, 1999
47	Glyn Milburn, 1995
47	Odell Barry, 1964
46	Deltha O'Neal, 2000
46	Vaughn Hebron, 1998

Game
8	Chad Jackson, at San Diego, 12/28/2008
8	Triandos Luke, at Kansas City, 12/19/2004
8	Kevin Kasper, at Kansas City, 10/20/2002 (OT)

Kickoff Return Yardage
Career
3,324	Vaughn Hebron, 1996–1998
2,523	Floyd Little, 1967–1975
2,355	Rick Upchurch, 1975–1983
2,250	Glyn Milburn, 1993–1995
2,218	Ken Bell, 1986–1989

Season
1,269	Glyn Milburn, 1995
1,245	Odell Barry, 1964
1,216	Vaughn Hebron, 1998
1,138	Chris Watson, 1999
1,127	Chris Cole, 2001

Game
211	Eric Decker, at Arizona, 12/12/2010
201	Randy Montgomery, at San Diego, 9/24/1972
197	Rick Upchurch, vs. Cleveland, 10/19/1975
185	Floyd Little, at Miami, 9/17/1967
182	Chris Cole, at San Diego, 10/21/2001

Yards per Kickoff Return
Career (min. 40 returns)
26.28	Abner Haynes, 1965–1966 (43–1,130)
25.42	Odell Barry, 1964–1965 (73–1,856)
25.13	Bill Thompson, 1969–1981 (46–1,156)
25.07	Reuben Droughns, 2002–2004 (46–1,153)
24.81	Vaughn Hebron, 1996–1998 (134–3,324)

Season (min. 15 returns)
28.50	Bill Thompson, 1969 (18–513)
28.47	Goldie Sellers, 1966 (19–541)
28.00	Al Frazier, 1961 (18–504)
27.10	Rick Upchurch, 1975 (40–1,084)
27.00	Glyn Milburn, 1995 (47–1,269)

Kickoffs Returned for Touchdown
Career
2	Goldie Sellers, 1966–1967
1	9 players

Season
2	Goldie Sellers, 1966

Game
1	11 times

Longest Kickoff Return for a Touchdown
105	Trindon Holliday, at Cincinnati, 11/4/2012
100	Nemiah Wilson, at Kansas City, 10/8/1966
100	Goldie Sellers, vs. Houston, 10/2/1966

DEFENSE

Interceptions
Most Interceptions
Career
44	Steve Foley, 1976–1986
43	Goose Gonsoulin, 1960–1966
40	Bill Thompson, 1969–1981
34	Tyrone Braxton, 1987–1993, 1995–1999
34	Champ Bailey, 2004–2012

Season
11	Goose Gonsoulin, 1960
10	Champ Bailey, 2006
9	Deltha O'Neal, 2001
9	Tyrone Braxton, 1996
9	Willie Brown, 1964

Game
4	Deltha O'Neal, vs. Kansas City, 10/7/2001
4	Willie Brown, vs. N.Y. Jets, 11/15/1964
4	Goose Gonsoulin, at Buffalo, 9/18/1960

Consecutive Games with an Interception
5	Champ Bailey, 2005
4	Tyrone Braxton, 1996
3	numerous times (last: Champ Bailey, 2006)

Interception Return Yardage
Career
784	Bill Thompson, 1969–1981
643	Mike Harden, 1980–1988
622	Steve Foley, 1976–1986
614	Tyrone Braxton, 1987–1993, 1995–1999
542	Goose Gonsoulin, 1960–1966

Season
179	Mike Harden, 1986
162	Champ Bailey, 2006
153	Nemiah Wilson, 1967
144	Chris Harris, 2012
140	Willie Brown, 1964

Game
105	Ray Crockett, at Oakland, 9/20/1998
98	Chris Harris, at Baltimore, 12/16/2012
93	Randy Gradishar, at Cleveland, 10/5/1980
91	Willie Brown, vs. N.Y. Jets, 11/15/1964
80	Darrent Williams, at Oakland, 11/13/2005

Most Yards per Interception Return
Career (min. 10 returns)
23.73	Wymon Henderson, 1989–1992 (11–261)
19.60	Bill Thompson, 1969–1981 (40–784)
19.48	Mike Harden, 1980–1988 (33–643)
18.06	Tyrone Braxton, 1987–1993, 1995–1999 (34–614)
17.60	Jim McMillin, 1960–1962, 1964–1965 (10–176)

Most Interceptions Returned for Touchdown
Career
4	Tyrone Braxton, 1987–1993, 1995–1999
4	Mike Harden, 1980–1988
3	Champ Bailey, 2004–2010
3	Tom Jackson, 1973–1986
3	Randy Gradishar, 1974–1983
3	Bill Thompson, 1969–1981
3	Nemiah Wilson, 1965–1967

Season
2	Chris Harris, 2012
2	Champ Bailey, 2005
2	Deltha O'Neal, 2002
2	Jimmy Spencer, 2000
2	Mike Harden, 1986
2	John Rowser, 1976
2	Nemiah Wilson, 1967

Longest Interception Return for Touchdown
98	Chris Harris, at Baltimore, 12/16/2012
93	Randy Gradishar, at Cleveland, 10/5/1980
80	Darrent Williams, at Oakland, 11/13/2005
80	Ray Crockett, at Oakland, 9/20/1998
79	Jimmy Spencer, vs. Seattle, 12/10/2000

Fumble Returns
Longest Fumble Return for Touchdown
88	Bob Swenson, at San Francisco, 11/18/1979
86	Louis Wright, at Buffalo, 12/2/1979 (78 yds. after lateral from Randy Gradishar)
80	Bill Thompson, vs. Oakland, 10/22/1973

Sacks
Note: Sacks first became an official statistic tracked by the NFL in 1982. Broncos sack totals prior to 1982 are derived from play-by-play analysis.

Most Sacks
Career
97.5	Simon Fletcher, 1985–1995
79.0	Karl Mecklenburg, 1983–1994
75.0	Barney Chavous, 1973–1985
73.5	Rulon Jones, 1980–1988
64.5	Lyle Alzado, 1971–1978

Season
18.5	Von Miller, 2012
17.0	Elvis Dumervil, 2009
16.0	Simon Fletcher, 1992
13.5	Simon Fletcher, 1993
13.5	Simon Fletcher, 1991
13.5	Rulon Jones, 1986

Game
4	Elvis Dumervil, vs. Cleveland, 9/20/2009
4	Simon Fletcher, at San Diego, 11/11/1990
4	Karl Mecklenburg, at Pittsburgh, 12/1/1985
4	Karl Mecklenburg, vs. New Orleans, 9/15/1985
4	Barney Chavous, at Seattle, 12/21/1980
4	Dave Costa, at Buffalo, 9/7/1970
4	Rich Jackson, at Cincinnati, 10/19/1969

Consecutive Games With Sack
10*	Simon Fletcher (1992–1993)
8	Simon Fletcher (1991)
7	Lyle Alzado (1974–1975)

* NFL Record

Multi-Sack Games
Career
20	Elvis Dumervil, 2006–2012
20	Simon Fletcher, 1985–1995
16	Barney Chavous, 1973–1985
15	Paul Smith, 1968–1978
13	Lyle Alzado, 1971–1978

WINNING TRADITION
Super Bowl Wins
2	1997 (XXXII), 1998 (XXXIII)

American Football Conference (AFC) Championships
6	1977, 1986, 1987, 1989, 1997, 1998

AFC Western Division Titles
12	1977, 1978, 1984, 1986, 1987, 1989, 1991, 1996, 1998, 2005, 2011, 2012

Playoff Berths
19	1977, 1978, 1979, 1983, 1984, 1986, 1987, 1989, 1991, 1993, 1996, 1997, 1998, 2000, 2003, 2004, 2005, 2011, 2012

Winning Seasons
25	1973, 1974, 1976, 1977, 1978, 1979, 1981, 1983, 1984, 1985, 1986, 1987, 1989, 1991, 1993, 1996, 1997, 1998, 2000, 2002, 2003, 2004, 2005, 2006, 2012

Streaks
Most Wins, One Season
14	1998
13	2012
13	2005
13	1996
13	1984

Most Consecutive Wins
14	1997–1998
11	2012
10	1984
9	1996
8	1985–1986
8	1976–1977

Most Consecutive Home Wins
24	1996–1998
13	2004–2006
12	1983–1984
9	1988–1999

Most Consecutive Road Wins
7	1976–1977
6	2012
6	1998

Most Consecutive Games Without a Win
14	1963–1964
9	1967
8	1970–1971
8	1960

Most Consecutive Home Losses
7	1967–1968
6	1963–1964
5	1982–1983
5	1965–1966
5	1962–1963

Most Consecutive Road Losses
12	1963–1965
6	2010
6	1992
6	1990–1991
6	1966–1967
6	1965–1966
6	1961

Most Consecutive Postseason Wins
7	1997–1999
2	1990
2	1988
2	1987
2	1977–1978

Most Consecutive Postseason Losses
5	1978–1984
3	12/31/2000 through 1/9/2005
3	1/12/1992 through 1/4/1997

Most Consecutive Postseason Home Wins
6	1987–1992
4	1997–2006

Most Consecutive Postseason Road Wins
2	1998

Most Consecutive Postseason Home Losses
1	4 times (last: vs. Baltimore, 1/12/2013)

Most Consecutive Postseason Road Losses
3	2000–2005
3	1978–1983

TEAM RECORDS
Scoring and Total Offense
Most Points
Season
501	1998
485	2000
481	2012
472	1997
395	2005

Game
50	vs. San Diego, 10/6/1963
49	vs. Kansas City, 11/14/2010
49	vs. Philadelphia, 10/30/2005
48	vs. Tampa Bay, 11/7/1976
48	at Houston, 10/14/1973

One Half

38	vs. Seattle, 11/26/1989 (first)
38	vs. New England, 11/11/1979 (first)
38	vs. Tampa Bay, 11/7/1976 (second)

One Quarter

28	vs. Philadelphia, 10/4/1998 (first)
26	at N.Y. Jets, 12/3/1967 (second)
24	10 times

Largest Margin of Victory, Game

43	vs. N.Y. Jets, 9/19/1976 (46–3)
37	at Phoenix, 12/16/1989 (37–0)
37	vs. Oakland, 10/5/1962 (44–7)
35	vs. Kansas City, 12/30/2012 (38–3)
35	vs. San Diego, 12/21/1997 (38–3)
35	vs. New England, 11/11/1979 (45–10)
35	vs. Tampa Bay, 11/7/1976 (48–13)

Most Touchdowns

Season

62	1998
58	2000
57	2012
55	1997
47	1996

Game

7	vs. Kansas City, 11/14/2010
7	vs. Philadelphia, 10/30/2005
6	14 times (last: vs. Kansas City, 12/7/2003)

Fewest Points Scored

Season

148	1982 (9-game season)
196	1966
203	1971
240	1964
251	1961

Game

0	at L.A. Raiders, 11/22/1992 (24–0)
0	at Philadelphia, 9/20/1992 (30–0)
0	at New Orleans, 11/20/1988 (42–0)
0	at Chicago, 9/9/1984 (27–0)
0	at San Diego (23–0), 10/8/1978
0	at San Diego, 12/15/1974 (17–0)
0	at Kansas City, 12/6/1970 (16–0)
0	at Oakland, 9/10/1967 (51–0)
0	at San Diego, 10/29/1961 (37–0)

Largest Margin of Defeat

52	vs. Kansas City, 9/7/1963 (59–7)
51	at Oakland, 9/10/1967 (51–0)
46	vs. Kansas City, 10/23/1966 (56–10)
45	vs. Oakland, 10/24/2010 (59–14)
43	at Kansas City, 10/29/1967 (52–9)

Most Field Goals Made

Season

31	2001
31	1995
30	2009
30	1994

29	2004
29	1999

Game

5	vs. Miami, 10/13/2002
5	at Kansas City, 11/16/1997
5	vs. Buffalo, 9/3/1995
5	vs. Seattle, 11/20/1983

Highest Percentage on PAT attempts

1.000	21 times (last: 2012, 55 of 55)

Most Total Offensive Plays

Season

1,152	1985
1,115	2000
1,092	1996
1,090	2012
1,077	1988

Game

95	at Green Bay (at Milwaukee), 9/20/1987 (OT)
88	at Seattle, 10/29/1978 (OT)
86	at Chicago, 12/12/1976
86	vs. San Diego, 11/30/1975 (OT)
84	vs. Oakland, 10/16/1995
84	at Kansas City, 12/4/1994 (OT)
84	at L.A. Raiders, 10/28/1984 (OT)
84	vs. Boston, 12/3/1961

Most Yards Total Offense

Season

6,366	2012 (1,832 rush, 4,534 pass)
6,333	2008 (1,862 rush, 4,471 pass)
6,332	2004 (2,333 rush, 3,999 pass)
6,092	1998 (2,468 rush, 3,624 pass)

Game

567	vs. Atlanta, 10/31/2004 (68 rush, 499 pass)
564	at Cleveland, 11/6/2008 (123 rush, 441 pass)
564	vs. Philadelphia, 10/30/2005 (255 rush, 309 pass)
548	vs. Baltimore, 10/20/1996 (222 rush, 326 pass)
543	vs. N.Y. Jets, 9/19/1976 (251 rush, 292 pass)

Most Yards Gained per Play

Season

6.21	2008 (1,019–6,333)
5.92	2004 (1,070–6,332)
5.88	2000 (1,115–6,554)
5.85	1998 (1,041–6,092)
5.84	2012 (1,090–6,366)

Game

9.53	vs. Dallas, 9/13/1998 (54–515)
8.33	vs. Kansas City, 12/7/2003 (61–508)
7.94	at Cleveland, 11/6/2008 (71–564)
7.83	vs. Philadelphia, 10/30/2005 (72–564)
7.77	vs. New England, 12/17/1972 (62–482)

Fewest Yards Total Offense

Season

2,837	1982 (9-game season; 1,018 rush, 1,819 pass)
2,947	1967 (1,265 rush, 1,682 pass)
3,168	1966 (1,173 rush, 1,995 pass)
3,332	1964 (1,311 rush, 2,021 pass)
3,811	1961 (1,091 rush, 2,720 pass)

Game

-5	at Oakland, 9/10/1967 (48 rush, -53 pass)
26	at Houston, 9/3/1966 (33 rush, -7 pass)
82	at Philadelphia, 9/20/1992 (52 rush, 30 pass)
128	at Washington, 10/12/1992 (26 rush, 102 pass)
130	at Chicago, 9/9/1984 (53 rush, 77 pass)

Rushing

Most Rushing Attempts

Season

601	1978
554	1989
546	2011
543	2003
542	2005

Game

60	vs. San Diego, 11/30/1975 (OT)
59	at Kansas City, 9/24/1978 (OT)
59	at Chicago, 12/12/1976
57	at Seattle, 10/29/1978 (OT)
57	at Cleveland, 10/24/1971

Most Rushing Yards

Season

2,632	2011
2,629	2003
2,539	2005
2,468	1998
2,451	1978

Game

356	at Chicago, 12/12/1976
328	vs. San Diego, 11/30/1975 (OT)
301	at Seattle, 11/26/2000
299	at Oakland, 11/6/2011
292	at Oakland, 11/24/1974

Most Yards Gained per Rush

Season

4.96	2002 (457–2,266)
4.84	2003 (543–2,629)
4.82	2011 (546–2,632)
4.81	2008 (387–1,862)
4.70	1998 (525–2,468)

Game (min. 10 rushes)

9.52	vs. Chicago, 11/23/2003 (21–200)
9.00	at San Diego, 12/28/2008 (10–90)
8.44	vs. Kansas City, 12/7/2003 (32–270)
8.13	vs. New England, 12/18/2011 (31–252)
8.09	vs. Arizona, 12/29/2002 (32–259)

Most Rushing Touchdowns

Season

26	1998
25	2005
21	2002
21	2000
20	2003
20	1996
20	1985
20	1974

Game

5	vs. Kansas City, 12/7/2003
4	7 times (last: vs. San Francisco, 12/23/2000)

Fewest Yards Rushing

Season

1,018	1982 (9-game season)
1,091	1961
1,173	1966
1,195	1960
1,265	1967

Game

13	at Oakland, 10/22/1972
14	vs. Miami, 11/2/2008
19	at Tennessee, 10/3/2010
20	at Dallas, 12/10/1961
26	at Washington, 10/12/1992

Passing

Most Pass Attempts

Season

626	1994
620	2008
617	1985
594	1995
588	2012

Game

59	at Green Bay, 10/10/1993
58	vs. San Diego, 11/19/2000
57	vs. Indianapolis, 9/26/2010

Most Pass Completions

Season

402	2012
388	1994
386	2008
359	2002
354	2000

Game

37	vs. Indianapolis, 9/26/2010
36	vs. San Diego, 9/14/2008
36	vs. San Diego, 11/19/2000
36	vs. San Diego, 9/4/1994

Highest Completion Percentage

Season

.684	2012 (402–588)
.648	2002 (359–554)
.633	2007 (326–515)
.633	1993 (350–553)
.623	2008 (386–620)

Game (min. 10 attempts)

.917	at L.A. Raiders, 11/2/1986 (11–12)
.875	vs. San Diego, 9/27/1981 (21–24)
.870	vs. Kansas City, 12/10/1978 (20–23)
.824	at Indianapolis, 12/21/2003 (14–17)
.808	at Tennessee, 12/25/2004 (21–26)

Most Yards Passing (net yards)

Season

4,534	2012
4,471	2008
4,243	2000
4,045	1995
4,038	2010

Game

499	vs. Atlanta, 10/31/2004
472	vs. Indianapolis, 9/26/2010
459	vs. Kansas City, 11/18/1974
443	vs. San Diego, 11/19/2000
441	at Cleveland, 11/6/2008

Most Yards per Pass Attempt

Season

8.23	1981 (485–3,992)
8.09	1974 (329–2,660)
7.85	2004 (521–4,089)
7.85	2000 (569–4,464)
7.76	1998 (491–3,808)

Most Yards per Pass Completion

Season

15.79	1968 (179–2,826)
14.94	1976 (168–2,510)
14.77	1969 (192–2,835)
14.60	1967 (150–2,190)
14.46	1974 (184–2,660)

Fewest Yards Passing (net yards)

Season

1,682	1967
1,819	1982 (9-game season)
1,863	1977
1,995	1966
2,021	1964

Game

-53	at Oakland, 9/10/1967
-7	at Houston, 9/3/1966
1	at Pittsburgh, 9/4/1983
6	vs. N.Y. Jets, 11/15/1964
8	vs. Oakland, 9/3/1978
8	vs. San Diego, 11/30/1975 (OT)

Most Touchdown Passes

Season

37	2012
32	1998
28	2000

Game

5	vs. Kansas City, 11/14/2010
5	vs. San Diego, 11/19/2000
5	vs. Minnesota, 11/18/1984
5	vs. Buffalo, 10/28/1962
4	24 times

Most Interceptions Thrown

Season

45	1961
40	1962
35	1960
34	1975
32	1964

Game

8	at Houston, 12/2/1962
6	vs. San Diego, 9/21/1980
6	vs. San Diego, 11/30/1975 (OT)
6	at San Diego, 9/24/1972
6	vs. Buffalo, 11/19/1961
6	at Houston, 11/26/1961
6	at Green Bay (at Milwaukee), 9/26/1971

Interception Avoidance Percentage

Season

.015	2005 (7–465)
.018	1993 (10–553)
.019	2012 (11–588)

First Downs

Most First Downs

Season

383	2000
380	2012
357	2002
354	2008
351	2004

Game

34	vs. San Diego, 9/14/2008
34	vs. San Diego, 11/19/2000
34	vs. Kansas City, 11/18/1974
32	vs. Kansas City, 12/30/2012
32	at Cincinnati, 10/22/2000

Punting

Most Punts

Season

105	1967
101	2011
96	1984
96	1978
96	1968

Game

12	at Buffalo, 10/25/1981
12	vs. Cincinnati, 10/6/1968
12	at Oakland, 9/10/1967
11	at Seattle, 11/30/1992 (OT)
11	vs. Seattle, 10/20/1985 (OT)

Fewest Punts
Season

45	1982 (9-game season)
46	2008
54	1995
55	2002
60	2007
60	1997
60	1990
60	1972
60	1962

Game

0	vs. Oakland, 9/30/2012
0	vs. Buffalo, 12/21/2008
0	vs. San Diego, 11/16/2003
0	at Minnesota 11/4/1990
0	vs. Dallas, 10/8/1961

Most Yards per Punt
Season

47.4	2011 (101–4,783)
46.7	2008 (46–2,150)
46.5	1999 (84–3,908)
46.3	2012 (67–3,099)
46.2	1998 (67–3,097)

Game (min. 4 punts)

57.2	vs. L.A. Raiders, 9/26/1988 (OT) (5–286)
56.6	vs. Seattle, 11/24/1984 (5–283)
56.2	at Arizona, 12/12/2010 (5–281)
55.8	vs. San Diego, 12/16/1990 (5–279)
55.8	vs. Cincinnati, 9/18/2011 (6–335)

Most Net Yards per Punt (Since 1976)
Season

42.1	2012 (67–2,822)
47.4	2011 (101–4,058)
38.5	1990 (60–2,313)
38.1	1997 (60–2,283)
38.0	2005 (73–2,771)

Game (min. 4 punts)

52.8	vs. L.A. Raiders, 9/26/1988 (OT) (5–264)
52.3	vs. San Diego, 11/11/2001 (6–314)
52.3	at Houston, 12/4/1977 (4–209)
51.2	vs. San Diego, 12/16/1990 (5–256)
51.0	vs. Cincinnati, 9/18/2011 (6–306)

Fewest Yards per Punt
Season

35.1	1976 (84–2,945)
36.4	1978 (96–3,494)
37.3	1960 (70–2,610)
39.0	2002 (55–2,145)
39.2	1977 (91–3,563)

Punt Returns

Most Punt Returns
Season

63	1970
58	1977
54	1999
53	1988
51	1981
51	1978
51	1976

Game

8	at Carolina, 11/11/2012
8	vs. Chicago, 12/11/2011
8	vs. San Diego, 12/27/1987
8	vs. Baltimore, 10/22/1978
8	vs. San Diego, 11/30/1975 (OT)
8	at Kansas City, 10/6/1974
8	at Buffalo, 9/20/1970

Most Punt Return Yards
Season

712	1977
640	1976
583	1996
582	1978
556	1970

Game

168	vs. Carolina, 11/9/1997
167	vs. Pittsburgh, 11/6/1977
150	vs. San Diego, 12/27/1988
128	vs. Oakland, 9/12/2011
128	vs. San Francisco, 9/19/1982

Most Yards per Punt Return
Season

14.5	1982 (21–305)
13.5	1997 (41–555)
13.5	1967 (26–351)
13.1	2001 (31–405)
12.9	1963 (30–387)

Most Punt Return Touchdowns
Season

4	1976
3	1997
2	2011
2	2003
2	1986
2	1982

Game

2	vs. Carolina, 11/9/1997
2	vs. Cleveland, 9/26/1976
1	25 times

Kickoff Returns

Most Kickoff Returns
Season

78	1963
76	1964
75	1994
71	2008
71	1965

Game

10	at Arizona, 12/12/2010
10	at Indianapolis, 10/31/1988
10	vs. Boston, 10/4/1964
10	at San Diego, 12/22/1963

Most Kickoff Return Yards
Season

1,801	1963
1,758	1964
1,731	1965
1,576	2001
1,558	1966

Game

295	vs. Boston, 10/4/1964
289	vs. Kansas City, 9/7/1963
272	at Arizona, 12/12/2010
238	at Kansas City, 10/8/1963
219	at Indianapolis, 10/31/1988

Most Yards per Kickoff Return
Season

26.9	1966 (58–1,588)
25.3	1967 (60–1,518)
24.5	2011 (39–956)
24.5	1975 (59–1,446)
24.4	1965 (71–1,731)

Most Kickoff Return Touchdowns
Season

3	1966
1	8 times (last: 2012)

Game

1	11 times

Turnovers
Most Fumbles Committed
Season

36	1984
36	1966
35	1979
34	1988
34	1983
34	1963

Game

6	vs. Washington, 11/18/2001
6	vs. Philadelphia, 10/29/1989
6	vs. Cleveland, 10/19/1975
6	at Boston, 11/6/1966
6	vs. L.A. Chargers, 10/16/1960

Fewest Fumbles Committed
Season
15	2009
15	1969
18	2008
17	1998
19	2005

Most Takeaways
Season
55	1984 (31 int., 24 fum.)
53	1964 (32 int., 21 fum.)
47	1987 (28 int., 19 fum.)
47	1983 (27 int., 20 fum.)
46	1981 (23 int., 23 fum.)
Game
10	at Detroit, 10/7/1984 (7 int., 3 fum.)

Fewest Takeaways
Season
13	2008 (6 int., 7 fum.)
18	2011 (9 int., 9 fum.)
18	2010 (10 int., 8 fum.)
19	1982 (12 int., 7 fum.) (players' strike; nine-game season)
20	2004 (12 int., 8 fum.)
20	2003 (9 int., 11 fum.)

Most Giveaways
Season
65*	1961 (45 int., 20 fum.)
54	1962 (40 int., 14 fum.)
52	1960 (35 int., 17 fum.)
48	1975 (34 int., 14 fum.)
47	1966 (30 int., 17 fum.)
* NFL Record
Game
9	at Houston, 12/2/1962 (8 int., 1 fum.)
9	vs. Buffalo, 11/19/1961 (6 int., 3 fum.)

Fewest Giveaways
Season
16	2005 (7 int., 9 fum.)
20	1998 (14 int., 6 fum.)
21	1997 (11 int., 10 fum.)
23	2009 (13 int., 10 fum.)
24	2003 (18 int., 6 fum.)

Consecutive Games with a Takeaway
36	1982–1984

Consecutive Games without a Giveaway
4*	2005
* Ties NFL record

Best Takeaway Ratio
Season
+21	1984 (55/34)

+20	2005 (36/16)
+19	2000 (44/25)
+13	1964 (53/40)
+12	1977 (39/27)
Game
+8	at Oakland, 10/16/1977 (8/0)

Worst Takeaway Ratio
Season
-25	1961 (40/65)
-17	2008 (13/30)
-17	1982 (19/36)
-16	1975 (32/48)
-16	1966 (31/47)
Game
-9	vs. Buffalo, 11/19/1961 (0/9)

Penalties
Most Penalties
Season
132	1978
116	1997
116	1979
115	1998
114	1999
Game
15	vs. Tampa Bay, 11/7/1976
14	at Kansas City, 9/20/1993
14	vs. Oakland, 10/17/1976
14	at N.Y. Jets, 10/28/1973
13	at San Diego 9/24/1995
13	at Green Bay, 10/10/1993
13	at Seattle, 10/22/1989 (OT)
13	at Seattle, 12/8/1979

Most Yards Penalized
Season
1,092	1978
1,023	1998
1,006	1997
1,006	1979
986	1976
Game
160	vs. Tampa Bay, 11/7/1976
148	at Seattle, 10/14/2001
146	at Kansas City, 12/16/2001 (OT)
134	vs. Pittsburgh, 11/6/1977
132	at Oakland, 10/17/1976

Fewest Penalties
Season
48	1967
54	1982 (9-game season)
54	1960
60	1961
64	1962
Game
0	vs. Kansas City, 9/17/2006 (OT)
0	at Chicago, 12/18/1993

0	vs. Kansas City, 12/16/1967
1	17 times

Fewest Yards Penalized
Season
478	2006
501	1960
512	1967
516	1982 (9-game season)
548	1963
Game
0	vs. Kansas City, 9/17/2006 (OT)
0	at Chicago, 12/18/1993
0	vs. Kansas City, 12/17/1967
0	at Boston, 9/21/1962
5	7 times

Total Defense
Fewest Points Allowed
Season
148	1977
198	1978
206	1976
226	1989
226	1982 (9-game season)
Game
0	17 times (last: Denver 24, N.Y. Jets 0, 11/20/2005)

Fewest Touchdowns Allowed
Season
18	1977
21	1978
22	1991
25	1989
25	1982 (9-game season)
25	1976

Fewest Field Goals Allowed
Season
8	1977
12	1976
13	1995
13	1961
14	2005
14	1998
14	1997
14	1987
14	1965

Fewest Total Yards Allowed
Season
3,169	1982 (9-game season; 935 rush, 2,234 pass)
3,705	1970 (1,351 rush, 2,354 pass)
3,734	1976 (1,709 rush, 2,025 pass)
3,775	1977 (1,531 rush, 2,244 pass)
3,819	1971 (1,834 rush, 1,985 pass)

Game

60	at Cleveland, 10/24/1971 (24 rush, 36 pass)
66	vs. Chicago, 12/5/1971 (73 rush, -7 pass)
70	vs. San Diego, 11/2/1969 (50 rush, 20 pass)
92	vs. New England, 11/11/1979 (58 rush, 34 pass)
96	vs. San Diego, 11/16/2003 (40 rush, 56 pass)

Lowest Average Yield Per Play

Season

4.01	1977 (931–3,775)
4.14	1976 (919–3,734)
4.38	1978 (1,016–4,448)
4.39	1972 (876–3,851)
4.42	1970 (838–3,705)

Game

1.12	vs. Chicago, 12/5/1971 (59–66)
1.25	vs. San Diego, 11/2/1969 (56–70)
1.30	at Cleveland, 10/24/1971 (46–60)
1.61	vs. New England, 11/11/1979 (57–92)
2.06	at Phoenix, 12/16/1989 (49–101)

Most Interceptions Made

Season

32	1964
31	1984
31	1978
28	1987
28	1967

Game

7	at Detroit, 10/7/1984
7	at Oakland, 10/16/1977
6	vs. Boston, 9/3/1967
6	at Houston, 11/14/1965
6	vs. N.Y. Jets, 11/15/1964
6	at Buffalo, 9/18/1960

Highest Interception Percentage

Season

.073	1964 (32–440)
.071	1978 (31–438)
.065	1960 (27–387)
.064	1962 (27–423)
.061	1987 (28–456)
.061	1976 (24–391)
.061	1967 (28–459)

Most Yards on Interception Returns

Season

510	1984
491	1977
483	1962
465	1965
459	1964

Game

133	at Buffalo, 9/18/1960
126	at Oakland, 11/13/2005
123	at Oakland, 9/20/1998

117	vs. Oakland, 10/5/1962
111	vs. San Diego, 12/27/1987
111	at Detroit, 10/7/1984

Most Interceptions Returned for Touchdown

Season

5	2000
5	1997

Game

2	vs. Kansas City, 9/10/1989
2	vs. Tampa Bay, 11/7/1976
2	vs. Oakland, 10/5/1962

Most Sacks

Season

57	1984
52	2012
52	1991
50	1999
50	1992
50	1970

Game

10	at Cincinnati, 10/19/1969
9	vs. N.Y. Jets, 9/1/1996
9	vs. Chicago, 12/5/1971
9	vs. Buffalo, 11/19/1961
8	vs. Seattle, 12/20/1992
8	vs. Seattle, 11/26/1989
8	vs. N.Y. Jets, 11/15/1964
8	vs. Oakland, 11/29/1964

Most Safeties Caused

Season

3	1990
2	2012
2	1999
2	1986
2	1982
2	1970
2	1967

Game

2	at Seattle, 1/2/1983
1	30 times

Lowest Opponent Punting Average

Season

39.0	1960 (67–2,611)
39.4	1982 (42–1,653)
40.5	1961 (77–3,120)
41.0	1989 (84–3,440)
41.1	1985 (94–3,868)

Game (min. 4 punts)

24.3	at Cincinnati, 11/1/1998 (3–73)
25.0	at Kansas City, 10/27/1985 (5–125)
26.0	vs. Oakland, 11/22/1999 (7–182) (OT)
27.3	at Cleveland, 10/1/1989 (6–164)
30.0	at Kansas City, 10/20/2002 (5–150) (OT)
30.0	vs. Buffalo, 11/27/1960 (6–180)

Lowest Opponent Punt Return Average

Season

4.81	1978 (47–226)
5.48	1995 (25–137)
5.97	2012 (33–197)
6.07	1991 (28–170)
6.13	1968 (46–282)

Lowest Opponent Kickoff Return Average

Season

17.14	1961 (42–720)
17.44	1989 (72–1,256)
17.68	1991 (62–1,096)
17.76	1993 (63–1,119)
17.91	1983 (46–824)

Fewest Opponent First Downs

Season

176	1982 (9-game season)
199	1970
206	1971
217	1977
222	1976

Game

3	vs. San Diego, 11/30/1975 (OT)
5	vs. San Diego, 11/16/2003
5	vs. Green Bay, 10/17/1999
5	at Chicago, 12/12/1976
6	at Cleveland, 10/24/1971
6	vs. Oakland, 11/20/1966

Most Opponent Penalties

Season

139	2005
138	1983
137	2003
134	1994
130	1997

Game

20	vs. Oakland, 12/15/1996
16	vs. Baltimore, 12/11/1983
16	vs. Chicago, 9/26/1978

Most Opponent Penalty Yards

Season

1,118	1997
1,096	1983
1,062	2004
1,034	1986
1,033	1979

Game

188	vs. Houston, 10/6/1985
157	vs. Oakland, 12/15/1996
147	vs. Chicago, 10/16/1978
145	at Seattle, 12/8/1979
140	at Houston, 10/26/1969

INDEX